W9-CPO-900

GARLAND STUDIES IN

ENTREPRENEURSHIP

edited by

STUART BRUCHEY
ALLAN NEVINS PROFESSOR EMERITUS
COLUMBIA UNIVERSITY

A GARLAND SERIES

WOMEN'S RESOURCES IN BUSINESS START-UP

A STUDY OF BLACK AND WHITE WOMEN ENTREPRENEURS

KATHERINE INMAN

GARLAND PUBLISHING, INC.
A MEMBER OF THE TAYLOR & FRANCIS GROUP
NEW YORK & LONDON / 2000

331.481
I 57

Published in 2000 by
Garland Publishing, Inc.
A member of the Taylor & Francis Group
19 Union Square West
New York, NY 10003

Copyright © 2000 by Katherine Inman

All rights reserved. No part of this book may be reprinted or reproduced or
utilized in any form or by any electronic, mechanical, or other means, now
known or hereafter invented, including photocopying and recording, or in any
information storage or retrieval system, without permission in writing from
the publisher.

10 9 8 7 6 5 4 3 2 1

Library of Congress Cataloging-in-Publication Data

Inman, Katherine, 1952–
    Women's resources in business start-up : a study of Black and white women
entrepreneurs / Katherine Inman.
        p.   cm.—(Garland studies in entrepreneurship)
    Includes bibliographical references and index.
    ISBN 0-8153-3391-9 (alk. paper)
    1. Women executives—United States.   2. Afro-American women executives.
3. Women-owned business enterprises—United States.   4. New business
enterprises—United States—Finance.   5. Business women—United States.
6. Entrepreneurship—United States.   I. Title.   II. Series.
HD6054.4.U6155 1999
331.4'816584121'0973—dc21   99-29726
                                                             CIP

Printed on acid-free, 250-year-life paper
Manufactured in the United States of America

This work is dedicated to the memory of E. S., whose story is presented here in the character of "Bernice." Her courage and commitment in helping others were an inspiration to me as I am sure they have been for others who knew her. May her memory live on in the work that she did, and may it remind us to help others less fortunate than ourselves.

Contents

Preface

Women-owned businesses are the fastest growing segment of new business start-ups, and black women's businesses are a larger share of black-owned businesses than white women's businesses are of all white firms. Most studies compare men's and women's businesses, but few examine differences among women. By choosing to examine only women entrepreneurs, I felt I could make a significant contribution to the entrepreneurial literature by making comparisons not only based on race, but also on location. I found a large literature on African American business owners, but little of this work addressed the experiences of black women. Further, the literature on women entrepreneurs in general focused almost entirely on women in urban centers, ignoring the experiences of rural women, black or white.

In the course of my work, I found this to be a critical shortfall in understanding the full range of women's entrepreneurial experiences and differences in their resources and social networks. This was particularly true of rural African American women. Including women from small towns and cities in my sample brought an almost structured element of social class into the work, so different were rural and small city black women's experiences from most of the other women in the study. For black women, life in the rural South frequently begins with hard work and offers little to look forward to in paid employment but low wages and menial jobs. Self-employment becomes a way to increase income and create meaningful work alternatives. Women in this study told stories of struggle and hardship that reflected the reality of their daily lives in rural settings. Out of these struggles frequently was born the desire to use their businesses to improve the lives of those around them. As they were able to lift themselves out of hard times and limited opportunity, so, too, did they choose to help others in their communities.

Empirical literature suggests that entrepreneurs need skill (human capital) and financing to start successful businesses. The literature on woman-owned businesses has found that women are often inadequately prepared for business ownership, lacking training and experience, funding, and access to male business networks. In addition, women's non-economic goals for business often contribute to lower earnings. Existing literature fails to adequately identify resources women do have. Particularly for rural women, where lower earnings mean fewer financial assets at the outset of business ownership, social networks become crucial in aiding and facilitating the start-up of women's businesses.

This study examines African American and European American women's experiences in garnering resources for business start-up. I have included both traditional sources of human and financial capital, such as formal education and bank loans, and less traditional, or "invisible" resources, such as informal training, family labor, and income from previous or concurrent employment. Data are taken from 61 qualitative interviews with 65 black, white, and Hispanic women in three rural communities, one small city, and one large metropolitan area in the South. All the women started or bought businesses, and all were at least half owner or controlling partner at the time of the interview. I examine women's reasons for starting businesses, circumstances surrounding start-up, and resources in start-up, including human, financial, and social capital. I explore how motivations and resources affect each other, and how race, locale, and age affect women's resources in business start-up.

Most studies of entrepreneurship occur within the context of neo-classical economic theories of rational choice. In this framework, individual actors are assumed to make economic decisions maximizing personal profit without influence from non-economic relationships. I introduce theorists who broaden rational choice theory to include non-economic motives, situation-based decision-making, opportunities and constraints faced by individuals based on membership in disadvantaged groups, and actions based on conflicting pulls from multiple group memberships. I broaden these theoretical frames further to apply to women and to business ownership. I find that feminist and black feminist theories are better suited than traditional rational choice theories to explain women's entrepreneurial choices and the environments in which they make choices. For instance, rural black women make choices to start businesses in response to limited employment options available to them in the context of small town patterns of disadvantage and discrimination. Social capital and social embeddedness theories are better suited than traditional rational choice theories to explain how women mobilize resources for businesses within contexts of disadvantage. Again, rural black women draw upon family and community ties for information, cost-saving labor, and donations to help start their businesses.

I would like to express my gratitude to, and admiration for, all the women who took part in the study. The information and insights they provided have led me to a deeper understanding of entrepreneurship and social theory and a great regard for those who have been bitten by the entrepreneurial "bug." It is my hope that their experiences will provide practical guidance and inspiration to others who wish to pursue business start-up.

K. I.
January 1999

Acknowledgments

Research for this book originated from my dissertation, a work I completed in partial fulfillment of my Ph.D. in sociology at the University of Georgia in the fall of 1997. Many people contributed directly and indirectly to this work, and I can't begin to thank them all enough. I can only acknowledge those who helped the most and send the rest a giant, collective "THANK YOU."

First and foremost, I would like to thank Dr. Linda Grant, my major professor, for her guidance and her unfailing generosity with her time and knowledge. Without her help I would not have completed this study. I would like to thank Elizabeth Watts-Warren and Roosevelt Warren for their help in finding the rural African American business owners. Sharon Lumpkin also aided me in identifying African American owners in small city settings. To all the women who agreed to participate in this study, I owe heartfelt thanks. Their stories fascinated me and inspired me to bring their experiences to life on paper so others might learn from them.

I thank Dr. Gary Green, who suggested the research topic, and members of my committee for their care in reading my proposal and final dissertation. Their suggestions deepened my understanding of the work and encouraged me to refine and affirm the importance of my findings. In particular, I would like to thank Dr. Josephine Beoku-Betts, who inspired me to do something important; Dr. James Coverdill for pushing me to think about what I was doing; Dr. William Finlay for telling me I was trying to do too much; and Dr. Dawn Bennett-Alexander for insisting that I continue.

Many thanks go to those who work at the University of Georgia Small Business Development Center's Business Outreach Services. I thank Jennifer Horton for allowing me to use the SBDC facilities to carry out the daily work of interviewing respondents, analyzing data, and writing up results of the study. Her friendship and support were unfailing and made the study affordable. Thanks also go to Candee and Vicky for their friendship and support in answering questions, helping with computers and printers, and contributing many other small, important gifts. Thanks to Donna for her support with the SBDC library, and to Beth and Becky for their support and encouragement.

I would like to thank the editors at Garland for soliciting, reviewing and accepting my work and would especially like to thank Damon Zucca for initially contacting me and helping me with preparation of the manuscript. I would also like to thank the following people for the help they so willingly gave: Linda Kundell and Deborah Tootle for telling me I could do it; Sandy Gary and Clara Roesler for transcribing interviews; my parents for their encouragement and support; Anne L. for keeping me sane; and Terry for transcribing, doing dishes, cleaning house, taking me on walks, keeping me focused, making me laugh, and showing me there was life after graduate school.

List of Figures and Tables

List of Abbreviations

AA	African American
CEO	Chief Executive Officer
CPA	Certified Public Accountant
CRA	Community Reinvestment Act
EA	European American
EOL	Economic Opportunity Loan
IRSEP	Imperfectly Rational Somewhat Economic Persons
MESBIC	Minority Enterprise Small Business Investment Company
NAACP	National Association for the Advancement of Colored People
PR	Potential Respondent
RC	Rational Choice
SBA	Small Business Administration
SBDC	Small Business Development Center
SBIC	Small Business Investment Company
SE	Social Embeddedness
SC	Social Capital

WOMEN'S RESOURCES IN BUSINESS START-UP

CHAPTER 1

Introduction

Entrepreneurial pursuits are emerging as an increasingly important aspect of women's economic activities in the U.S. As one of the fastest growing segments of small business ownership, women offer a rich variety of experiences and information that has as yet been largely untapped. A vast sociological literature has developed on women and work, yet little research has focused on women and small business ownership. In addition, sociological research has virtually ignored the entrepreneurial experiences of African American women, a group that is entering business ownership in record numbers.

Existing studies typically focus on women's business earnings in comparison with men's business earnings and sample a white, middle-class business population. This framework does not apply to many first-time and minority women business owners. Women's businesses are often newer and smaller than men's businesses, and women frequently start businesses for non-economic reasons, with profit becoming a secondary or tertiary motive. In addition, women entrepreneurs can be disadvantaged in the resource mobilization process in ways not applicable to white, middle-class male entrepreneurs.[1] This is especially true for African American women and women in rural areas where resources are limited.

I chose to focus on women because most studies compare women and men in the context of male measures of success. Women do not necessarily share the same reasons and goals for starting businesses. To compare women's with men's experiences from a male perspective does not adequately illuminate women's experiences or develop a woman-centered understanding of the entrepreneurial experience. Furthermore, the differences among women themselves become lost in male-female comparisons. Black women's experiences are mediated by effects of race as well as gender and are different from white women's perspectives. To combine women's experiences in a general comparison with men-owned businesses is to obscure racial effects among women and detract from a greater understanding of all women's entrepreneurial activities.

Women business owners from both urban and rural settings are included in the study. Observing first hand the differences between the bustling life of the city and the quieter rural existence, and the needs and pulls of each upon the other, has made me aware of the need for a more regionally integrated approach to social research. The economic differences alone can be astronomical, with the cost of living so much higher in large metropolitan areas than in truly rural areas. Opportunities for education and training, for work and businesses, and for social and cultural events are much more limited in rural areas. The South in particular is likely to have different opportunity structures for black and white women business owners across rural and urban settings.

This study seeks to fill some of the empirical and theoretical gaps concerning women's business ownership. In a comparison of black and white women's business ownership experience, I examine women's social, human, and financial capital as resources in business start-up.[2] I also examine how these resources differ according to the circumstances surrounding business start-up and each woman's goals or motivations for her business. Women who enter business ownership voluntarily, as the natural outcome of a chosen career or the fulfillment of a life's dream, are likely to draw upon different sets of resources, built through different means, than women who become entrepreneurs involuntarily. Those who never intended to become self-employed must depend on whatever skills they have built by the time they unexpectedly become business owners. Those who plan for their businesses are likely to put thought and effort into building skills and knowledge needed for success in their enterprises.

I base this research on interviews with 65 African American and European American women business owners in three rural communities, one small city, and a major urban center in the Southeast.[3] I interviewed women owning businesses ranging from hair salons to law firms, travel agencies to chemical manufacturing plants. Many of the businesses were in traditional, female-dominated occupations, and some were in non-traditional occupations for women, or occupations usually dominated by men. Some women were professionals and some were in trades. Although not a selection criterion for my sample, I interviewed women of widely different ages, and with different educational, class, and family backgrounds. All of the interviews used for this study were with women who had started or bought their businesses, and all but 11 were working full time in their businesses at the time of the interview.

I begin by providing some background on small business ownership, women's experiences in the paid labor force, and women's entry in business ownership. I present a rationale based on existing empirical and theoretical literature for a study of women's resources in start-up and for a comparison of black and white women's resources. Finally, I provide an overview of the study format and define key terms and concepts used throughout the study.

SMALL BUSINESS OWNERSHIP: AN OVERVIEW

As noted by Light and Rosenstein (1995), classical sociological theory predicted the decline and near extinction of small business ownership during the twentieth century. Weber (1958; 1978), while suggesting that European capitalism grew out of a Protestant work ethic, predicted that maturing economic markets would promote the evolution of small entrepreneurial firms into large bureaucratic organizations. Schumpeter (1943; 1988; 1991) suggested that large firms would take over and departmentalize the numerous tasks of small firms. Thus, innovation and research, product development, technology and risk assessment, and marketing would all find homes under the roof of a single, large organization. Marx (1965) examined how the accumulation of capital favors large firms with greater economic strength, access to capital, and the benefits of economies of scale. His writing suggested that larger firms would eventually take over smaller firms because of their unequal advantage in a competitive market.

Throughout the twentieth century, until the early 1970s, these theorists accurately portrayed the life of small business ownership. As a proportion of over-all employment, self-employment waned, as did interest in the study of small business ownership.[4] After that year, however, entrepreneurship experienced a renaissance unparalleled in modern times. In the 1980s, non-agricultural small business ownership increased from 7.0 percent (in 1979) to 8.3 percent of the total U.S. population (Light and Rosenstein 1995:13). Women and minorities entered business ownership at unprecedented rates. Between 1970 and 1983, women entered self-employment at a rate five times greater than men, and three times greater than women entering wage and salaried jobs (Becker, 1984). By 1992, over 34 percent of all U.S. non-farm, self-employed workers were women, according to the 1992 Economic Census. According to the Census Bureau's *Survey of Minority-Owned Business Enterprises* (1996b), the number of black-owned businesses increased 46 percent between 1987 and 1992. Making up 3.1 percent of total business ownership in 1987, black-owned businesses increased to become 3.6 percent of firms in 1992 (see Mergenhagen 1996:24). These figures do not include those self-employed in the informal or underground economy. When these entrepreneurs are included in figures of self-employment, the proportion of self-employed workers increases even more (see Guttman 1977; Portes and Stepick 1985).

What is responsible, one might ask, for such a turnaround, and why have white and minority women been increasing rapidly as owners of small businesses? Researchers suggest several possible explanations for the recent boom in small business ownership. First, technological developments, especially in personal computers, have made many tasks easier for small firm owners. Small firms innovate better than large firms (Acs and Audretsch 1990; Hartley and Hutton 1989; Stein 1974). With the latest computer technology and fewer regulations, small firms can adapt more easily than large firms to changing trends, employing what Piore and Sabel (1984) termed "flexible specialization" (see also Scott 1988). They can move faster to produce new products and fill market niches. Economists and market analysts are still debating whether the reduced costs associated with externalizing certain production transactions to smaller firms are worth the risk of relying on potentially unreliable markets outside the control of the larger firm (see Williamson 1987, 1994). Yet sub-contracting remains a major source of revenue for small firms.

Lastly, government has played an important role in supporting small business development (see Bates 1974, 1975, 1993a, 1993b; Weiss 1988). Federal direct lending programs have experienced varying degrees of success in their efforts to foster minority businesses (see Bates 1979; U.S. Comptroller General 1981; Dominguez 1976; SBA Review Board 1978). Government set-aside programs appear to have fared better in promoting development of successful minority firms through market competition (Bates 1985b, 1985c). This has been particularly important for women and minority entrepreneurs who have sought, through business ownership, to create opportunities for themselves beyond the secondary economy of the dual market system[5] (Light and Rosenstein 1995). Many government programs have targeted these groups.

WOMEN AND WORK

Since the turn of the century, women have moved into the labor market in large numbers and, particularly since the 1960s, have entered a wider variety of occupations than ever before (see Kilson 1977; Sokoloff 1992). Historically, black women have moved into jobs and occupations left vacant by white women, who have moved into more desirable positions (Malveaux and Wallace 1987). Black women moved from private household work into female-dominated clerical work as white women left for higher positions in management and male-dominated occupations. Black women rose into management and professions in the inner city and public sector as white women deserted to the private sector in suburbs and office parks. Recent figures indicate that women, both black and white, are now entering small business ownership at a faster rate than any other group in the U.S (Becker 1984; U.S. Department of Commerce and U.S. Bureau of the Census 1996b).

Women are faced with barriers and contradictory goals, both in their working lives and their personal lives. Women's increased independence from men means that men provide less financial support to their families, making women's job earnings necessary for their own and their children's support. Higher divorce rates mean more women are single mothers, a status fraught with conflicting pushes and pulls between job and family. Increased living costs frequently make second incomes for married couples a necessity, not a luxury. For African American women, who have always worked and who expect to work, these changes may come as no surprise.

Self-employment, while increasingly an option for women, is not without contradictory choices and goals as well. Women choose to start businesses under many different circumstances for many reasons, sometimes voluntarily and sometimes involuntarily. While some women may pursue a career or trade that naturally leads them into business ownership, others are forced or nudged out of paid employment by recession, restructuring, or discrimination. Goals and expectations women form in childhood or adolescence may not be achievable in adulthood. Women's access to resources change, opportunity structures change, and new opportunities and barriers dictate a completely different life path from the one originally envisioned (Gerson 1985).

Most studies juxtapose the male entrepreneur, whose wife supports him with her unpaid labor, with the self-employed female who starts her business in the home to accommodate both economic and family responsibilities. These represent the extremes in small business ownership.

Some women do not have these conflicts because they are childless and single, so viewing their entrepreneurial activities through a work/family balance lens is limiting. This study examines women's choices and actions in business start-up, whether based on internal preferences and desires or in response to external events.

WOMEN AND BUSINESS OWNERSHIP

Small business ownership has allowed women to transcend limited opportunities for career advancement in paid employment. Entrepreneurship has provided them with a sense of autonomy, achievement, and career satisfaction and allowed women with families to accommodate work while fulfilling childcare and other domestic responsibilities. It has provided older women with economic options not otherwise available to them in an economy that puts a premium on youthful workers and limits older women workers to low-paid jobs. Business ownership has allowed African American and other minority women to avoid discrimination on the job and to achieve occupational mobility.

The process of starting a business requires more effort and responsibility than getting a job or choosing investments. It requires a commitment of time, money, and other resources that can drain the entrepreneur's energy, tax her health, and test her family and personal relationships. She must have not only occupational training about the goods or services she provides, but also finance and management skills with which to operate her business. She must rely on personal, social, and business relationships for help with business, information, leads, referrals, and financial support more than she would in paid employment. Lastly, she might have to rely on personal funding sources or employ inventive financing alternatives to fund her business.

According to Bates (1989b), three ingredients for a viable business include skill, capital, and markets. This study addresses the first two, skill and capital, as necessary resources for starting a business.[6] Although the literature on women-owned small businesses is growing, studies have not examined how factors affecting resource mobilization in business start-up vary by race. Contingencies faced by African American and European American women may be distinctly different, both from each other and from problems explored in the traditional literature on small business ownership. Much prior research has used models derived from white males' experiences to compare men- and women-owned businesses. These are inadequate for capturing the complexities of black and white women owners in business start-up and operation. I have therefore undertaken a study of African American and European American women business owners to better understand the problems and opportunities of business start-up and operation from the perspectives of these women.

WOMEN'S BUSINESS GOALS AND RESOURCES FOR START-UP

Existing empirical research (reviewed in Chapter 3) suggests that women entrepreneurs lack adequate resources in starting new businesses. Three findings in particular are important to this study. They are:

1. women are inadequately prepared for business ownership, lacking business skills and/or training in their occupational fields (Bender 1980; Bowen and Hisrich 1986; Hisrich 1989; Watkins and Watkins 1983);
2. women lack significant financial start-up capital and access to credit, limiting the scale at which they start and operate their businesses (Bowen and Hisrich 1986; Hisrich and O'Brien 1981; Humphreys and McClung 1981); and
3. women lack access to white male business networks through which entrepreneurs receive business information and referrals (Aldrich 1989; Aldrich, Reese, and Dubini 1989; Aldrich and Sakano 1995; Bowen and Hisrich 1986; Loscocco and Robinson 1991).

Further, these studies find that inadequate training and limited access to male business networks contributes to women's lack of access to commercial financing, indicating a connection between skills, financing, and network opportunities.

These resources—human resources, financial resources, and business and social networks—play a vital role in starting a business. Yet existing studies fail to examine in detail what resources women *do* have in starting their businesses. Lacking formal business ties, women might rely on less formal social ties for information and referrals. Unable to obtain commercial funding, they might tap personal or family sources of financing. Existing studies shed little light on differences between black and white women's access to conventional resources, nor do they explore differences in black and white women's alternative sources of information and referrals, skill-building strategies, and financing.

A fourth generalization from the entrepreneurial literature is that women's business goals are frequently tied to non-economic personal goals. This is important to this study in that women's intentions and goals for their businesses can affect the levels of social, human, and financial resources they bring to business start-up. A woman starting a home-based business to combine economic and domestic responsibilities might finance her venture with a smaller loan, particularly if she wanted to limit the size of her business. Likewise, the woman who is pushed into entrepreneurship during a recession, never intending to own a business, might be prepared with different skills than the woman who intentionally starts a business to practice her chosen trade.

In addressing these issues, I seek to determine women's motives and goals in business ownership, the circumstances surrounding the start-up of their businesses, and how these motives, goals, and circumstances affect the mobilization of education, training, and financial resources for their businesses. I compare the experiences of African American and European American women, and of women living in different sizes of communities. I also seek to examine women's business ownership experiences based not solely on economic action but on a larger web of social affiliation in which women business owners are embedded. I illuminate previously "invisible," personal-life connections and resources, and seek to accurately portray women's business ownership experiences without abstracting their economic lives from their personal lives. By examining differences among women, I develop an understanding of how criteria such as race, age, and locale affect entrepreneurial activities and thereby avoid using white women's experiences as the norm for all women's entrepreneurial pursuits.

STUDY FORMAT AND DATA ANALYSIS

Data for this study can be examined several ways. First, differences by demographic characteristics of the business owners, such as race, locale, age, and other characteristics, can be identified. These differences can indicate variations in opportunities and environments experienced by women of different racial backgrounds or ages, or by women who start and operate businesses in different sized locales. Second, women business owners may be grouped into categories based on similar experiences or motivations for business that owners encounter regardless of demographic differences. Examination of women's experiences based on these categories of similarity provides information about women's common experiences and does not necessarily take into account racial or other demographic differences. Differences in how women gain human and financial resources for business ownership can be explored according to factors of commonality across race, age, or other demographic characteristics. A black woman and a white woman whose business service jobs were restructured might have more resources in common than the same black woman might have with a black hair stylist.

A third step in examining the data is to combine these two perspectives by identifying demographic differences and similarities *within* the grouped categories. I have organized this study to include all three of these perspectives in examining the data. First, I included variations in race, locale, and (to a lesser extent) age as important demographic differences in my sample. Then I looked for patterns of similarity based on women's reasons and motivations for business start-up. I wanted to discover if, regardless of differences in opportunity based on demographic characteristics, some women had similar experiences in starting their businesses, and whether women garnered resources differently according to motivations for business (i.e., based on the categories of similarity).

The women in the study fell into two general groupings. One group consisted of women who had an internal drive or motivation to start a business. For the most part, intrinsic motivations pulled them towards entrepreneurship. Sometimes their aspirations focused on a particular trade or career, but other times it was focused simply on business ownership. Many of these women had planned their education, training, and/or work experiences to set them on a path towards business ownership. Other women, in contrast, had an external drive or motivation to start a business. They had been pushed or pulled out of their positions in the paid labor force by external circumstances or persuasion, and they had not planned initially to have a business. For whatever reasons, they had decided to start a business rather than search for a new job. These two groups were differentiated still further based on factors such as prior business experience, training in a particular trade or profession, the need for supplemental retirement income, or a calling to fill a community need.

I found that black and white women did have some similar experiences within subgroups, and their experiences and efforts to mobilize resources differed somewhat between the motivational sub-groupings. Even so, differences occurred within and across the sub-groups to indicate that race and locale continued to be important factors affecting women's resources and motivations for business ownership. Women of different race and social class backgrounds tended to be unevenly distributed across these subgroups. For instance, most of the women pursuing trades were black, while two thirds of the professionals were white. Only urban black women pursued professions; black women in rural areas largely pursued personal service occupations, reflecting limited occupational opportunities available to them. Greater access to occupations did not always indicate greater advantage, however. White women, with greater occupational opportunities across all locations, experienced effects of down-sizing and restructuring in urban, small city, and rural locales, while only urban black women, with similar access to a wide variety of occupations, experienced these same disadvantages.

Differences in race occurred among older owners. While older black women had worked full time all their lives, older white women had taken time off to raise families. These women had different goals for starting businesses later in life, and they had accumulated different resources for start-up. Middle-aged and older black women also demonstrated a strong commitment to uplifting the race by using businesses to provide their communities with basic survival and services such as education-oriented childcare, elder care, and job opportunities for youth and single mothers. Some white women demonstrated a similar commitment to helping other women, but used their businesses to provide economic, networking, and spiritual support.

By organizing and examining the data this way, I was able to combine comparisons based on similarities with analysis of differences based on race and locale that persisted across sub-groups of similarity. This pattern of analysis provides a picture of how far black women entrepreneurs have come in gaining parity with white women entrepreneurs and areas where more work is needed. Lack of educational and career opportunities clearly affects black women's business opportunities in rural areas, yet being African American has both positive and negative effects. Black women in small and larger cities have access to minority loan programs and minority advocacy organizations that are unavailable to white women in the same areas. Black women still encounter obstacles to commercial financing, however, when they challenge white-defined boundaries of appropriate behaviors for their racial group, especially in rural areas. Even so, some rural black women in this study were able to obtain small loans more easily then their urban counterparts by building reliable reputations and business relationships with local bankers and opening businesses that did not threaten existing white businesses. This detailed view of black and white women's experiences illuminates the complexity of their entrepreneurial motives and strategies as they encounter existing barriers and available opportunities.

Definitions of Major Terms and Concepts

Small business was defined using the Small Business Administration's definition as being firms with fewer than 500 employees, including workers at all establishment locations. Only a few of the businesses in the study, however, had more than 10 employees.

Businesses were defined as *woman-owned* if one or more women owned 51 percent or more of the business. For this study, I attempted to include only women who 1) started their businesses themselves; 2) operated their businesses themselves; 3) worked full time in their businesses; and 4) received the bulk of their income from their businesses. These factors were not always possible to determine before each interview. While most of the women fit these definitions, there were a few exceptions. One of the rural white women bought an existing restaurant rather than started her own. Some of the women, particularly rural African Americans, worked only part time or had another source of income in addition to their business income.

For the purposes of this study, I use *partner* to mean a woman's business partner, and the term *spouse* or *companion* to mean a married or unmarried romantic partner. When a woman had both a "partner" and a "companion," I use the more specific term *business partner* for the sake of clarity.[7]

I use the terms *capital* and *resources* interchangeably throughout this work. I define *social capital resources* as the relationships with individuals, groups, or organizations through which women entrepreneurs gain help, information, skills, knowledge, referrals, and money to start and operate their businesses. I define *human capital resources* as women's formal education and training; their job training and experience; and any other informal knowledge, training, or skills they have gained that help them start and operate their businesses. I expand the traditional definition of *financial capital resources* to include a broad array of monetary and non-monetary resources women use to finance their businesses. Traditional monetary forms of financial capital include commercial sources, such as bank loans, lines of credit, etc.; and non-commercial (or personal/private) sources, such as personal and family savings, investments, pension funds, personal loans from a friend or family member, etc. To this I add non-traditional, or alternative, finance sources. These might include donated equipment, supplies, rents, or labor; trades; in-kind services from kin and family; and other informal, cost-saving measures or exchanges that reduce women's need for monetary resources.

Entrepreneurship is different from paid employment in that two skill sets rather than one are needed to operate a business. While employees sell occupational *or* management skills, business owners need both. Skills associated with production of a good or service must be combined with knowledge of business operations to successfully operate a business. Research on women entrepreneurs' human capital must include an examination of both these aspects of women's training and experience. In discussing women's human resource, I distinguish between these two skill sets and describe them as 1) *occupational skills*; and 2) *business skills, business management skills*, or *financial management* skills. Occupational skills include all training and experience related to the product or service the entrepreneur is selling. Business or financial management skills include training and experience related to a range of business operations, including but not limited to accounting, tax preparation, office and personnel management, and payroll.

Organization of Chapters

In Chapter 2, I review theoretical and empirical literature on entrepreneurship, and applications of these perspectives to issues of gender and race. In Chapter 3, I review and synthesize the multi-disciplinary literature on women-owned businesses. In Chapter 4, I review the research design and methods used in the study. In Chapters 5 through 9, I report the results of the study. Chapter 5 discusses circumstances surrounding start-up and women's goals and motivations in business. In Chapter 6, I discuss women's human capital resources. In Chapter 7, I discuss women's financial capital resources. In Chapters 8 and 9, I examine how women's social resources aided them in building human and financial capital.

These chapters (5 through 9) examine processes of resource accumulation and mobilization. Because of the diverse and complex nature of the social networks women draw upon in starting their businesses, I do not attempt a separate analysis of social capital. Rather, I examine how social capital affects, and is affected by, accumulation and mobilization of human capital and financial capital. Chapter 10 considers the implications of my analysis for theoretical understanding of women's small business establishment and suggests avenues for further research. Finally, I consider the implications of the study for policies aimed at enhancing entrepreneurial activities for women of all racial backgrounds.

All figures and tables are in Appendix A. Figure 1 is the only figure in the study, and I refer to it in several chapters. Table 1 includes a list of owners, their businesses, and owner and business characteristics. Table 2 includes a list of owners and their client bases. I refer to these tables throughout the study. All other tables are numbered by chapter and sequence within the chapter, for example Tables 3.1, 3.2, and 3.3 refer to tables referenced in Chapter 3. Appendix B contains copies of the consent form, verbal interview questionnaire, and mailback survey form used to collect data for the study.

NOTES

[1] Light and Rosenstein (1995) distinguish between "resource disadvantage" and "labor market disadvantage," saying of the first that members of certain groups, such as blacks, enter the labor market with fewer resources than other group members because of past inequalities (i.e., slavery). Labor market disadvantage "arises when groups receive below-expected returns on their human capital for reasons unrelated to productivity" (p.154). The authors note that the two forms of disadvantage are often linked, as ". . . today's resource disadvantage can reflect yesterday's labor market disadvantage" (p. 154).

[2] See "Study Format" section at the end of this chapter for definitions of terms and concepts.

[3] Two papers based on data for the rural and small city African American women have been presented at professional meetings. The first, entitled "The Importance of Place in Motivations and Options of African American Small Business Owners," was presented at the 1998 Southeastern Women's Studies Association meeting in Florida. The second, entitled "Building from Kin and Community: Business Start-up Strategies of Rural African American Women," was presented at the 1998 annual meeting of the American Sociological Association in San Francisco, California. Both papers were co-authored by Dr. Linda Grant. A paper based on data from the first 15 cases, including black and white women from the small city, was presented at the 1996 annual meeting of the Southern Sociological Society in Richmond, Virginia. It was entitled "Networks and Money: How Women Finance Small Businesses" and was sole-authored by myself.

[4] During that time, however, according to Blackford (1991:xiii), "While their relative share of America's industrial output declined, small businesses continued to grow in absolute numbers, even in manufacturing."

[5] According to labor market theorists (for example, Saint-Paul 1996), the U.S. economy is bifurcated into two "economies," the primary economy and the secondary economy. These are the twin legs upon which the dual economy stands. The primary economy consists of core jobs and industries that are essential to the society and/or economic system in which it rests. These jobs usually pay high salaries, carry prestige and career mobility potential, and are dominated by white men. The secondary economy consists of jobs and industries that produce non-essential goods and/or services in support of the primary economy. Women and minorities frequently fill these jobs which are typically low-paying retail and service positions with little potential for advancement.

[6] As can be seen later in the study, potential markets may affect the amount of capital obtained by the business owner and may be affected by the type and amount of skill the owner maintains.

[7] In a few cases, women had business partners who were also their husbands or companions. In this case, I clearly state that the two different relationships are with a single person.

CHAPTER 2

Society and the Economic Actor
Theories of Women's Labor Market Involvement

Much of the scholarly literature on entrepreneurship has been developed by economists and those in the fields of public policy or business management (for instance, see Birch 1979; Lenzi 1996; Malizia 1996; Miller 1990; Ross and Friedman 1990). These scholars use mainstream economic theories to examine business survival or failure, business growth, and job creation. Sociologists have been less likely to study entrepreneurship. When doing so, they focus primarily on micro-level social or cultural characteristics of the individual entrepreneur that motivate him or her to start a business and become successful (i.e., Bender 1980; De-Carlo and Lyons 1979; Goffee and Scase 1985; Humphreys and Mc-Clung 1981). Alternately, they focus on macro-structural factors affecting small firm survival and growth, sometimes with an emphasis on high growth, or very successful firms (i.e., Eisinger 1988; Harrison 1994; Piore and Sabel 1984).

Rational choice theory (RC) has been used extensively in economic and business management literature to explain entrepreneurial choices for profit-maximization, with economic growth the logical and desired outcome (Coleman 1994). When applied to women's entrepreneurial choices, it has been used, implicitly or explicitly, in the same manner that it is applied to male-owned businesses: as an explanation of growth, or, more frequently for women, lack of growth. A major focus has been on how women's non-economic life circumstances, motives, and goals affect the choices women make for their businesses. The most common theme suggests that women are pulled away from entrepreneurship by domestic responsibilities and must limit the size of their businesses to fulfill family obligations (i.e., Goffee and Scase 1985).

While this is true in some cases, many women no longer fit this nuclear family stereotype. Women are working in jobs in the paid labor market in larger numbers than ever before. They enter business ownership from positions in the paid labor force (whether married and/or with children or not) and for a variety of reasons. Therefore, traditional economic theory is inadequate to explain all women's entrepreneurial activities.

RC theory has not been used to examine women's resources and their resource mobilization processes when starting businesses. With the tremendous increase in women's business ownership that has occurred in the last two decades, it becomes imperative to examine both formal and informal resources that are available to women starting new businesses. To do so requires a broad examination of women who own many types of businesses and who are in many different life situations. While most studies focus on white middle class women owners, inclusion of black women allows a better assessment of what resources are available to women based on gender and what resources are available to women based on racial ties. It also provides a baseline of non-white women's entrepreneurial activities, which have rarely been researched by scholars in any field.

Recent revisions of traditional economic theories proposed by sociologists, African American, and feminist scholars provide frameworks better suited to the analysis of women's entrepreneurial choices and their initial access to, and mobilization of, resources. These frameworks expose structural constraints encountered by minorities and women when starting their businesses that are not necessarily a consideration for white male entrepreneurs. They also illuminate alternative resources available to women and minorities that counteract structural disadvantages in society. Below, I review traditional RC economic theories and discuss their contributions and limitations for the current work.

DEVELOPMENT OF RATIONAL CHOICE THEORY

Classic theories of economic action examine the degree to which society influences the economic actor. Most economists agree with the sociological view that economic behavior in pre-industrial societies (and to an extent in current tribal societies) was mediated by the social relationships and cultures in which individuals were embedded. These forces determined to a large degree their economic actions and transactions. In contrast, modern societies are seen as having removed economic activity from daily life. People are assumed to make economic decisions independently from their family and social relationships and instead base their actions on what economists have labeled "rational choice" (Coleman 1994).

Rational choice (RC) is the theoretical perspective most commonly applied to entrepreneurial involvement. Increasingly, social scientists who study economic action have been stretching the boundaries of classical economic theory in ways that redefine this "rational choice" model upon which much of traditional economic discourse rests. Whereas neoclassical theory suggests that individuals act purely out of self interest to maximize personal financial gain, even economists who support this perspective realize that more than the bottom line is involved in individuals' economic choices. Lack of information, uncertainty about the future, and change in plans and desires all contribute to making "rational choice" actions of the "Rational Economic Man" seem not so rational. As Folbre (1994:20) writes,

> In this new world, inhabited by Imperfectly Rational Somewhat Economic Persons, or IRSEPs, the future is uncertain. Information is costly. Even when it can easily be acquired, it takes time to process and analyze. Sometimes there is little basis for rational assessment of the possibilities. Habit, tradition, and cultural stereotypes provide individuals with shortcuts. The actual practice of decision-making doesn't always conform to the theory of rational behavior.

Early Movements to Broaden Traditional Economic Theory

In their attempts to better explain economic action and broaden the concept of rationality to include non-economic motives, scholars have made several theoretical expansions of the rational choice model. Macro-structural factors such as economic circumstances, political climates, and labor market conditions must be considered in explanations of economic choice and action. Likewise, micro-structural considerations can affect choice and action: education, training, and experience vary from one individual to the next, limiting or expanding access to information, resources, and power. Thus, those who are in structural positions to implement economically efficient solutions might not have the money, information, labor, or the political backing to do so. Lastly, personal and societal attitudes, norms, and preferences might affect individual action.

Gender norms have long constrained women in their occupational and employment choices, and there is evidence that these constraints still operate, despite women's significant inroads into industries and occupations traditionally filled by men (Reskin and Roos 1990).

Economists' Theories of Rational Economic Action. One of the first economists to expand rational choice theory to include factors and behaviors previously considered non-economic, Becker moved economic theory from the marketplace into the arena of family relations and personal preferences. In doing so, he expanded economic theory to encompass productive behavior in the home (Becker 1965; Michael and Becker 1973); education as an investment in self (Becker 1964, 1975, 1993 editions); marriage and children as investment and consumer choices (Becker 1960; Becker 1981, 1991 editions; Becker and Lewis 1973; Becker and Tomes 1976); and discrimination as an economically measurable preference of employers (Becker 1957, 1971 editions).

While Becker expanded the range of factors and behaviors that could be theoretically included in an economic model, his view was that of an economist trying to fit broader social life into economic boxes to create models economists could use in cost analyses of individual behaviors. According to his view, all social activity could be explained as maximization of profit. Social activities and personal choices that did not directly produce or increase resources could still be viewed as economically rational if they could be shown to *indirectly* produce or increase resources. Thus, a shop floor worker who took night classes in management to qualify for a better job would be acting rationally by spending money on the class because doing so would eventually lead to greater earnings.

This view does not leave room for truly non-economic behaviors, such as those based on tradition, culture, emotion, or other socially constructed systems of action that may result in reduction of resources, or in economic disincentives.[1] It only begins to take into account barriers to economic action based on irrational preferences such as discrimination, and then only describes the point of view of the actor who discriminates. Still, Becker's consideration of activities outside the marketplace as being rationally and economically based has enabled scholars to expand rational choice theory to include other non-economic factors. His view on human capital as an investment in self provides an important vantage point from which to examine the development of women's (and men's) skills and knowledge as resources for starting and operating their businesses.

More Recent Developments in Economic Theory

More recent movements to expand economic theory have come from sociologists studying "social capital" and "social embeddedness." A closely related theory, social embeddedness places the actor within the context of a "web" of social relations. Social capital describes the structure of those relations and conceptualizes the activity that passes through that structure as a resource.

Social Embeddedness Theory. Moving away from Becker's tendency to put a price on all social activities, Granovetter (1973; 1974, 1995 editions; 1982; 1992) revived the concept of social embeddedness and placed economic life in a less prominent position, as embedded in social life. Rejecting both economic and sociological positions,[2] he suggested that the economic actor is embedded in a network of social relations that shifts and changes, and that can significantly affect an individual's choices and actions.

In a landmark work, Granovetter (1974, 1995 editions; see also 1973) found labor market mobility to depend largely upon information passed through social contacts. He found that the majority of individuals moving from one job to another obtained information about the new position from personal contacts. Without the dissemination of this information, personal characteristics of individuals did little to explain success in job placement. Thus, the social networks in which individuals are "embedded" facilitate career mobility.

Particular kinds of network ties provided greater access to significant job information than other ties. Granovetter distinguished between "weak" ties (ties to acquaintances outside one's immediate circle of family and friends); and "strong" ties (ties with family, friends, and well-known coworkers). Strong tie connections create tight-knit groups of people who know each other well, while weak ties connect individuals from different groups to those in other groups and networks. Densely knit, strong tie groups, Granovetter theorized, were likely to share information within the group. These ties provided individual group members little information they would not already know, or could not get elsewhere within the group. Weak ties, however, were more likely to provide new information from more distant sources. When weak ties were maintained to a group with more resources (knowledge, wealth, information, class standing, etc.), valuable information could be passed through the weak tie from the relatively more resource-rich group member to the resource-poor group member. Granovetter (1982; see also Lin 1982) defined these as "bridging weak ties."

Although Granovetter included only men in his sample and studied how network ties aid job seekers, social embeddedness theory is an important perspective for understanding women's entrepreneurial activities. Social contacts often aid the owner with physical set-up, monetary and non-monetary resources, information, and referrals. Personal relationships, particularly with family members, may influence and be influenced by the new owner's decisions and actions in business start-up. Women with strong ties to male executives would have access to business information and advice not available to those without such ties. Similarly, women with strong community ties might call on community members for aid in setting up businesses. These strong ties also bridge the gap between women and resources and might be considered "bridging strong ties" for women. Personal relationships, however, can also constrain or limit business activities. Women devoting their attention to new businesses might be less available to their families than are women employed by someone else. Conversely, women might choose to open certain businesses with flexible time schedules so that they *can* spend more time with their families.

Granovetter's strong family and friendship ties and his weak business ties generally correspond to private and public spheres of life, as suggested by Daniels' (1988) work on women's "invisible careers" in the voluntary sector. According to Daniels, women make important contributions to public life by organizing and fund raising in cultural, political, health, and educational arenas while remaining largely unrecognized for their efforts. Despite progress into public life, this failure to recognize women's work may continue to occur because "women still belong mainly to that world of support, privacy, and invisibility that makes the frontstage of public affairs possible for men" (Daniels 1988:271). An important finding in Daniels' work is that women's public voluntary efforts are largely achieved through activities and influence in the private arena. This has important implications for the current study. It suggests that women have personal contacts with publicly recognized individuals. They utilize strong family and social friendship ties to public figures to accomplish tasks contributing to their public voluntary activities. Rather than seek out strangers to get the job done, they rely on those they know personally for referrals and contributions. Although the women in Daniels' study were almost all white and from upper and upper-middle class backgrounds, their experiences and strategies can be applied to women of other class, racial, and ethnic backgrounds. If actors are embedded in social networks, as Granovetter suggests, women entrepreneurs are likely to first seek aid, information, and resources through immediately available family and friendship contacts, moving to less well-known sources only when closer ties fail to yield what is needed. Although women from different backgrounds might have fewer family ties to public figures than women in Daniels' study, they might have some, and they are just as likely to have friends and family members who work in occupations with relevant knowledge to aid them in business start-up.

Knowledge of public figures in private life leads to a blurring of the boundaries between public and private arenas. Actors who depend on privately known individuals for public resources are less likely to keep those boundaries in sharp focus. Women already bridge the gap between their children and families in the private sphere and husbands' worlds of work in the public sphere. They are likely to see all relationships—to children, to husbands, to friends and neighbors, to husbands' coworkers, to public figures (who, after all, have families of their own)—as equally important. Women's tendencies to blur the boundaries between public and private spheres and view the world instead as a web of non-hierarchical, contextual relationships in which they are a single node has been noted by other authors (i.e., Cheney 1987; Gilligan 1982; Warren 1987, 1990). While some women may be more comfortable acting in the private sphere, as did several women in Daniels' (1988) study, their fears may directly correspond to how public the arena is in which they must act, and the meaning of "public" and "private" may vary depending on context or locale. In rural areas, public life is more tightly tied to private relationships. At the same time, separation of racial groups may result in different understandings by race. For blacks, "public life" may mean "white life," while the entire black community may constitute an extended private sphere. Rural whites may hold a ringside seat to the public life of the town. In larger cities, private life may be more narrowly defined as immediate family and friends, and the public arena may remain at a greater distance, making access more difficult.

Social Capital Theory. The term "social capital" was coined by Loury (1977, 1987) and popularized further by Coleman (1988, 1990). A theory positing multiple levels of social relationships, Coleman (1988:S98) defined social capital "by its function." He wrote,

> It is not a single entity but a variety of different entities, with two elements in common: they all consist of some aspect of social structures,

and they facilitate certain actions of actors—whether persons or corporate actors—within the structure. Social capital comes about through
changes in the relations among persons that facilitate action.

Social capital may take different forms, including the exchange of
services, the flow of information, or a system of norms affecting individuals' behavior, causing them to forego self-interest and act in the interest
of others or of the collective. Social capital facilitates some actions but
constrains others (see Coleman 1988; 1990; Duncan 1996; Flora and
Flora 1993; McLanahan and Sandefur 1994; Putnam 1993a, 1993b). Social networks form one aspect of social structure through which social
capital may flow. Existing organizations form another dimension. Created for one purpose, they can be used for another purpose, providing a
source of social capital in the process. For example, advocacy organizations that help women prepare loan applications might also become conduits for locating clients.

One of the properties of social organization that can create social
capital in a group or community is the existence of multiplex relationships between two individuals (Coleman 1988; see also Gluckman
1967). Multiplex relationships occur when individuals are linked by and
through more than one relationship. For instance, the business owner
who hires her neighbor becomes not only a friend but also an employer,
while the neighbor becomes an employee as well as a neighbor. If the
two belong to the same church or civic group, a third relationship exists
between them, and so on. Multiplex relationships, more so than simplex
relationships (persons linked by only one relationship), have the potential to create social capital by facilitating information flows; for instance,
passing on information about the business while at church. They also
allow obligations incurred in the context of one relationship to be repaid
in another. The employee who receives a favor, as a neighbor, from the
business owner may be called upon to work harder than another employee whose relationship with the business owner did not include other
ties. Multiplex relationships are likely to occur in Granovetter's strong
tie groups.

Business Opportunities and Social Relationships. General studies of women's networks suggest that women have significantly smaller,
mostly kin-based, primarily female social networks, while men maintain
contact with other men through formal and informal business ties (Fischer
and Oliker 1983). Extending Granovetter's (1973) theory of "weak ties"

into the sphere of business ownership, these "weaker" ties with friends and acquaintances afford men more diverse business-related contacts. Women who lack as many "weak" ties to men in the economic sphere are disadvantaged when seeking business opportunities and financing. With primarily "strong" ties to relatives and close female friends, women have less access to a broader range of indirect ties, since most of their close-knit contacts know each other and have fewer reference contacts outside the strongly bonded group (see Granovetter 1982).

"Strong" ties, however, can become resources that benefit the entrepreneur. As mentioned above, women's strong family ties to men in business or the public sphere might yield important aid in starting businesses. Further, social capital and social embeddedness are viewed differently in black communities than in white communities. Boorman (1975) theorized that if unemployment is low in a group (such as whites), group members will invest their time in weak ties involving mostly non-kin others. When unemployment is high in a group (such as African Americans), group members will invest in strong relationships for mutual support and survival. Groups with above-average unemployment, such as the young, the poor, the less educated, African American, and other minority groups, rely on strong ties for survival. Extending this view to business ownership, the strong ties of the African American community might reflect still-important investments in survival and avenues through which cost saving, volunteer labor might aid the entrepreneur in business start-up. Yet it may also signal an inability on the part of African Americans to connect with and benefit from weak ties to others outside their communities. Without such connections, African American women business owners are limited in gaining skills and information needed to operate their businesses.

Research shows that African American women are frequently embedded in strong ties to a black community that provides a market for their products. White women, often less focused on a particular group as a market, provide services "to everyone." Black women often exchange in-kind services such as child care, while white women pay for daycare. Black women may have strong, work-involved black role models to follow, and, because of their community ties, may follow a cultural ethic of "giving back" to the community (Higginbotham and Weber 1992).

While these are positive instances of social capital within the African American community, black women may lack social capital in other respects. Especially when they live in rural areas, African American women might have minimal experience working with whites. As a result, they may know little about how to deal with white customers or suppliers. This is an impediment if the owner wishes to expand her customer base to include white clients. Information about opportunities and business conditions might flow more freely through the strong ties of an African American community. But at the same time, such information might be limited by those same strong ties, ties that enclose the community and discourage weak ties to the "outside" white community. Without a flow of new information through weak ties, community members have little chance of hearing about potentially lucrative business opportunities (Granovetter 1982).

Social Capital and the Creation of Human Capital. Social capital has been found to influence economic resources through education (Coleman 1988). By attending school and earning degrees, individuals invest in themselves and build "human capital" (Becker 1964, 1975, 1993 editions). Investment in human capital increases productivity and earnings by increasing skills, knowledge, and problem solving abilities.[3] Social capital, defined as "the set of resources that inhere in family relations and community social organization and that are useful for the cognitive or social development of a child or young person" (Coleman 1990:300), can be an important resource in building human capital. Within the family, the level of human capital possessed by parents and other close relatives is important in the creation of human capital in children. However, if parents' educational skills and resources are used primarily outside the family, at work, and are not shared with children in the family, the potential support for children's education goes unrealized.

Human Capital: Education, Training, and Job Experience. Becker (1964, 1975, 1993 editions) differentiated between formal educational training and on-the-job training and introduced the notion that human capital is inseparable from the individual. This becomes important in job training, where job skills can be broken down into general and specific training. Becker theorized that general training provides skills that can be transferred across a range of jobs.[4] Gaining general business skills, as well as occupational skills, becomes important to the business owner to be able to transfer as much knowledge as possible from school and job settings to the operation of her business.

Job Training. In addition to formal education, job training is an important form of human capital. Research suggests that a significant amount of training takes place on-the-job (Thurow 1972). Therefore, access to jobs that provide training in occupation and/or business-related skills becomes important for the aspiring entrepreneur. Formal educational training is one means to gain these skills, especially in highly technical trades and professions. But to gain experience, future business owners may also need to spend time in a work setting. Formal education and degrees may serve as credentials to obtain placement in important job positions, giving the entrepreneur access to further on-the-job training.[5]

Human Capital and Access to Financial Capital. Not only does human capital provide both occupational and business skills with which to operate the business, but it also has the potential to influence financing. It might affect whether a prospective business owner receives a loan and the size of the loan. In his examination of loans to minority entrepreneurs, Bates (1993b: 55) found that "entrepreneurs with college educations have the greatest access to traditional financial capital sources such as commercial banks." In addition, those would-be entrepreneurs with more education are more likely to have built up significant wealth holdings from previous employment and investments, making them more desirable as loan clients than those who have not. Receiving larger loans, more educated entrepreneurs have a better chance at success than those with smaller loans or those with no loans[6] (see also Bates 1993a).

Contributions and Limitations of Mainstream Economic Theory

Theories of social and human capital provide a needed backdrop in assessing background characteristics influencing women's decisions to start a business. Women who have more educational training and work experience related to their businesses stand a better chance of obtaining commercial loans for start-up than those with less education and experience (Bates 1993a). Likewise, women who have access to (and who use) organizations set up to help owners start businesses may be more likely to succeed than women without such access.

Becker, Coleman, and Granovetter contribute to a departure from purely economic reasoning, but do not specifically address differences in women's experiences in their analyses. Race and gender issues are considered only tangentially in these theories. Coleman and Granovetter allow room for structural inequalities potentially affecting social networks and leading to differential opportunities based on gender and race, but do little to explore the ramifications of such inequalities.

The major contributions of these theorists lie in their depictions of how social structure facilitates individual action. In a network theory of individual outcomes, Granovetter's actors find jobs through the structure of social networks. Applying this theory to business owners, entrepreneurs would find business opportunities through a similar network structure. Using Coleman's theory of social capital, children learn more from parents who have higher and/or better educations. They learn more when they live in communities with more advanced social organization and infrastructure (good schools, community cultural activities, etc.). Again, applying social capital theory to business ownership, women who start businesses in urban settings benefit from membership in social and business organizations not available to their counterparts in rural areas. Even Becker, intent on measuring individual choice and action outside the marketplace, examines how the individual invests time in human capital (available through existing social structure) to increase personal income. Thus, women seek business and management training in order to make their businesses more efficient and productive. They reap the benefits of their new knowledge when it is applied in their businesses.

A FEMINIST CRITIQUE OF RATIONAL CHOICE THEORY

While the male theorists discussed above examined how social structures facilitate individual action, their theories have only limited applicability to non-white, non-male actors. Because of structural and normative barriers, disadvantaged groups face roadblocks to action not usually encountered by white, middle-class men. Therefore, I draw upon the works of two feminist scholars, Gerson (1985) and Folbre (1994), to elaborate a framework for understanding women's entrepreneurial activities. These theorists broaden the discourse on rational economic choice to include African American and European American women's experiences as economic actors. They also provide a more detailed critique of the structural constraints that affect women as a group.

Agency and Choice: Situation-Based Interests

In her study of women's decisions concerning work and family, Gerson (1985) presents a dynamic theory of structured choice in which women's choices

> develop out of a negotiated process whereby they confront and respond
> to constraints and opportunities, often unanticipated, encountered over
> the course of their lives. The process is dynamic, not fixed. It depends

on how women define and perceive their situations as well as on the objective circumstances that structure these perceptions. Because the structural arrangements that channel women's motivations, perceptions, and behavior are ambiguous and contradictory, decision making involves a difficult struggle to define and act on situational interests (Gerson 1985:213).

Like Granovetter, Gerson has moved away from Parsons' theories of childhood socialization, considering them incomplete. Rather, she uses them as a base to develop an expanded theory of individual agency whereby women make choices amid shifting structural constraints and opportunities; re-evaluate intentions and goals based on current "situational interests"; and create unique life paths through a series of choices and life stages. This theory of agency is similar to Glade's (1967) approach to entrepreneurial action based on micro-level analysis of situational opportunity structures that change over time. Glade's actors "recognize the new opportunities and take advantage of them without losing them to others" (Martinelli 1994:486). Like the male theorists discussed above, however, Glade's primary focus was on opportunity and competition. Barriers existed only as "structural or environmental features" that took the form of "conditions defining the potential opportunity structures (Glade 1967:250). He recognized that a structure of differential advantage existed, making some actors more able and likely to recognize and take advantage of existing opportunities. He used this analysis, however, simply to explain why a specific group (an ethnic minority group, for instance) in one location succeeded in business while the same group in a different environment failed to produce large numbers of successful entrepreneurs. He did not closely examine specific barriers and opportunities affecting individual entrepreneurs' access to resources, nor did he address personal preferences as influences on economic actors.

The choices women make over time are both toward opportunities and preferences and away from barriers and dislikes, and themselves become structural factors from which future choices are made. The press of discrimination and of gender norms defining more stringent family obligations for women and men may make women's choices qualitatively different, and more constrained, than men's. A woman's choice may not coincide with her preferences; it may simply be the best she can do under the circumstances. Still, choices are a key part of the process that structures the direction a woman will take, the arena in which she will operate, and the relationships she will develop.

Gerson finds that not all women end up doing what they thought they might or wanted to do in their lives. For some women, barriers and opportunities emerge that are unrelated to their original life goals and that take them places they never thought they wanted to go. Others find that their preferences change once their goals are achieved. They either move on from their original life plan to form and achieve new goals, or remain resigned or ambivalent within their original plan. Still other women achieve their original goals and are happy to remain on life paths they had laid out for themselves in their youth.

Like the women in Gerson's study who ended up in particular employment sites, women in this study came to business ownership from different paths. Some "always wanted" their own business, while others pursued a career, a trade, or a line of work that led them to own a business as personal and economic circumstances changed. Others had not planned to own a business but were pushed towards ownership through job loss, burn-out, restructuring, or other mid-life reassessments or crises. These women's choices for business ownership were not motivated solely by the lure of economic gain, but stemmed from varying situational factors. Like those in Gerson's study, not all the women in this study intended to become business owners, and some would choose employment over business ownership if that option were available. Still, all the women made decisions based on personal preferences given the options available at the time.

Collective Interests and Action Based on Group Membership

Moving beyond single-group identification, Folbre (1994), a feminist economist, broadens the view of structural opportunity and constraint affecting human economic action by theorizing that multiple group membership and loyalties, such as those based on class, race, and sexual orientation, influence individual women in their economic choices and actions. She develops a complex theory of collective action based upon given and chosen group memberships. Rather than solely claim, as Becker did, that non-market activity can be reduced to economically based rational choice, Folbre recognizes the inherent conflict between women's personal self-interest and their altruistic interests in children and family. She expands the term "rational" to include non-economically based reasoning and, like Gerson, suggests that personal preferences structurally affect action outcomes by channeling individuals toward some choices and away from others throughout the actor's life course. In addition, cultural rules and norms and existing asset distributions define what she calls "boundaries of choice."

According to this theory, those with fewer financial assets may be more limited in their economic choices than those with greater financial assets. Similarly, those women preferring to stay home to raise children may do that if they have financial support to do so. Preferences and existing assets may not always coincide, making both work and child rearing a simultaneous necessity.

Outside the family, Folbre also recognizes that women are born into and become involved with a variety of groups. For instance, actors are born into "given" categories of race or gender, but may choose to move into other groups, such as chosen families or interest groups. They may even move into a lower or higher social class-based group through choices made about education, career goals, or marriage. Folbre includes women's alliances with others along lines of race, class, gender, and other distinguishing characteristics as factors in their negotiation of collective interests, in the choices they make, and in actions taken. Because people belong to more than one group, they occupy more than one position in the structure and can feel pushed and pulled by conflicting interests, loyalties and boundaries. Still, individuals come to identify with other group members, creating "common identities and interests that are conducive to collective action" (Folbre 1994:51). This may be particularly true when a given group, such as a racial minority, faces structural constraints that result in unequal treatment and uneven access to resources or assets, leading ultimately to inequitable outcomes for group members.

Pushes and Pulls: Self-Interest and the Good of Others. Folbre's theory of action based on multiple group membership is consistent with Granovetter's theory of embeddedness, including as it does women's relationships with family and other significant groups. Inherent in Granovetter's concept of strong and weak ties is a conflict between the self-interest and self-promotion pursued through use of weak ties for personal gain, on the one hand, and the more altruistic choice to forego self interest and act in the interest of others, on the other. The normative aspect of Coleman's social capital theory suggests a similar conflict. This conflict poses a particular dilemma for women, who are socialized to put family welfare before personal gain. Both black and white women may face a choice between helping to create family and community social capital through strong ties and pursuing personal gain through weak ties in business.

When women do forego their personal interests to act on behalf of their families, differences may become apparent between black and white women's approaches to normative behavior. When black women act on norms that call for them to forego their own interests to act for the good of others, they do so on behalf of their immediate families, which tend to be based on larger extended kin networks than white women's families. But they may also do so on behalf of their given racial and class-based groups or communities. Thus, black women business owners may consciously serve their communities by hiring and training unwed teen-aged mothers, whose job prospects would otherwise be poor. In doing so, they are acting as what Collins terms "community othermothers," looking out for the welfare of the community's young people (Collins 1991:119-123). Similarly, African American women attorneys may spend their lives working to change institutional stereotypes of the black community and black population. Such strategies maximize a value important in black women's culture and are evident also in civic associations, the ethic of "uplifting the race" (see Collins 1991:147-151; Higginbotham and Weber 1992; Woodard 1997:166-171).

When the business owner pursues individualistic goals, placing more of her time, effort, and resources developing business acquaintance and weak tie relationships, she moves away from her strong tie group, leaving them with fewer resources than they would have if she stayed and invested her time in the group. For the white owner, this may mean less time spent with her family and/or more meals eaten outside the home. She may send her children to daycare or after school programs, and/or hire a maid to clean and cook.[7]

For the African American owner, moving away from strong ties may mean spending less time not only with her family, but also with her community. Since the African American community has collectively fewer educational and financial resources than the European American community, this loss can be significant to the smaller African American community. As black women move up into management and business positions, those around them may respond negatively (Collins 1991:61), or may want a hand up. African American norms and expectations of extended resource sharing across kinship groups may lead either to continued ties and shared responsibilities with less fortunate family and community members, or to alienation from an extended community inclusive of working class members (Blauner 1992; Etter-Lewis 1993; Woodard 1997).

Multiple strong ties, however, also provide a safe, stable web from which the business owner may draw physical aid, economic support, and spiritual nourishment. Disadvantages imposed on blacks via race discrimination by the larger society inspire the growth of group solidarity. Solidarity in turn spurs development of resources unique to the African American community that are made available to community members. The conflict between self-interest and social capital may be minimized by maintaining a balance between strong family and community ties, on the one hand, and business relationships, on the other. African American women interviewed for this study, for example, found ways to "give back" to their communities: by owning businesses that provide uplifting public services (e.g., education-oriented daycare); by providing employment opportunities for at-risk youth or single mothers; or by volunteering for community service projects.

Group Membership and Interlocking Oppression. The pushes and pulls of multi-group membership are also consistent the inter-connectedness of oppression based on race, class, and gender, as examined by feminist, African American, and black feminist scholars (see Andersen and Collins 1992; Brewer 1988; Collins 1986: Davis 1981; Higginbotham 1983; Mullings, 1986). Higginbotham (1991:226) identifies a common base to these (and other) "axes of oppression," that of "social relations of domination." While each base of oppression (whether race, gender, class, or other disadvantaged statuses) is significantly different from the others, they all share a common ideological feature: the acceptance of hierarchical thinking paired with valuation based on dualities (see Warren 1987). Thus, in the ideology of dominance, "good" is better than "bad," "white" is better than "black," "upper" is better than "lower." Those who make up the rules are higher on the hierarchical scale, constituting a group called "us" that is better than, and therefore has the right to dominate, the lower, less powerful group called "them."

Recognizing similarities based on a common ideology of domination does not mean that race, class, and gender oppressions are all alike, nor that women of different racial or age groups experience class oppression in the same way. While racial and class oppressions tend to foster group solidarity, contributing to the creation of concrete communities, gender oppression combines with the structure of nuclear families to create very different outcomes. Women who remain in heterosexual relationships may seek support from other women, but they remain in direct, intimate relationships with members of the dominant group. Furthermore, gender oppression occurs across ethnic, racial, class, age, and most other groups, complicating and obscuring clear-cut instances of oppression based on these other statuses. Only through careful examination of women's individual experiences is it possible to determine the characteristic upon which oppression occurs.[8]

Structures of Opportunity and Constraint

Like Gerson, Folbre includes in her work personal preferences in a context of larger circumstances. Folbre, however, explicitly includes asset distributions, rules, and norms, as well as preferences, in her definition of economic structure. Her actors include groups as well as individuals. Her action sites include families as well as markets, states, and firms. Inclusion of the personal with the public, of ties to given as well as chosen groups, supports a theory of ambivalence and structural constraint that may help explain individual action within the bounds of uneven access to resources based on a race or gender status. Folbre's work is applicable to other minority and/or disadvantaged groups. African American and European American women are simply the populations under study in this work.

Using this framework, one can begin to understand how new business owners may have limited access to financial and/or educational resources as a result of structural constraints related to gender or race. Limited access to capital and production of capital historically has disadvantaged the African American community in comparison to the white community in providing private aid to finance new businesses.[9] African American women starting their businesses usually have fewer personal sources of finance to draw upon than their white counterparts. In turn, limited resources have an impact on women's decisions about starting new businesses. Their families may have little excess income to spare for building capital through investments or for supporting new businesses. Therefore, they may have to seek outside funding, usually from commercial sources. White women, although sometimes also limited in personal financing, might be more able to draw upon aid from family members (Granovetter's strong ties) with investments and high incomes (Bearse 1983; Bradford 1990; Terrell 1971). With greater initial financing, white women may start businesses at a higher level than black women.

To counteract this shortfall in the African American community, efforts have been and are being made in larger metropolitan black communities to build capital and organize support groups for black business start-up and operation (Reynolds 1995; see also Pronet Group, Inc.

1996). African American women in areas where these organizations exist may have greater access to larger amounts of capital than black women in smaller, rural communities.

African American and Black Feminist Theories. The works of African Americans and black feminist scholars have contributed to the discourse surrounding rational economic choice by presenting the African American standpoint. From that standpoint, these theorists critique European American-based theories as incorrectly claiming to represent "everyone." For instance, in the neoclassical economic theories, the self-interested consumer makes profit-maximizing choices. In contrast, black women have historically viewed economic action (or work in the paid labor market) as a task necessary to their family's survival. Profit beyond survival is desirable, but can be a lesser concern. African American women's wages have been viewed historically not only as personal income, but as necessary components of family income when black men's incomes were inadequate to support to their families (Blauner 1992; Collins 1991).[10] African American women historically have done work avoided by whites and black men as menial and undesirable (Dill 1980; 1988; Glenn 1985; Higginbotham 1983; Jones 1985; Rollins 1985; Wallace 1980). From their perspective, work is not necessarily something they wanted to do, but rather as something they had to do (Collins 1991). More so than middle-class white women, some of whom may still see work as a personal economic choice, black women (as well as immigrant and working-class white women) have been taught to expect to work and earn a living throughout their lives (Burlew 1982; Murrell et al. 1991). Thus, when labor markets offer few employment options, African American women may found businesses not just to create employment for themselves but also to employ others in their communities.

As significant contributors to family income, black women's relationships within families may be different from white women's. Historically, West African women in agricultural societies combined family and work responsibilities by carrying their children with them to work, whether in the fields or the marketplace (Sudarkasa 1981). During enslavement, this relationship persisted. In addition, enslaved Africans developed broad, community-based family relations and relied on extended kinship ties to resist separations and the dehumanizing effects of slavery (Gutman 1976; see also Collins 1991). This development of the concept of family that includes extended kin and the broader African American community has enabled black women to rely on social networks of kin relations for exchange of child care and other services, both economic and non-economic (Day 1986; Malson 1983; Martin and Martin 1978; White 1985). It has also allowed them to view motherhood and paid employment as compatible activities that can be undertaken together (Murrell et al. 1991), not necessarily as competing priorities.

As job opportunities have increased for African Americans, a new black middle-class has emerged. These developments have changed the lives of individual women and their relationships within the black community. Black women in management positions, who may themselves have worked their way up from working class origins, may not be completely comfortable managing other workers. Still subordinate to the ownership class, they may be called on to support dominant norms and ideologies when, in fact, they would rather challenge them (Collins 1991). Due to persistent racism, their positions and incomes may not be as secure as those of their white counterparts (Blauner 1992; Pinkney 1984). These women's ambivalence, combined with concerns about job security, may lead them to consider business ownership as a viable alternative to other employment. They face a further choice of serving the African American community or a larger, predominantly white, market.

The Effects of Discrimination on Human and Financial Capital. In what may have been the first attempt to introduce into rational economic choice theory a viable model of the economic affects of personal preferences, Becker introduced the notion of a "psychic cost" to tastes or preferences in an economic model of discrimination (Becker 1957, 1971 editions). He put forth an economic formula designed to measure the cost to production of preferences practiced to benefit (nepotism) or handicap (discrimination) a given group. While this may be considered a "production cost" to the white factory owner, it becomes a "survival cost" to the black worker against whom the white owner discriminates.

> Employers use a range of more or less rational criteria in choosing workers, including individuals' characteristics and the potential cost to the employer of training them.
>
> Because employers rarely have direct and unambiguous evidence of the specific training costs for specific workers, they end up ranking workers according to their background characteristics—age, sex, educational attainment, previous skills, performance on psychological tests, etc. Each of these is used as an indirect measure of the costs necessary to produce some standard of work performance (Thurow 1972:73).

The first to describe this method of job assignment in the labor market as a "job queue," Thurow (1969:48) pointed out that arbitrary preferences such as discrimination against women, blacks, and other minorities can affect the choices employers make in assigning jobs to workers. These assignments in turn can affect the amount and types of training these disadvantaged workers receive on the job (see also Reskin and Roos 1990). Black women, often pushed into lower paying, less technical, and less desirable jobs, receive less on-the-job training than white women. This can leave them less prepared for business ownership than white women, or prepared only for service sector businesses. A wider range of occupational options is available to white women. With less education and training, black women may also have less access to commercial financing.

Contributions from Feminist and African American Theorists

The female and African American theorists broaden the view of how social structure provides both opportunities for, and impediments to, the action of individuals, both as single actors (Gerson) and as members of groups (Folbre). White women business owners with connections to white male business networks can find doors opening to them that others miss. What are viewed as rational economic choices for white men become necessary survival choices for black women. As Collins (1991:45-46) points out, "Black women's work remains a fundamental location where the dialectical relationship of oppression and activism occurs."

Gerson and Folbre, while including women, do not address women's entrepreneurial activities. Gerson's sample is limited primarily to white women with varying class and educational backgrounds. Arguing against explanations based mostly on childhood socialization and role model theories (Granovetter's "over-socialized" theory of action), Gerson suggests an alternative theory of personal outcomes. She asserts that individual aspirations, motivations, and ambivalence interact with, and sometimes overcome, cultural norms and socialization to create life paths that develop over time according to situational changes. She does little to develop an explanatory model of larger structural constraints, suggesting only that they exist and affect women's decision-making process. Folbre provides a model that accommodates structural constraint, differential access, and collective action based on common interests, while maintaining a balance with the personal through inclusion of individual preferences and goals. She provides a framework that can accommodate African Americans as a group. However, like most other economists and sociologists, she does not apply her ideas specifically to business ownership and the mobilization of resources to start businesses by women of different races.

African American and black feminist theorists provide needed insight into the experiences of African Americans, particularly African American women. This perspective of black women's standpoint is needed to expand a theory of rational choice as applied to business start-up and resource mobilization. However, many of these theorists have not applied their perspectives to business owners. Bates' research on black-owned businesses touches on black women's entrepreneurial experiences but provides no extended analysis. Instead, he groups black women with black men or focuses exclusively on black men. Careful analysis of black women's entrepreneurial activities and comparison of their activities with those of white women is needed.

DEALING WITH DISADVANTAGE: DRAWING ON "INVISIBLE" RESOURCES

African American and European American women historically have been disadvantaged in employment and the economic sphere. Even so, and perhaps as a result, they are starting businesses as an unprecedented rate, and they are succeeding in their efforts. It therefore becomes important to ask how success is possible given these setbacks. Several lines of inquiry contribute insight on strategies used to deal with and overcome disadvantages due to unequal treatment based on gender and racial status. These are reviewed below.

Theories of Minority and Immigrant Entrepreneurship

Light and Rosenstein (1995) discuss three theoretical frameworks applied in efforts to explain relatively high levels of entrepreneurship in minority and immigrant populations. Empirical studies related to these theories focus primarily on immigrant entrepreneurs (mostly Asian), but they nevertheless provide important theoretical insights for studies of African American and women's business ownership. All three frameworks embrace Folbre's theories of action based on group membership.

Cultural Theory. Cultural theory suggests that immigrants who were entrepreneurs in their country of origin carried skills and talents to their new country, becoming business owners as a means to make a living in a new land. Bonacich's (1973) theory of "middleman minorities" fits this framework. While this may be the case for some minority groups, such as Gypsies (see Sway 1988), for others it is not so. Studies of Korean and Cuban immigrants show that not all of them were business owners in their home countries. More frequently, labor market disadvantage in the U.S. is the basis of their entrepreneurial pursuits (Light 1979; Light and Bonacich 1988; Min 1984). In addition, theories of labor market disadvantage begin to explain non-immigrant, African American business ownership as well as women's entrepreneurship. Women, both black and white, who experience discrimination in the workplace may choose business ownership as a means to gain status and an independent income and to escape discrimination in other employers' workplaces.

Reactive Ethnicity. A second theoretical framework from Light and Rosenstein (1995) is what the authors call "reactive ethnicity." Following the studies of labor market disadvantage above, this theory suggests that subordinate groups respond to loss of status, or lower status, by becoming entrepreneurs. With a lower return on human capital investments (education) in the labor market than in self-employment (for instance, due to discrimination in hiring), minorities turn to business ownership as a viable means to earn greater income. Women who experience similar labor market discrimination may likewise turn to business ownership as a means to earn greater returns on human capital investments.

On the surface, this may seem applicable to the experiences of African Americans as well as to women or immigrant Asians. However, blacks have historically experienced segregation and discrimination in the educational process, making investment in human capital harder for them than for white men and women.[11] It has not been until recently that blacks have been able to achieve higher education levels in significant numbers. Particularly in rural areas, but also in cities, limited educational opportunities for African Americans meant few educational resources upon which to capitalize, keeping them in the lower ranks of employment and business ownership. As blacks have achieved higher educational degrees, they have left ghetto areas and entered the economic mainstream in metro areas, lured by higher wages (Bates and Fusfeld 1984).

Building on reactive ethnicity theory, researchers have found that immigrant and minority groups tend to favor certain types of businesses (Hechter 1976; Light and Bonacich 1988) and provide group solidarity through networks of multiplex social ties, such as those described in Coleman's work on social capital above (Cohen 1969). Trust is built through many dimensions of relationship, allowing business owners in immigrant Asian communities to take part in informal business transactions that can reduce costs and increase market power (see Light et al. 1990).

These findings present fertile ground for application of reactive ethnicity theory to the experiences of African Americans. Blacks traditionally have owned businesses in a few industrial sectors, predominantly personal services and construction (Bates 1993b; Farmer 1968; Foley 1966; Pierce 1947). Lower education levels may have been a factor in keeping blacks who did start businesses in lower paying, less specialized industry sectors. However, with a long history of discrimination and isolation within the U.S., African Americans have long depended on their communities for support. With such networks already in place, black women are likely to turn to their communities for help in reducing outside costs when starting their businesses.

Resources Theory of Entrepreneurship. In an attempt to synthesize cultural and reactive ethnicity theories, a "resources theory of entrepreneurship" distinguishes advantages business owners may have based on their group status (see Fratoe 1986; Light 1984; Min and Jaret 1985; Myers 1983; Waldinger 1988 and others). While Folbre focuses on conflicting pulls and responsibilities women experience from multiple group memberships, resources theory focuses on the cultural, demographic, or economic characteristics or advantages a single group has that aids members who become business owners. These characteristics are considered "entrepreneurial resources" and are comparable to social capital as described by Coleman (1988, 1990) above.

Light and Rosenstein (1995:22-23) distinguish between "ethnic" and "class" resources. *Ethnic* resources are collective features of an ethnic group available to all members that are used by entrepreneurs within the group to their advantage in business. Some examples are revolving loan funds, entrepreneurial values or heritage, solidarity based on reactivity to low social status, reduced costs through social networks and social capital, or an available labor pool of co-ethnic workers. *Class* resources are social, cultural, or material advantages that are available to a group based on class membership. They are different from ethnic resources in that anyone, whether an ethnic minority or otherwise, has access to these resources as a result of their given or acquired class background. Thus, a middle class black family might have financial resources from investments, just as a middle class white family might.

The resources theory of entrepreneurship is directly relevant to a study of black and white women's resources in business start-up. It parallels Folbre's theory of uneven access to assets based on group membership, and it provides a framework for examining what resources are available to women based on racial and class backgrounds. It also broadens the picture of the "disadvantaged" entrepreneur by considering that some advantages might be available to her via group membership. This concept has not previously been brought to bear on studies of women's entrepreneurial pursuits.

Contributions and Limitations to Theory. Light and his colleagues are the only theorists of those discussed above to apply their work specifically to business ownership or the mobilization of resources in business start-up. However, they focus almost exclusively on immigrant populations, largely of Asian descent. They do not consider the African American entrepreneurial experience, nor do they address disadvantages or group solidarity and trust based on gender.

In examining minority responses to labor market disadvantages, however, they have pointed to how structures of discrimination inspire actors within disadvantaged groups to develop group solidarity and trust in the face of discrimination. The group then builds alternative resources to aid members' entrepreneurial pursuits. Group solidarity for women, as members of a disadvantaged group based on gender oppression, might be more difficult because of entwined personal relationships with men. Expressions of group solidarity for women business owners may mean drawing upon increasingly large numbers of female business associates for their knowledge and expertise. Networking among women may occur in an atmosphere of greater trust than women might feel when networking with male business associates. Similarly, black women may draw upon others in the African American community, including those in minority business organizations, for aid in planning, financing, and starting their businesses.

Innovation in Small Businesses

A major theme in the literature on small business ownership is the role of innovation in creating robust, high-growth entrepreneurial ventures. The first to distinguish "entrepreneurship" from "self-employment," Schumpeter (1934, 1943; see also Clemence 1989) claimed that true entrepreneurs are innovative in their businesses, while the merely self-employed are not. Much of the economic literature on small business ownership embraces this distinction (see Carland et al. 1984; Kallen and Kelner 1983; Kilby 1971; Wilken 1979). However, Light and Rosenstein (1995:1-5) dismiss it as being elitist, claiming that all business owners are innovative. While some business owners may make "frequent, original, and important" innovations, becoming elite entrepreneurial leaders (e.g., Henry Ford, Bill Gates, Oprah Winfrey, and Anita Roddick, founder of The Body Shop), the vast majority of business owners make small, infrequent, and insignificant innovations.

Entrepreneurs innovate in different ways.[12] While some make technological or product innovations, others improve quality of services or products or make market innovations (Wilken 1979). This diversity in entrepreneurial creativity points out an important avenue through which the new business owner may seek resources for starting a business. Especially for women, who may face significant barriers due to lack of resources, innovation through creative management of the social, human, and financial resources that are available to them provide adequate capital (both financial and human) with which to start businesses. For example, women with few resources to pay employees might hire family members in the early months of business and pay them less than non-kin workers.

APPLYING RATIONAL CHOICE THEORY
TO THE CURRENT STUDY

In this study, I apply the theoretical perspectives discussed above in assessing how past, present, and possible future circumstances influence women's entrepreneurial choices. In addition, I examine how these situational factors affect their access to and pursuit of resources for business start-up.

The Process of Choice

In general, the processes women go through in starting businesses can be described as follows. Women come to a point of choice in their lives, having built a variety of more or less adequate skills and assets. They face differing circumstances, have unique personal preferences, hold opinions on cultural norms, and interact in an array of relationships. In order to start their businesses, they draw upon their experiences, assets, and relationships in a variety of ways to mobilize resources, both in terms of knowledge and skills, and in financing, that help them open the doors and begin operation.

Once begun, operation of the business contributes to the owner's assets, allowing her business to survive and grow. In the growth process, the owner may continue to mobilize resources. New circumstances and relationships may add to her knowledge and skills. She may reinvest profits made in the business or mobilize additional financial resources to increase business size to keep up with perceived market demand. Figure 1 in Appendix A provides a visual depiction of women's resource accumulation process.

Components of Choice. Women choose to start businesses under varying degrees of constraint. While some women are free to choose if and when to start and what type of business they want with little outside influence, others are less able to do so. Some women have few personal financial resources and have limited ability to mobilize commercial credit. Others only choose business ownership when faced with the loss of their paid employment. Some would rather not have a business, but find it is the only way to practice their profession. Thus, "choice" of business ownership becomes a relative term.

Components of Capital Assets. Initially, owners start their businesses with both ascribed (or "given") assets and accumulated assets. Ascribed assets that typically influence business ownership include family background (income levels, parents' education levels, etc.), racial and ethnic heritage, and cultural norms. Over the course of their early lives, women accumulate other assets, such as their own early education and training, their professional training and experience, friendships and ties to community organizations, and monetary savings. Women then start businesses with a combination of given and accumulated assets, including social, human, and financial capital.

Social Capital. Social capital can be defined as the benefit a woman derives from her relationships. Through social ties to individuals, groups, and organizations, women gain help, information, skills, knowledge, referrals, and money to start and operate businesses. The new business owner may draw social capital from any number of relationships. An example of ascribed social capital would be educational support from parents, but other family support could be given as well, taking forms such as business advice, financial aid, or donated physical labor. Community organizations and churches could provide needed information, community support networks, or potential client bases. Other personal and business network relationships could also provide needed resources.

Human Capital. Human capital can be broken down into formal education and/or training, and less formal training and work experience. Formal education may be reflected in high school, college (two and four year), and graduate degrees, or may be take the form of trade school certificates such as those earned in cosmetology school. Training may also take place in the workplace, both during structured workshops and seminars, and informally as an individual performs her job.

Within each of these categories, formal and informal, (or education, training, and experience), the aspiring business owner must eventually become proficient not only with occupational skills, but also with skills that help her operate her business. According to the literature, few women start their businesses with adequate preparation in both occupational and business skills (see Chapter 3). However, most research examines only formal means of preparation (degrees earned and college majors). Because of this, I take a broader and more detailed view in examining the processes through which women learn the skills they need for their businesses.

Financial Capital. Research shows that most women start their businesses with relatively little commercial capital (see Chapter 3). Because of this, I deemed it important to examine a broader range of strategies women employ in financing their businesses. I have therefore broken down financial resources into commercial, personal, and alternative sources. Commercial (or external) resources include bank and credit union loans, mortgages, lines of credit, factoring, and other distinctive methods found to stabilize and/or utilize cash flow. Examples of personal (or internal) funding sources are personal savings, continued employment earnings, investments, and family monetary gifts and loans.

Alternative sources of financing are non-monetary and can be described as strategies that reduce costs for the business owner, either in the business, or in her personal life. These strategies often take the form of support from strong family and community relationships. They may surface as donations of supplies or equipment; donated labor from friends or relatives; home-based businesses that eliminate office rents; and husband's or companion's payment of bills at home. Other unique strategies to distribute costs over time have been discovered in the current work.

Closely related to these categories of financing are accumulated characteristics and abilities of the business owner that promote acceptance or disapproval on the part of commercial financiers. These characteristics facilitate or detract from the new owner's abilities to borrow commercial funds. Examples of these characteristics and abilities include a personal credit history, the ability to earn money, and the ability to produce collateral. Both ascribed and accumulated human and social capital can influence the production of these characteristics and abilities. For instance, responses of others to racial heritage can influence an individual's opportunities to build credit; level of education may influence an individual's chances for high-paid employment; and a past history of family investments may affect the new business owner's ability to produce collateral.

Degree of Choice. Women choosing to start businesses do so differently according to their life experiences and the circumstances surrounding their decisions for having a business. Some women plan, over the course of their lives, to have a business. They build up skills and assets over time in order to create a base with which to start their businesses. Other women have little idea, before making their decision, that they will one day own a business. The processes that women in these divergent circumstances experience with business start-up are bound to be very different. Similarly, women who first choose an occupation, then start a business in their occupation, are very likely to experience resource mobilization and business start-up differently from women who want to own a business and later decide what type of business they will have. Race will affect women's actions as it differentially and systematically affects background and opportunities.

RESEARCH FOCUS

I will examine data collected through interviews with black and white women business owners with various types of businesses in rural, small city, and urban centers in the Southeast. In the Chapters 5-9, I group the women according to their business and occupational motivations and circumstances in start-up. I then examine differences and similarities in the groups' processes of resource mobilization. This includes examination of formal education, job training, and work experience for both occupational and business skills at the time of start-up. It also includes examination of additional training or experience sought after start-up to aid the owner in business operations.

I examine methods of business financing for each group, including commercial, personal, and alternative cost-saving strategies. I analyze the social and business relationships the women use, and how the people in these relationships aid the women, in their decision-making and resource mobilization processes. I take into account differences by race, business location, type of business, and other demographic variations, as they become apparent. These differences should allow rich comparisons of women's experiences in business ownership and the contacts and processes through which they mobilize resources for start-up and operation.

NOTES

[1]Homans (1990:85) argued that rational choice theory is a "stripped down version of behaviorism" that does not address emotion the way behaviorism does and can only be used in limited situations. Behaviorism, according to Homans, can take into account personal history and unusual situations.

[2] The traditional positions taken by economists and sociologists on the nature of economic activity can be traced back to Adam Smith and Hobbes. Economists based their assumptions on an "under-socialized" notion of human action, where the actor is "atomized" in her universe alone and makes rational choices based on pure economic self-interest. Sociologists, following the tradition of Parsons' work on role theory and social learning theory (1951; 1958; Parsons and Shils 1951), put forth a somewhat "over-socialized" view of human action. In this view, the actor internalizes the norms and traditions of the culture into which she or he is born to the point where actions are structured by those internalized norms.

[3] Although the concept of human capital encompasses other personal resources such as health, I limit the discussion of human capital in this study to education, training, on-the-job experience, and other forms of knowledge and skill building.

[4] General training is more valuable to employees because they can take these skills with them to other jobs. Specific training, however, is more valuable to an employer because it provides skills that are only applicable to a particular job. When an employee is trained with skills specific to her job, she is more likely to remain in the job, allowing more return on the training investment.

[5] Becker (1964, 1975, 1993 editions: 19-20) pointed out this alternative theory of human capital suggesting that more education may not, in and of itself, necessarily increase production. Rather, more education may be an indication of a type of person who is inherently more productive and more likely to learn needed skills. In this view, called "credentialism," the educational degree becomes an indicator of underlying characteristics of the individual, such as a propensity to work harder and learn better than persons not holding a degree. Whether viewed as a symbol, or as real skills learned, degrees are used in evaluation of individuals for job positions (see also Thurow, 1972).

⁶ This would generally be true, unless the entrepreneur with no loan has other significant funding sources or chooses a type of business that needs little start-up financing.

⁷ Hertz (1986) points out that, even though the "couple" should be responsible for making such arrangements, it is more often the woman who actually does so and who takes over the chores if help is interrupted or unavailable.

⁸ In this study, black women experienced discrimination in prior job settings and in their businesses as blacks or as women and sometimes both, but they were not always able to clearly separate the two.

⁹ To paraphrase a commentator on National Public Radio's "All Things Considered," (Winter 1996) for example, she realized that her white friends had ancestors who built assets, leaving an inheritance to their children. In contrast, the commentator's African American ancestors *were* assets, as slaves to white landholders. They had to build a life from scratch. Private aid can take the form of individual savings or investments; loans or gifts from family or community members; or other non-commercial sources of finance.

¹⁰ With the strong ties of the African American community, black women's wages are not easily held in savings for the immediate family, but are often shared with those less fortunate in the extended family and community.

¹¹ Immigrants vary widely in levels of human capital, and some groups are more highly educated than U.S.-born whites (Portes and Rumbaut 1990).

¹² Schumpeter (1934:66) suggests five forms that entrepreneurial innovation may take: 1) introduction of a new good or quality of good; 2) introduction of a new method of production; 3) opening a new market; 4) discovery and utilization of a new source of supply or raw material(s); and 5) development of a new organization of an industry.

CHAPTER 3

Review of Research
on Women and Business

Women-owned businesses are the fastest growing segment of the small business sector in the U.S. Even so, women make up only one third of all self-employed workers. Between 1970 and 1983, women entered self-employment at a rate five times greater than men and three times greater than women who entered wage and salaried jobs (Becker 1984). Annual rate of increase of women business owners from 1972 to 1985 was 5.1 percent compared with an over-all annual increase in self-employment of 2.9 percent (SBA 1988b). A survey conducted by the National Foundation for Women Business Owners estimated that, between 1987 and 1996, women-owned businesses grew by 78 percent, a rate of nearly 2 to 1 over all U. S. businesses. In addition, revenues of women-owned businesses were projected to triple during that time (see Poole 1996). By 1987, 30 percent of all U.S. non-farm self-employed workers were women (Aronson 1991:61). By 1992, 34 percent of all businesses were owned by women. In the Southeast, all states except Florida lagged slightly behind this national average. According to 1992 census figures, nearly one out of every four U.S. workers was employed by a woman-owned firm (U.S. Department of Commerce 1996). (See Table 3.1 in Appendix A for more detail.)

White women predominate among women business owners. While the national average hovers just below 88 percent, white women in the Southeast own anywhere from 83 percent (Florida) to 95 percent (Kentucky) of women-owned firms. African American women own a greater share of women-owned firms in the Southeast than elsewhere in the nation. They own, on average, 3 to 13 percent of Southeastern woman-owned firms compared with the U.S. average of just under 5 percent of women-owned firms. Perhaps the most striking pattern in women's business ownership is found in a comparison of African American women-owned firms as a percentage of all African American owned firms. While women in general own about a third of all firms, black women own businesses at a rate, on average, of 10 percentage points higher when compared with all black firms. Nationwide, African American women own almost 45 percent of all black firms. Black women in most Southeastern states own nearly the same proportion of black firms, with only Louisiana, Mississippi, and South Carolina lagging below 40 percent (see Table 3.1 in Appendix A).

One factor contributing to the growth in women-owned small businesses is the growth in women's participation in the labor force in general, leading to more work experience and a greater tendency to choose self-employment. While greater participation and experience are certainly necessary, some researchers suggest that as more women enter the work force, more women face discrimination on the job. Making the choice to start their own businesses may be the way some women avoid subordination in paid labor and bypass barriers to their careers in the corporate world. Starting their own businesses allows them the autonomy to be their own manager and boss (Goffee and Scase 1985). African American and other minority women in particular find self-employment attractive for these reasons (Poole 1993; Poole et al. 1993).

Much of the literature on women-owned businesses focuses on comparisons of men- and woman-owned firms. Such studies usually conclude that women are less financially successful than men, citing four major reasons. First, women's businesses are newer and smaller, generating less profit than men's businesses. Second, women start businesses in lower-income-generating industries such as retail and personal services. Third, women lack relevant education and training for business operations. And fourth, women lack access to commercial financing, having less credit and fewer network ties in the white male business community. A general conclusion of this line of research is that women have various deficits that result in lesser success in business. This leads to the questions, if women are indeed so unprepared for business ownership, how do they manage to start businesses despite these shortcomings? For what reasons do they start businesses? How do the circumstances surrounding their decisions to start a business affect their business start-ups, particularly their skills-readiness and their financing? What are the processes they go through to gain needed skills and training? And finally, how do they finance their businesses?

EMPIRICAL BUSINESS LITERATURE: THE BIG PICTURE

In this chapter, I first present literature on business ownership in general, and on women-owned and minority-owned businesses. To give some sense of the obstacles that women face in starting new businesses, I will review empirical literature on business survival and success. I then provide information on macro-structural labor market forces affecting small business ownership by women. I present current literature on African American business ownership and provide background on African American women's experiences in mobilizing resources and starting their businesses. Finally, I narrow the focus to examine the literature on women's reasons for founding businesses, and the social, human, and financial resources they use in business start-up.

Business Performance: Survival and Success

Much of the literature on entrepreneurship is couched in terms of business survival and success. Because new and small businesses frequently suffer high failure rates, much attention has focused on why they fail, or, perhaps more to the point, how and why the ones that don't fail manage to survive. Since high failure rates generally plague all business start-ups, the literature on business survival is relevant to women-owned and African American-owned businesses alike. Statistics on business success, however, begin to reveal differences by gender and race based on owners' motivations for ownership and their access to educational financial opportunities.

Business Survival. Although the overall number of small businesses increased during the 1980s, this was so only because the number of new business start-ups was greater than the number of small business failures. Aldrich and Auster (1986) found that small businesses, including those owned by women, frequently suffer from liabilities associated with newness and smallness. According to Starbuck and Nystrom (1981), 81 percent of corporations do not survive their first 10 years. Aldrich and Auster (1986) compiled results from several studies that show failure rates as high as 50 percent in the first two years (Evans 1948; Mayer and Goldstein 1961). More recent studies of manufacturing (Hoad and Rosko 1964) and high technology firms (Roberts and Wainer 1968) reveal lower failure rates over slightly longer periods. New businesses lack clientele and well-defined organizational structures, while very small businesses may have trouble raising capital, competing for employees, and complying with government regulations and tax laws.

Researchers have found that if a business can last through the stress and hardship of its first two to five years, it is more likely to survive over the long term. Those that grow frequently do so at the expense of autonomy. Choosing to start a franchise, competing for government contracts and set-asides, or offering a buy-out are three survival strategies available to small businesses. Growth and prosperity are more likely to occur in larger firms (Aldrich and Auster 1986).

Economic "Success." Women's businesses are not immune to these failure rates. What has attracted more attention, however, is the lower income generation by women's businesses when compared with men's. In 1984, women sole proprietors working full time earned just over half as much (53 percent in mean annual income) as women working full time in the paid labor force, and only 37 percent as much as full time self-employed men (SBA State of Small Business 1986). Using median annual earnings on a five year average from 1980 to 1984, U.S. Department of Health and Human Services data shows that self-employed women earned 62 percent as much as wage earning women and only 42 percent as much as self-employed men (Aronson 1991:66-67). These differences may be due in part to newness of women's businesses.

Although 30 percent of U.S. firms were women-owned in 1987, women-owned businesses drew in less than 14 percent of small business sales and receipts. By 1992, women owned 34 percent of all firms nationwide but still drew in just over 19 percent of sales. Southeastern states varied around this mean from 14 percent in Tennessee to 27 percent in Georgia and 34 percent in Louisiana. African American women, owning nearly 45 percent of African American firms nationwide, drew in over 26 percent of sales by African American-owned firms (see Tables 3.1 and 3.2 in Appendix A).

Gaining Parity. Women who owned firms employing workers fared better than those who did not have employees. While women owned 26 percent of all firms with employees in 1992, they made nearly 19 percent of all sales nationwide. Sales in the Southeastern states again ranged around this national average, with lowest sales in Tennessee (just under 14 percent) and highest sales in Georgia (28 percent) and Louisiana (nearly 37 percent). In Georgia and Tennessee, women who owned firms with employees made greater average sales in 1992 than their share of receipts. Nationwide, African American women who owned firms with employees did better than women in general, owning 29 percent of all African American firms with employees and making nearly 24 percent of all African American sales nationwide. Sales for black women's firms in most of the Southeastern states hovered between 18 and 26 percent of all black sales of firms with employees.

Barriers to Economic Success

While the share of sales for women-owned businesses is increasing, major gains have been made in businesses that employ workers. However, these represent less than one fifth of all women-owned businesses. Overall, women still receive proportionally less than their share of income in business ownership.

Motives for Ownership. Researchers have used several theoretical approaches to explain this discrepancy. First, studies show that an increase in numbers of employees is not necessarily desired by many women business owners (Cromie 1987; Goffee and Scase 1985). Women frequently choose business ownership as a means to meet both career and domestic needs (Cromie 1987). Home-based businesses may allow women to combine earning money with fulfillment of domestic responsibilities such as childcare. Operating a business out of the home may demand less initial funding, a resource many women lack. Yet trying to do two things at once detracts from the amount of time women have to devote to their businesses, and this might result in lower earnings.

Personal Characteristics of the Owner. Research suggests that personal characteristics of the owner affect business earnings. Human capital skills gained through education, training, and job experience aid entrepreneurs in starting and operating businesses (Bender 1980). Women's lack of experience and training has contributed to lower earnings (Loscocco et al. 1991), and their educational majors are often mismatched with the types of businesses they wish to start (Bowen and Hisrich 1986; Hisrich 1989). However, some studies suggest that women entrepreneurs seek autonomy and are high achievers, taking risks with their businesses that can lead to higher earnings (Bender 1980; DeCarlo and Lyons 1979; Humphreys and McClung 1981).

Access to Commercial Capital and Government Contracts. Studies show that women, even those who start successful businesses, face difficulty in obtaining commercial loans (Bowen and Hisrich 1986; Hisrich and O'Brien 1981; Schwartz 1976). Women reported difficulty getting loans as the second biggest barrier they faced in starting a business, next to lack of previous business experience (Bowen and Hisrich 1986). This can occur for several reasons. First, women lack significant personal credit or loan histories making them less able to obtain business loans.[1] Second, women frequently lack access to male business networks. This limits their ability to build relationships within the business community and reduces access to information and referrals about lending and contract opportunities (Bowen and Hisrich 1986).

Minority and Small Business Administration loan programs may offset this disadvantage for some women, but do not automatically do so (Bates 1975, 1981, 1985b, 1985c; Small Business Administration 8(a) Review Board 1978). Evidence suggests that the number and share of Small Business Administration loans to women decreased in the 1980s (Committee on Small Business 1988). Lacking commercial financing, women must rely on personal savings or private loans. As a result, they start businesses with fewer resources and produce lower earnings.

Contracts and Set-Asides. Contracts and set-sides provide alternative avenues through which women may gain needed capital. Still, women are at a disadvantage when competing for federal government contracts and subcontracts. Just under a third of purchases under federal contract went to small businesses in 1990, including subcontracted services from larger companies using federal contract dollars (SBA State of Small Business 1991). Although the percentage of federal contracts going to women-owned businesses is increasing, it is still negligible.[2] Federal government contractors who are required to subcontract to small businesses are not required to report how many of their subcontracts go to woman small business owners, as they are required to report for minority-owned businesses (Committee on Small Business 1988). In addition, women may be excluded from networks through which government and other contracts are awarded (Loscocco and Robinson 1991). If access to government contracts and subcontracts are limited, women's business receipts may also be lower.

Labor Market Characteristics and Industrial Structure. Characteristics of businesses and labor market structures can affect business earnings. The type of industry and product market, and a firm's size and age can determine income levels (Kalleberg and Leicht 1991). Overall, women's businesses are newer and smaller than men's businesses. Women tend to start small and remain so, with more than 70 percent of woman-owned firms employing fewer than 5 workers (Humphreys and McClung 1981). Several women in this study continued to work at full or part time jobs to support their businesses financially, suggesting that the business may be still developing or a labor of love.

Market conditions have moved in a direction that favors small businesses. Shifts toward more labor-intensive industries, more subcontracting by larger firms, and greater innovation and marketability all provide opportunities for small businesses. While some of these conditions have had a positive influence on women-owned businesses, others have not. The structural shift from a majority of employment in goods to greater employment in services has been suggested as opening opportunities for women, since they have traditionally had more experience in the labor-intensive service sector. However, rapid growth in the service sector occurred earlier than the growth in women-owned businesses, so it cannot directly account for the growth of the latter (Aronson 1991).

Nevertheless, women frequently operate in the retail and service sectors, in what feminist scholars consider "reproductive" labor jobs (see Sokoloff 1980). In paid positions in these jobs, women often perform tasks for pay that mothers often provide without wages at home to care for their families, for example cooking or food service, clothing, or caretaking. In 1985, 25.3 percent of women-owned businesses were in retail trade nationwide, while 58.4 percent were in services (adapted from Aronson 1991:62). Women may gravitate toward the retail sales and service industries because these businesses require less start-up capital than others, a resource that women frequently lack. Women's socialization, training, and experience may steer them into these sectors. They also may open service and retail businesses because men are less interested in these sectors. Within these traditionally female- and minority-dominated industries (see "African American Business Experience" section below), both black and white women may hold lower income positions than white men within each sector (Loscocco and Robinson 1991).

Non-Traditional Occupations. Many studies show that the types of industries women choose significantly influence business performance (Aronson 1991; Loscocco et al. 1991; Tigges and Green 1992). Earning potentials are greater for self-employed women in non-traditional occupations than for women in traditionally female fields. By industry, the largest economic gains made by self-employed women from 1972 to 1985 were in industries where women had little prior participation: manufacturing, mining, construction, and wholesale trade (Aronson 1991). In 1983, receipts of women sole proprietors in construction, transportation, and communication were greater than receipts of self-employed men in the same sectors (SBA State of Small Business 1986). Despite this, women remain under-represented in "non-traditional" industries. Between 1971 and 1988, the number of self-employed women in the construction industry grew by a factor of eight nationwide, yet represented only 6 percent of all self-employed construction workers by 1988 (Aronson 1991:63). According to Bowen and Hisrich (1986:402), "The [Small Business Administration] believes that the lack of educational and work experience in technical and business fields traditionally dominated by males limits the opportunities for female entrepreneurs in these fields."

Thus, many factors contribute to women business owners' lower share of earnings. Using the criteria typically applied to measure business success, women's businesses that remain small may continue to turn in relatively small profits. They therefore may be considered less successful than businesses that grow rapidly in size and profits. Yet in their own eyes, these women might be successful in what they do.

The African American Business Experiences

Historically, self-employment has been an avenue for minorities and women to overcome discrimination. However, studies of women-owned businesses focus primarily on white, middle-class women. Studies that address African American business ownership usually focus on black men (e.g., Borjas and Bronars 1989; much of Bates' work), even though black women own nearly 45 percent of all African American firms nationwide (see Table 3.1 in Appendix A). This is ten percentage points higher than the national average for all women-owned businesses. Still, a review of African American business literature provides a "big picture" setting from which to examine the experiences of African American women business owners.

Much of the literature on African American and minority owned businesses compares black and minority businesses to white owned businesses (for example, Bates 1993a; Bearse 1983; Caplovitz 1973; Elliehausen, Canner and Avery 1984a, 1984b; Terrell 1971). Some of these studies group women with men of their ethnic group, and some exclude women altogether. African American business literature also focuses primarily on metropolitan areas, comparing businesses by location, whether in the inner city ghetto, the central business district, or the suburbs (Bates 1989). Rural areas are rarely included in studies of African American business ownership.

Racial Issues and Labor Market Barriers and Opportunities.
Since the Civil War, African American businesses, like women-owned
businesses, have been concentrated in the personal service and retail sectors (i.e., beauty and barber shops, Mom and Pop groceries, and restaurants) for two reasons. First, African Americans learned skills while
serving whites during enslavement that they put to use in starting businesses. Some of these businesses (restaurants, sewing and alterations
shops, cleaners) still catered to white patrons. Second, they founded
businesses to serve the black community, which most whites did not pa-
tronize (Bates 1993b; Pierce 1947; Foley 1966).

These were not the only skills learned in slavery. Taught by slave
masters in many trades, skilled slaves were allowed by their masters to
hire out their skills in return for a fee based on earnings. Protected by
slave masters, these skilled workers made up a majority of the skilled
tradesmen in the South prior to the Civil War (Bates 1993b:107). With
emancipation, skilled black laborers had to compete on the open market.
Facing harsh discrimination in licensing and craft unions, they lost skills
and businesses. Largely limited to serving the black community, blacks
retained retail and service skills and were largely limited to these sectors
throughout most of the 20th century.

The labor market opened up throughout the 1960s, 1970s, and
1980s, providing job opportunities for blacks in most sectors of the paid
labor force. Economic options for working class black women in clerical
work increased, but economic options for working class black men in
manufacturing declined. A growing service sector, which institutional-
ized domestic services to wealthier whites, now attracted both black
women and black men (Blauner, 1992). Black business ownership
shifted to include higher skill levels and more capital intensive businesses, particularly in business services (Bates 1983, 1987; Suggs 1986).
As African American businesses expanded their markets to include
racially mixed clientele, personal service businesses among African
American enterprises have begun to decline (Suggs 1986).

These trends affect African American women's family incomes and
their relationships to black men. While black women have traditionally
had access to low-paying jobs, their incomes were relatively secure. In
contrast, black men had access to less secure, higher paying jobs
(Collins, 1991). Without black men's incomes, or with reduced earnings,
more working class black women might fall into poverty or seek higher
paying opportunities, including business ownership. One rural black
woman in this study worked a full time job in addition to operating a

business, and her husband worked two full time jobs. Consistent with the literature on African American extended kin networks, her mother and an older child took care of younger children in the family.

Success and Failure. Literature on minority-owned businesses suggests that black-owned businesses had higher failure rates in the past for reasons similar to those affecting women-owned businesses. Black-owned businesses tended to be newer and smaller (Bates 1989b; Evans 1987). They were frequently "ghettoized" into low paying retail and personal services industries (Foley 1966; Pierce 1947). Blacks had less education (Caplovitz 1973) and had limited access to capital, both personal and commercial (Bates 1973a, 1973b, 1993a; Pierce, 1947). As their education and income levels increased, African Americans have started businesses in a broader range of fields, such as finance, insurance, real estate, professional and business services, and transportation and communications (Bates 1987; Suggs 1986). They have earned higher financial returns for their efforts and survived longer (Bates 1988). However, in the Southeast states, black women still lag behind white women in business sales (Tables 3.2 and 3.4).

Barriers to African American Business Success: Social, Human, and Financial Capital. Business ownership is partially determined by social resources. Social relationships can affect human and financial capital for the new business owner. A lower rate of self-employment among blacks has been linked to lower levels of social capital available from social support networks (Fratoe 1988). Specifically, younger black entrepreneurs have fewer role models than whites. Black business owners who rely solely on the African American community as a customer base may have fewer clients with lower purchasing power than those with a mixed racial or white client base (Fratoe 1988).

White business owners have been able to obtain more commercial capital than blacks, leaving African American owners little choice but to rely on personal savings or to start a business that requires little initial capital. Some business owners rely on family or friends for financial capital. Differences in amounts of personal and family wealth holdings among African Americans compared with European Americans, however, make this alternative more likely for whites than blacks. While 91.4 percent of white households had accumulated wealth in 1990, only 69 percent of black households had accumulated wealth (Bradford 1990). This discrepancy points out the lower assets available in the African

American community in general, and is another indication of how social capital can affect financial capital for the new business owner (see "Financial Capital" section below).

Human Capital. Historically, African Americans have had inadequate education and training opportunities and limited access to jobs. White business owners, with greater business experience, more education, and more wealth, have tended to have larger, more successful businesses (Bates 1993a; Caplovitz 1973; Terrell 1971). More recently, educational and training opportunities have opened up for blacks, particularly in professional and managerial positions in large metropolitan areas. This partially accounts for the growth in black businesses (Swinton and Handy 1983). Minority college enrollment increased dramatically in the 1960s and 1970s, especially in business-related fields (Bates 1993a, 1993b).[3] African American college graduates enter business ownership in more lucrative sectors, rarely starting personal service or small-scale retail businesses (Bates 1993b).

Labor Market Structure and Blacks' Education. Although in general, more education increases likelihood of self-employment (Bearse 1984), younger and better educated blacks have been lured into state and local government employment, and the private business sector, by agencies and corporations emulating federal affirmative action programs (Bates 1985a, 1985b). Greater earning power in the paid work force tends to discourage educated blacks from starting businesses (Bearse 1984). However, recent recessions have sparked corporate restructuring and down-sizing. African American women, hired later and with less seniority than white women and black and white men, may choose business ownership as a viable alternative to lay-offs or demotions.

Financial Capital. Like women, African American business owners find lack of access to financial capital to be a major constraint on the formation, growth, and diversification of their businesses (Bates 1993b). Personal wealth holdings are lower for blacks than for whites,[4] and discrimination by commercial banks presents obstacles to African American loan applicants. Using the Characteristics of Business Owners database of businesses with start-up between 1976 and 1982, Bates (1993a) found that more loan capital was given to owners with more equity, or personal wealth. With commercial banks offering the most loans, blacks were disadvantaged obtaining commercial financing. Business owners in inner city black communities faced bank redlining (see "Community Reinvestment Act" below) and other discriminatory practices as further barriers to capitalization (Bates 1993a). Ando (1988) found that, for large firms at least 2 years old in 1984, black firms had a harder time obtaining commercial financing, even after controlling for risk, than Asian, Hispanic, or white-owned firms. In that study loan acceptance rates for blacks were 25-35 percent lower than for any others (see Table 3.5 in Appendix A). Lack of financing has forced many blacks to start businesses in fields needing little start-up capital (Bates 1973b).

Education and Commercial Loans. As black business owners' education levels have increased, so have their chances of receiving commercial funding. African Americans with four-year college degrees have greater access to commercial bank loans than those without four year degrees. Controlling for personal wealth, owners who had more education received more loans. In addition, owners receiving the biggest loans had the highest incomes prior to starting a business (Bates 1993a). This raises a question of whether college graduates succeed because they get larger loans, or because they are more educated. If, as Becker suggests (1964, 1975, 1993 editions), higher education is an indicator of productive character rather than a measure of actual increased ability to perform, then financing may be the key to success. Education level may simply be a sign that the business owner obtained socially accepted credentials before moving into business ownership (see "Credentialism," below).

Government Efforts at Intervention. Efforts have been made to offset low rates of bank loan receipt by blacks through federal loan programs and set-asides. In addition, legislation has been enacted to ensure fair distribution of commercial loans without regard to where a business is located.

Loan Programs and Set-Asides. Bates (1993b) has extensively reviewed the literature on effectiveness of government loan programs, including the Economic Opportunity Loan (EOL) program; the Minority Enterprise Small Business Investment Company (MESBIC); the 8(a) program; and other SBA loan programs. Set-asides in general help to expand minority businesses both in size and type of business (Bates 1985a, 1985b). Bates (1981) asserts, however, that the EOL and 8(a) programs failed because they gave money to weaker minority businesses with less ability to repay their loans and made stronger firms ineligible for aid.

Although in this study some white women perceived that black business owners have an advantage in receiving financial loans and in market share due to set-asides, African American women had a very different perspective. Many women experienced difficulty in their loan application processes, particularly with larger loans. They were frequently turned away and were successful in obtaining loans only after a long process of struggle. Some women did not bother to apply, not wishing to "go through the hassle." A few of the women were exploring 8(a) status, but they reported that the paperwork required to qualify as a minority-owned business was prohibitive. Woolf (1986) found that, although black manufacturing firms were "somewhat more likely" to operate in sectors where government purchasing regulations contributed to a large government market share, the relationship was not statistically significant. Thus, government capital might not contribute significantly to African Americans' decisions to start businesses.

The Community Reinvestment Act. Congress enacted the Community Reinvestment Act (CRA) in 1977 "to ensure that financial institutions have a continuing and affirmative obligation to help meet the credit needs of their local communities" (SBA Office of Advocacy 1994:1). With 12 assessment factors included in the evaluation process governing CRA, implementation following the original enactment became a record-keeping headache. As a result, revisions of the regulations affecting implementation of the Act were proposed in 1993 and adopted in 1994.

These revisions included a Presidential request to focus on lending to low- and moderate-income individuals and to those in low- to moderate-income neighborhoods. The main purpose of the revisions was to increase loans to such individuals and neighborhoods. Before revision, "redlining" was a common practice among commercial loan officers. Redlining is the practice of systematically refusing loans to individuals living in low-income neighborhoods. In the revised Act, the twelve assessment factors were replaced by three evaluation tests, making lending practices easier to document and to evaluate. The three tests included

(1) lending to low-and moderate-income individuals and neighborhoods, small businesses, and small farms; (2) the ability to service low- to moderate-income neighborhoods, including accessibility of branches and other services promoting greater access to capital; and (3) the amount of qualified investments made by a financial institution in organizations and initiatives that foster community development (SBA Office of Advocacy 1994:3).

Under these regulations, "a financial institution [is] judged on its geographic servicing area, where it makes the bulk of its loans" (SBA Office of Advocacy 1994:3). Adoption of the new CRA regulations occurred at approximately the same time as the data collection for this study, so they did not affect loan opportunities for women in the study. Future funding opportunities for African American women may increase, however, as a result of CRA.

CONTRIBUTIONS OF THE LARGER
LITERATURE TO THE STUDY'S FOCUS

By studying woman-owned businesses, this study broadens understandings of what constitutes a "successful" small business and calls into question the traditional criteria for evaluating business success. Whether "success" is measured in dollar figures or in growth in numbers of employees, black and white women's small businesses fall short when compared with models of success based on experiences of white males. While economic success is important, it may not be the only measure by which to judge the performance of a woman-owned business. Success may mean something completely different from economic profit to women business owners. Almost every woman interviewed considered her business to be a success, including those working only part time in their businesses. Whether their intentions were to become independent, earn money for retirement, or simply utilize a skill or talent, these women viewed the fact that they were doing what they set out to do as a sign of success.

The contributions made by the larger literature on small business survival and success lies in its display of the differences in men's and women's reasons for starting businesses, and in the examination of difficulties women face in mobilizing resources for their businesses. Little access to financial capital (both personal and commercial), inadequate training, job discrimination and subsequent minimal job experience, and restricted network opportunities all play a part in limiting women's opportunities to start businesses. Black entrepreneurs experience similar barriers when starting their businesses.

Little is known about African American women's business experiences, including their motives for business ownership. Nor is much known about their occupational choices or their efforts to break out of limiting occupational ghettos in which they have long worked. Self-employment is one avenue that both women and minorities have used to overcome discrimination and to enter mainstream economic life. Just as women have moved into positions abandoned by men, blacks have moved into jobs and occupations vacated by whites (Malveaux and Wallace, 1987). In the 1970s and 1980s, black and white women increasingly entered the labor force in a wider range of professions than ever before (Kilson, 1977; Sokoloff, 1992). Black women moved from private household work into female-dominated clerical work as white women left those jobs for higher positions in management and male-dominated professions. Black women rose into management and professions in the public sector and in cities as white women deserted to the private sector in suburbs and office parks. With greater educational attainment, more black women are now moving into private sector management and higher paying industries (Trent 1984).

Black women are also entering business ownership in record numbers. Whether practicing a traditional skill or plying a trade learned in prior employment, black women may choose business ownership as a means to become independent, as a strategy to avoid further job discrimination, and/or serve the needs of the African American community. In doing so, what resources do they tap? Through what process do they mobilize resources?

LITERATURE ON WOMEN'S MOTIVES AND RESOURCES FOR BUSINESS

Women start business under widely differing circumstances. Some look forward to owning businesses for most of their lives. Others choose entrepreneurship when suddenly faced with unexpected career changes. Such widely differing circumstances influence the type and amount of resources women have in starting businesses. The following review of the literature more closely examines black and white women's reasons for starting businesses and their experiences with accessing and mobilizing human, social, and financial resources for business start-up.

Women's Reasons for Starting Businesses

Starting one's own business may be a response to blocked opportunity, an attempt to reconcile conflicting responsibilities, or the manifestation of a desire to be one's own boss. Cromie (1987) found that women choose self-employment for autonomy, a sense of achievement, job satisfaction, and career satisfaction (see also Schwartz 1976). Making money is significantly lower on women's lists of motivations for entrepreneurship than on men's (also Cuba et al 1983). Dissatisfaction with previous job and job displacement also are important reasons for women's self-employment (Hisrich and Brush 1983; Shapero and Sokol 1982). In addition, women frequently report business start-up as a response to lack of opportunity in the labor market (Bender 1980; Cromie 1987; Humphreys and McClung 1987). Mid-life changes such as children's leaving home, change of jobs, or lay-off during a recession can also lead women to start businesses (Scase and Goffee 1980).

African American women have always been more likely to work, and have always expected to work more, than middle class white women (Burlew 1982; Murrell et al. 1991). Historically, black women worked along side black men in the fields of slavery. More recently, black women, their husbands (when present), and all extended kin are likely to earn less and have fewer savings due to inequality in employment wages, than earnings and savings available to white women, their husbands, and kin. Such disadvantages make black women's earnings essential. One study suggests that black women choose non-traditional work more often than white women, perhaps because they are more motivated by finances than white women (Murrell et al., 1991). At the same time, black women have larger kin networks from which to draw support of all kinds (Day 1986). These differences may combine to influence African American women's educational expectations and aspirations, and their choices of strategies in starting businesses.

Domestic Responsibilities. The argument that women may start their businesses as a means to accommodate both work and children is a common one. Operating out of the home, women start low-cost businesses that might require less attention than larger ones in order to meet both the needs of their children and their own need for rewarding work (Cromie 1987). Estimates vary as to how many women small business owners are married, but the average seems to be between 50 percent and 60 percent (DeCarlo and Lyons 1979; Hisrich and Brush 1983; Humphreys and McClung 1983). Thus, over half of all women entrepreneurs are likely to have significant household responsibilities if a traditional division of labor in household tasks is assumed. Results of a Roper poll indicate that while men "help out" in 41 percent of all married households, women do all, or nearly all housework in another 41 percent of married households. Men and women share chores equally in only 15 percent of these households (Roper 1985).

A more recent study (Goldscheider and Waite 1991) found that married, non-working women do 83 percent of the housework in their homes, while married, employed women do 70 percent of the housework in dual-career homes. For women with children, domestic responsibilities are greater. Even when men participate equally in childcare, they often avoid doing their share of other household chores (Gerson 1993:226). Thus, despite progress spurred by the women's movement toward equality and shared responsibility within the household, women still carry an overwhelming majority of the unpaid reproductive labor load within the domestic sphere.

Raising Children While Working. Most women these days see work and family as being compatible. While differences are small between black and white women, black women see little conflict between career plans and family responsibilities. They are less likely to take time off to have children than white women, perhaps because of the necessity for income and because of more extensive kin support to help care for children. Black women in non-traditional careers, however, put off marriage longer and have fewer children than black women in traditional careers. White women in traditional careers express the most need to take time off for children (Murrell et al. 1991).

Women who continue to work while raising children, including those who own their own businesses, have found ways to cope with the stress and time constraints of adding work responsibilities to domestic and childcare duties. Some rely on supportive husbands, parents, family members, and in-laws (Lieber 1980). Others turn to friends and neighbors, or hire an array of professional household helpers (Lieber 1980; Martin and Keyes 1988). In doing so, they pass on unpaid labor tasks to paid laborers, almost always women and often minority women and/or women of lower class standing (Hertz 1986; Rollins 1985; Romero 1992; Sokoloff 1980). Almost all working mothers experience time conflicts between their home and work roles that affect business operations and relationships (Lieber 1980). Many women simply can't remove the strain of a double load of responsibility. Women who start and operate businesses out of their homes might be responding to this strain by bringing home life and work closer together (Crosby 1987).

Support from Husbands. Husbands' positive attitudes may be essential for women who are balancing self-employed careers with marriage and family responsibilities. Spousal support, financial, emotional, and practical (i.e., help around the house), might determine whether or not women start their own businesses. Sexton and Kent (1981) found that more than half of their respondents reported husbands as being most influential in the start-up of their business. Without spousal support, married women might still experience work and family role overloads (Crosby 1987).

Structured, Situation-Based Choices. In addressing women's employment in general, Gerson (1985) suggests that some women with few family responsibilities encounter opportunities in the work place that lead them to emphasize careers over domestic life. Even women whose original intent is to marry and raise children sometimes find that lack of a willing or desirable partner, combined with positive career opportunities, sway their focus toward work and away from family. In contrast, some women whose original intent is to follow a career path find that marriage to a husband desiring children, along with blocked opportunities at work, encourages them to embrace family as their "career."

These studies suggest that women may not straightforwardly "choose" one life path over another. Outside circumstances and opportunities play a significant role in women's career and business choices. Women experience a variety of life events and make different choices based on perceived opportunity. For example, two women in this study stated that they had not wanted to start their own businesses. They would rather have worked for others in established businesses. Such positions were unavailable, so they started their own businesses. They responded to real contingencies in real life situations.

Roles, Norms, and Values. Patterns of women's socialization and norms about gender interact with circumstances in women's lives to produce distinctive responses to opportunities related to business ownership. Noting that most business owners operate truly small or even marginal businesses, Light and Rosenstein (1995:213) identify two types of survivalist entrepreneurs. "Value entrepreneurs" are mostly white females who choose low wage self-employment over low wage paid employment. They prefer the independence and status of a work situation in which they can accommodate their family and professional lives (see Bates 1987). An example might be a woman who chooses to operate a home daycare over paid employment in a clerical job. In contrast, "disadvantaged entrepreneurs" seek self-employment as a means to earn higher incomes than they would in paid employment due to labor market disadvantage (Light 1979; Min 1984). For example, a woman might quit her low-paying clerical position to start a business selling office equipment. Thus, self-employment becomes a solution to poverty (Green and Pryde 1990). Differing circumstances according to race may result in the difference between choosing business ownership out of one's values and choosing ownership out of need.

Gender Roles and Entrepreneurial Ideals. In a study of predominantly white women business owners in England, Goffee and Scase

(1985) found that self-employed women have widely varying motivations depending on their outlook on traditional gender roles and entrepreneurial ideals. In that study, women's values combined with their needs to create different motivational outcomes. These outcomes affected women's goals and how they operated their businesses.

For instance, women with high values for both entrepreneurial ideals and traditional gender roles ("conventionals") tended to have a high profit motive as long as money was made using traditionally "female" skills and the business did not interfere with domestic responsibilities. Their income was a needed supplement to overall family income. Yet they minimized business growth in order to maintain a high domestic profile. These women did not rock the boat when faced with economic need. They embraced their role as traditional workers both at home and in their businesses, and found ways to fulfill both their economic needs and their domestic responsibilities within the boundaries of gendered labor roles.

Women with high entrepreneurial ideals and low values for traditional gender roles ("innovators") were also in pursuit of profit. Like their male counterparts, they were business oriented, frequently highly educated, and driven by a need to achieve. They drew on technical skills learned in school and prior employment and were highly involved in their businesses. As a result, their social lives sometimes suffered. They operated their businesses in an egalitarian manner with little hierarchical structure, a style that Goffee and Scase found inhibited business growth. They depended instead on an atmosphere of trust and expected commitment and hard work from their employees in return. Because they often lacked female role models, Goffee and Scase's innovators often followed men's models. Whether or not they considered themselves feminists, they attracted attention as women who had "made it" in a man's world.

Women with low entrepreneurial ideals and high values for traditional gender roles were Goffee and Scase's "domestics." These women had a low profit motive but a high commitment to family. They entered self-employment for self-fulfillment and personal autonomy, often employing a talent in a craft or artistic endeavor. Having little need for income, these women kept their businesses small in order to minimize conflict with their domestic responsibilities.

Women with low interests in both entrepreneurial ideals and traditional gender roles were considered by Goffee and Scase to be "radicals." These women, often feminists, started businesses as a means to overcome subordination and to improve women's position in society. Radicals had very little profit motive, and some turned all profits over to women's groups, or to funds aimed at providing services for disadvantaged women. Business ownership was a political choice, an attempt to gain freedom from male influence through self-financing. Radicals rejected the image of themselves as entrepreneurs, yet strived to provide role models for other women by creating a sphere of female autonomy. They often combined work with their personal lives, sometimes working as a collective with other like-minded people.

Not all women are interested solely in the *amount* of money they make in owning their own businesses, although most sociological research on entrepreneurship has assumed, explicitly or implicitly, that earnings are a primary motivation for all business founders. Other factors, such as self-fulfillment or covering domestic responsibilities, may take precedence over earnings. Income from self-employment may be more attractive than no income or than lower income from wage labor. Women in three out of four groups in Goffee and Scase's work consciously limited growth of their businesses. Women in the fourth group also adopted management styles conducive to limiting growth, though not intentionally. Thus, women may start businesses for non-monetary reasons, or combine earning money with other non-economic goals.

Human Capital: Training, Skills, and Experience

More education and prior work experience predict financial success for women who own their own businesses (Bender 1980; Cuba et al. 1983; Loscocco et al. 1991). Before 1960, more women than men received high school degrees. However, of the men who completed high school, more completed college degrees (Becker 1993). As earnings have increased for college graduates, college enrollments have increased. Women have increasingly entered fields previously dominated by men. From the late 1980s on, women have earned more B.A.'s and M.A.'s than men have (Digest of Educational Statistics 1997). By the early 1990s, women made up one third of all majors in law, medicine, and business, and enrollment in home economics had declined (Becker 1993).

Although a majority of women entrepreneurs now have completed a college degree, their education may be poorly matched to the types of businesses they operate, or to business ownership at all (Bowen and Hisrich 1986; Hisrich 1989). In one study, Hisrich (1989: 12, 14) reported that 29 percent of female entrepreneurs had some college or technical training, 31 percent had a college degree, and 34 percent had a graduate degree. Yet their college majors included social sciences (24 percent),

English literature (12.8 percent), fine and applied arts (12 percent) and humanities (10.4 percent). Only 15.2 percent of women entrepreneurs majored in business, accounting, or a related field. Thus, few women had financial and management training when starting their business. Hisrich and Brush (1983) and Watkins and Watkins (1983) reported similar patterns. Because of lack of training, bankers perceive women as bad credit risks and have been reluctant to advance them loans (see Finance section below) (Humphreys and McClung 1981).

Although African American women may have less access to education and training than European American women (Higginbotham 1985) educational and career aspirations and expectations for those black women are generally higher than those of white women (Kelly 1975; Murrell et al. 1991). Black women plan significantly more education above the minimum requirements than do white women, especially when preparing for a non-traditional careers (Murrell et al. 1991). This may be due to the motivation and encouragement many African American women receive from their families and communities to pursue education (Collins 1990; Higginbotham and Weber 1992; McAdoo 1978).

Employment Opportunities and Experience. As opportunities have opened up for women in new fields and as the economy has changed from a focus on production to a focus on service industries, more women are entering business ownership at a younger age. The average age of women starting businesses in 1970 was 52. By 1986, the average age was 41 (Aronson 1991:7). Even so, many women have previous work experience in their occupational fields. Two thirds of the women in Hisrich and Brush's (1983) study had prior experience working in the area of their business. Yet as many as 83 percent of women business owners may have no prior experience as business owners (DeCarlo and Lyons 1979). Women are more likely than men owners to be first-time entrepreneurs. This, combined with little training in business, increases the likelihood that women entering business ownership are unprepared to manage the financial and personnel aspects of their businesses.

Credentialism. "Credentialism," an alternative theoretical view of the role of education, suggests that degrees are merely indicators symbolizing underlying characteristics of individuals who attend school. Those who earn college degrees are assumed to be more productive than those who don't earn degrees. This view was widespread in the 1970s when an "over-educated" population saw low growth in earnings tied to education. During the 1980s, growth in earnings picked up as new technologies were developed, and a concern emerged over the inadequacy of the U.S. educational system (Becker 1993). With the growth in technology, especially in computers and communications, schooling has again become viewed as an important place to acquire technical knowledge and skills. In the current study, women business owners, particularly those in highly technical businesses, view education and training as a needed resource. They see business skills, in particular, as a vital resource and express a desire to gain more such skills through education.

Social Resources

A growing body of work has been directed at networks of self-employed women (see "Women's Business Networks" below). While some is theoretical rather than empirical (Aldrich 1989; Smith-Lovin and McPherson 1993), most of this work centers on the type and form of women's networks without examining specifically the ways in which such resources are mobilized.

Women's Business Networks. Studies of women's business networks differ in their outcomes. Women receive little encouragement to start their businesses (Kalleberg 1985). Once businesses are started, women lack adequate network contacts. Aldrich and colleagues have conducted several studies of entrepreneurial network contacts. In early works, the authors found that networks affect the "life chances" of businesses (Aldrich and Zimmer 1986; Zimmer and Aldrich 1987). Comparing men and women owners, they found that men have more opportunity to meet higher status individuals (Aldrich 1989), while women have more restricted business ties (Aldrich, Reese, and Dubini 1989). These findings support those of Loscocco and Robinson (1991), who found that women are excluded from networks through which government contracts are awarded.

Aldrich and his colleagues' findings suggest that women business owners may be at a disadvantage when tapping social capital to mobilize human and financial capital, a hypothesis supported by later findings that women are left out of men's informal networks (Aldrich and Sakano 1995). However, women form distinctive types of networks that only rarely have been examined by researchers. Recent studies have examined to whom women go for business advice (Aldrich, Brickman, and Reese 1995); whether women rely on strong or weak ties for business information and aid (Aldrich, Brickman, and Reese 1995); the degree to which women's business contacts are embedded in their social networks (Staber and Aldrich (1995); and whether networking pays off in increased business performance (Aldrich and Reese 1993).

In a study of young businesses in the Research Triangle Park area of North Carolina, Aldrich and Reese (1993) found no evidence to support theories that networking increases business survival or business income. They attributed these results, seemingly contrary to prior research findings, to the volatility experienced by extremely young firms and to difficulties in accurately measuring business failures.[5]

A second study found that both men and women seek business advice from men, but women do so less often. When available, women contact other women for financial and legal advice. In addition, women pay less for legal, loan, and expert advice than men do because they have more social ties to providers of these services. Women are as active as men in three out of four network areas (financial, loans, and expert advice), lagging only in pursuit of legal advice. Both women and men use weak ties (friends and business associates) for help. Both seek expert advice in their fields from contacts they already know. Neither men nor women use family members as channels to find aid or advice, and both willingly seek advice from strangers when necessary (Aldrich, Brickman, and Reese 1995).

Social Embeddedness Network Models. Departing from neoclassical theories in which business owners' networks are based solely on economic interests, Staber and Aldrich (1995) adopt a social embeddedness model of business networks based on Granovetter's (1985) work. In a mixed sample of men and women owners from Canada and North Carolina, they found that owners in both regions held a core of friends and family at the center of their networks. These relationships were densely embedded and characterized by the long-term development of loyalty and trust. Only a small percentage of these ties were business-oriented, and these were also of long duration. Third party "brokers" introduced owners to network contacts, but women had fewer brokered introductions. This research suggests gender barriers in making network contacts that could favor men over women in business networking circles (Staber and Aldrich 1995:462).

These strong, core networks of business owners in Canada and North Carolina are reminiscent of kin networks in immigrant populations and in strong African American communities (Day 1986; Malsen 1983). They are also similar to Light and Rosenstein's ethnic and class

resources, which can be seen as social resources created out of the benefits of belonging to ethnic or class-based groups. African American
women business owners who rely on child rearing support networks in
the African American community are benefiting from an ethnic resource
available to African American women as an ethnic/racial group. Such resources are based on extensive kin network support systems in which
childcare, activities supporting childcare, child rearing tasks, socialization help and advice, and collective help in emergencies are available.
This network forms an informal mutual aid system that benefits all black
mothers who work.

Building upon Aldrich and his colleague's work, Brush (1992) and
others suggest that women perceive and approach business ownership
differently than men. According to this view, women see their business
and social contacts as " 'cooperative networks of relationship' rather than
separate economic units. In this conception, business relationships are
integrated rather than separated from family, societal, and personal relationships" (Brush 1992:16).

This view is consistent with psychological studies of gender differences in self-concept and relationships with others (Gilligan 1982) and
with studies of women's activities in the volunteer sphere (Daniels
1988.). Daniels writes of the "seamless" quality of women's lives where
boundaries between work and family are blurred. White women may
turn to social and kin relationships for aid with their businesses in much
the same way black women rely on supportive kin networks (see
"African American Women's Networks" below). The aid sought, however, might depend on social class, individual women owners' kin, and
social location of these relatives in business circles.

Financial Resources

In *Banking on Black Enterprise*, Bates (1993:48) found that "the size
of an owner's financial investment is the most powerful single determi-
nant of both the size and the likely survival of a small business." Bearse
(1984) found that owners with greater assets (whites and Asians) were
more likely to start businesses than those with fewer assets (blacks).
For those with limited access to capital, starting a successful business is
difficult.

Access to credit was a barrier for women entrepreneurs in the 1970s
(Schwartz 1976) and the 1980s (Brush and Hisrich 1985). Women reported difficulty getting loans as the second biggest barrier they faced in
starting businesses, next to lack of previous business experience (Bowen

and Hisrich 1986). Women in non-traditional businesses have more difficulty obtaining commercial funding than do women in more traditional
businesses (Hisrich and O'Brien 1982). All women have trouble gaining
information about government programs (Brush and Hisrich 1985). As a
result, women sole proprietors borrow less money and depend on personal savings and assets to finance their businesses (U.S. Small Business
Administration 1988b). According to Brophy (1989:56), only eight percent of women business owners use more than two sources of funding.

Discrimination in Lending. There may be several reasons for
women's limited access to credit. As first time business owners from
lower-paying service occupations, women might lack a credit history or
enough collateral to obtain a large bank loan. Many women have experienced credit discrimination in the past (Brush and Hisrich 1985;
Schwartz 1976), and are still discouraged from applying for business
loans (Tigges and Green 1992).

Women face additional structural barriers in financing their businesses, including discrimination based on the perception that all women
start low-growth firms (see *Types of Businesses Started by Women*
below). Those who don't may have trouble convincing bankers of their
greater aspirations. In addition, lenders perceive women to be weak in
business operations and financial skills, considered by many to be
"male" skills that women have difficulty mastering. Their lack of confidence is evident to bankers, who assume that women cannot operate a
business well enough to merit a loan. However, studies suggest that
women acquire needed skills, so this rationale is probably not valid
(Brush and Hisrich 1985).

Networks and Financing. Much of the research on women's networks focuses on personal and social network ties as they relate to employment in the paid labor force (Campbell 1988; Marshall and Barnett
1992; Miller, Lincoln, and Olson 1981) or in business operations (see review of Aldrich and colleagues work above). The literature on minorities' network ties and financing focuses primarily on immigrant
entrepreneurs and rotating credit associations (for instance, Light, Im,
and Deng 1990). Although such associations are becoming more common in urban African American communities, community-based financing of black businesses has tended to be less formal than the
organizations set up in Asian communities. African American business
networks in metropolitan areas can provide support and financing for

black women starting businesses. For instance, one woman in Woodard's (1997) study "piggy-backed" on a line of credit belonging to a business associate to finance her business. In exchange, she gave him part ownership in her business. Kin-based networks available to black women can also provide financial aid for business start-ups. However, personal wealth in the African American community is lower than personal wealth of European Americans and Asians and is even slightly lower than personal wealth of Hispanics (Bearse 1983; Bradford 1990; Day, 1986; Terrell 1971). Especially in rural areas, kin-based aid is more likely to come in the form of information or physical labor.

Literature on female entrepreneurship focuses on white, middleclass women only or includes all women in one category without examining differences among them. This strategy ignores potentially significant differences in women's networks and financial resources by race, age, and locale, leaving open the question of how these potential differences might affect different women's business chances and experiences. Do African American and European American women have similar financial resources? How might race and/or age affect networks and access to financial resources? Do differences in community size affect women's opportunities for commercial funding? Research examining the number and types of contacts a woman has does not address the complexity of the business and personal networks women business owners may build.

Loan Structures and Characteristics of Businesses. The structural problems women face in financing their businesses are twofold. First, financing takes different forms, including venture capital (investments by stockholders or other high-stakes investors), debt capital (commercial loans), and government subsidized or guaranteed loans. Each type of financing is appropriate for different phases of business start-up and operations. Second, the types of businesses women tend to start are frequently looked on unfavorably by lenders, especially for certain types of financing. If the studies cited below are correct, women's motives in starting their businesses will clearly affect their success in obtaining commercial financing for their businesses.

Types of Businesses Started by Women. Brophy (1989) identifies three types of "entrepreneurial ventures" that women pursue based on their motivations for business ownership. "Lifestyle" ventures are those pursued by women who want the autonomy and independence of being their own boss. Income is viewed as secondary, except to provide enough for a comfortable life. "Smaller profitable" firms are those where income is a greater consideration. The owner wants to produce a profit, yet also wants to remain in control. She will not allow the firm to grow in size to the point where she must give up managerial control to others. The "high growth" firm is one in which high growth in sales and profit are expected and desired. The high growth firm may be profitable enough to attract venture capital and sell stocks on the public market.

Although female entrepreneurs vary in motives, women start lifestyle and low-growth businesses more frequently than firms with high-growth potential. This choice affects their ability to obtain commercial funding in start-up. In making lending decisions, banks weigh risk factors against the rate of return on a loan. Because of the potential for a high return on their dollar, they prefer lending to high-growth firms. Rather than making start-up loans, banks prefer to make growth loans after businesses are established. To limit risk, they seek owners who present good business plans backed with good management skills.

In assessing women as potential business owners, bankers look primarily at management experience and track records. Women tend to work for extended periods as paid employees in the same field in which they start their businesses. This gives them valuable employment experience, a positive characteristic when applying for a loan. However, evidence suggests that they nevertheless face difficulties obtaining commercial funding (Ronstadt 1984).

Types of Financing. Brophy (1989) identifies three types of financing: equity, special equity, and debt financing. Equity financing is used most often in business start-up and involves "selling a percentage of the ownership of the firm and sharing control over the direction the firm takes" (Brophy 1989:65). It often takes the form of venture capital. Because of the high risk involved in starting a new business, venture capitalists set high standards and require as much as 50 percent per year in returns. This creates a bias favoring high-growth firms, so that loans are inaccessible for women starting low-growth and lifestyle firms. In addition, women are excluded from networks passing on information about government programs (Brush and Hisrich 1985) and might also be excluded from networks for gaining information about venture capital.

Special equity sources take the form of grants and come from numerous programs created to aid small business start-ups. The federal Small Business Administration has sponsored several of these programs, including the Small Business Investment Company (SBIC) and the Minority Enterprise Small Business Investment Company (MESBIC). At

the state level, grants and venture capital sometimes come from programs managing employee pension funds. These public funds have often
been a funding source for minorities (Bates 1975) but have been less
available to women (Committee on Small Business 1988; Loscocco and
Robinson 1991).

Banks often see debt financing, or commercial bank loans, as more
an option for business growth than business start-up. Risks of commercial credit are high when an owner does not yet have income from her
business. Nevertheless, businesses in the retail and service sectors (often
the location of women's businesses) present certain qualities that fit with
requirements of commercial credit better than businesses in other industry sectors. Retail and service firms require little money to start, and they
have the potential to generate sales and profits rapidly. Depending on
cash-flow and the lag between out-going services and incoming receipts,
these businesses can be financed with commercial loans and leasing
agreements (Brophy 1989:69).

The three sources of financing discussed above clearly serve different segments of the entrepreneurial population. Venture capital, with its
competitive, high risk/high return intensity would typically attract entrepreneurs motivated by profit and the need to achieve. Publicly available
equity capital goes primarily to minority entrepreneurs. Women, as well
as some minorities, most often seek commercial debt capital. With little
access to information about venture capital and minimal regulatory support for securing public equity resources, women turn to the only other
commercial source available to them. Even so, they frequently have difficulty securing commercial financing and are sometimes under-funded or
denied loans altogether.

SUMMARY

Despite an apparent lack of financial and business experience, women
are starting new businesses in record numbers. Women entrepreneurs
come to business ownership for many reasons, not all of which are financial. Differing and conflicting commitments and priorities in women's
lives can affect the economic performance of their businesses. Lack of
business and financial training and related work experience can lead to
low profit margins. While new businesses in general may face inherent
liabilities in the market structure, women who start new businesses may
face additional disadvantages that are built into labor market structures.
Business networks dominated by men provide little financial support, re-

sources, or other support to women. Limited financial and educational resources and gender-typed socialization lead women to start businesses in lower paying labor sectors (and lower paying occupations within those sectors) of the economy, which in turn diminish their chances of adequate funding. Additional disadvantages of race, class, and location may set African American women back even further.

Research on women entrepreneurs focuses primarily on these barriers, outlining them and measuring the extent to which one more than another disadvantages women owners when held to a white male standard of success. This literature leaves unexamined how women's business motives, goals, and intentions, and the circumstances surrounding start-up, affect the resource mobilization process, and vice versa. Nor does it thoroughly analyze how women succeed in gaining skills and funding necessary to start businesses. Studies have also neglected to examine differences in women owners' resource mobilization by race and locale.

Research on motives and business intent has focused primarily on how gender roles and responsibilities shape women's desires and goals for business. It has yet to examine how women follow professional or trade careers as the main thrust in business ownership, or entrepreneurial careers as the first priority in their lives. Little work has examined rural and/or African American women's situation-based entrepreneurial motives, nor has there been a systematic study of older women's business goals.

Work on women entrepreneur's educational resources has been limited by relatively shallow measures of attainment. Women's education levels and college majors supply some information about women's skill readiness for business ownership, but cannot give a full, in-depth picture of their total skills and knowledge. Training opportunities and job experiences, as well as less formal sources of knowledge, must be included to complete the picture of each woman's human capital resources.

Lack of access to commercial capital has been the dominant theme in the literature on women entrepreneurs. Little research, however, has compared women who are successful in obtaining loans with those who are not. Such work is necessary to understand what characteristics and abilities are necessary to bring about success in the loan application process. In addition, little work examines alternative funding sources and cost saving strategies women use in starting businesses. Research has largely ignored differences in women entrepreneurs' access to commercial financing by race or locale, nor have studies examined women's personal funding resources, whether built in prior employed positions or invested from family reserves.

Research on women owner's network contacts focus primarily on type and form of network ties, with little examination of what transpires within relationships. The main thrust has been women's lack of ties to white male business contacts. Little work examines women's expressive, or "strong" ties to family and kin and how human and financial capital might be passed through these ties. Nor have studies thoroughly examined women's business contacts to determine what help they do provide. Much work discusses African American women's extended kin relationships and services provided in-kind, but little focuses on African American women business owners and how they mobilize donated labor, human, financial, and other resources through kin and community networks, especially in rural areas.

This study addresses these discrepancies by providing detailed examination of women entrepreneurs' situations, motives and goals for business, and how these affect resource mobilization. Educational experiences as well as job training and experience, professional and industry-structured training, and informal learning are examined. The study examines women's financial resources in depth, including commercial and personal resources, as well as cost reduction strategies. Most importantly, I examine the interaction between women's social contacts and their human and financial resource mobilization. I detail what occurs in their relationships to further or discourage them in establishing their businesses. I compare women's experiences and resources by race, urban/rural locale, and somewhat by age. By studying successful women business owners (those in business at the time interviewed) I focus on strategies and actions that have been useful to women in garnering human and financial resources and that have allowed them to succeed in establishing businesses.

NOTES

[1] Alternatively, they may have "too much" credit. One woman in this study said she was told by the bank that she had too much credit—she was paying back more debt than her income appeared to be able to support.

[2] In 1987, less than 1 percent of federal contract dollars went to women business owners (SBA 1988b).

[3] However, between 1976 and 1986, college participation *increased* for black women while *decreasing* for black men (American Council on Education 1988).

[4] In 1971, personal wealth of blacks was one fifth that of whites. At that time, blacks tended to hold wealth in homes and autos, while whites held more

wealth (one third to blacks' one tenth) in financial assets, such as savings and monetary investments (Terrell 1971). By the early 1980s, blacks still lagged behind whites, Asians, and Hispanics in personal wealth (Bearse 1983; El-liehausen, Canner and Avery 1984a, 1984b). By 1990, black family wealth holdings lagged behind white's wealth holdings by $.09 on every $1.00 (Bradford 1990).

[5] They did not include follow-up interviews to determine whether some owners may have closed their businesses to open other, larger businesses.

CHAPTER 4

Research Design and Methods

This study compares black and white women's resources in business start-up and how the circumstances surrounding their decisions to start and their goals for business affect these resources. This chapter reviews the research design and methodology that is used in the study to determine how business and community environments shape women's business experiences by race.

STUDY DESIGN

To better understand women's motives for business ownership and their resource mobilization processes, I used qualitative, in-depth interview techniques to delve into the details of business ownership. I chose to examine many kinds of businesses in order to get a broader picture of women's resource needs and sources. As women move out of traditional occupations and businesses into more lucrative industries, their needs and opportunities change. Larger businesses require more financing, both for start-up and growth and for more complex accounting systems. Commercial lenders require more proof of reliability and credit-worthiness. Women are more likely to hire service providers and full time employees to handle tasks for which they have had no training. In doing so they move towards either a more managerial role or the occupational provision of a good or service. They have less need for knowledge of both production of a good or service and skills related to operating a business.

The South provides an excellent setting within which to study black and white women entrepreneurs. A higher proportion of African Americans and a higher proportion of black women's businesses than in other parts of the U.S. provides an adequate sampling frame to examine black and white women's businesses. In addition, a high proportion of rural blacks allows comparison across urban and rural settings that might not be possible in other regions. This has been especially important for understanding opportunities and barriers that exist for black women in different sized communities and effects of different sized client bases on all women's businesses.

Qualitative Methods

One of the benefits of conducting a qualitative study is the freedom given to the researcher to examine the respondents' experiences more closely than is possible in a quantitative study. While quantitative methods provide measures indicating trends, they cannot adequately describe the quality of women's education and training or how women's social contacts provide information, skills, and other aid for business start-up. Education levels and job experiences, while quantifiable in terms of degrees and job titles, can be misleading if not also accompanied by the stories women tell about their training experiences. One woman's business training may provide her with little useful knowledge for operation, while another's job apprenticeship could provide first class skills upon which to base a business. Quantitative measures of network density and type reveal little of what actually takes place between the entrepreneur and her contacts that helps her with her business. In-depth qualitative interview techniques allow women to tell their own stories and provide detailed information on learning and financing processes, including who helped, why, and how. Such details would be lost in a quantitative study.

Another benefit of qualitative research is the opportunity to examine how women's resources intersect and interact to provide what they need to start and operate businesses. A quantitative study may ascertain those parts of women's experiences that are solely due to one factor or another, but when resources combine, multi-collinearity makes analysis difficult. A qualitative study can reveal how women's choices, abilities, contacts, and resources combine over time to provide support and opportunity in environments of limited access through other means.

Qualitative methods are particularly well suited to the exploration and comparison of cultures or sub-cultures in contemporary society. In undertaking a study that compares African American and European American women entrepreneurs, I find it natural to use intensive interview methods to explore how women choose and start businesses. To understand their experiences, it is necessary to understand the contexts within which they work, make decisions, and seek resources for start-up. Where quantitative methods rely on simplified measures of global trends, the in-depth qualitative interview can delve into respondents' lives and the myriad of contingencies upon which they base decisions (Lofland and Lofland 1995).

Study Focus

My first intent in this study was to compare African American and European American women business owners. As the study progressed, however, I discovered more cultural variations than I had originally anticipated. First, and perhaps foremost, I studied the American South, a region different from my native Midwest. Having lived in the South for more than twelve years, I became an entrenched participant, but in many ways remained an observer. While many of the participants of the study were Southern by birth, several were not, making their experiences in the South similar to mine in some respects. Second, the study focuses on small businesses. The worlds of business and economics, like politics, build their own cultures and draw into their sphere of operations the uninitiated. Women who have not previously been involved in business cultures enter for the first time, perhaps with dreams of independence, wealth, and autonomy. The third cultural comparison is one between rural and urban dwellers. Different opportunities available in different locales are important in studying resources available to entrepreneurs in different sized communities.

Finally, I make the comparison between African American and European American women. As a white woman, I initially feared I would be unable to interest black women in the study. To ensure an adequate pool of information for both black and white women, I wanted to interview equal numbers of each race. To gain access to the black community, I asked two black women acquaintances to provide a list of black women business owners, one in the rural areas sampled, and one in the small city. Both complied, giving me the base of my first interviews with African American women in these areas. I ultimately was able to interview almost as many black women as white.

While some black women refused to be interviewed (see Table 4.1 in Appendix A), I found that many black women wanted very much to participate. Several said they wanted to help out the educational process, and one explained that she saw herself as a role model for other black women. She wanted to take part in the study to further that end. Racial comparisons are a central organizing theme of the study, but variations by age, family background, and class status also affect women's outlooks, opportunities, and choices as founders of small businesses. I found that many black and white owners had similar concerns, motivations, and experiences, making them likely allies.

In all, I conducted 65 interviews between June 1994 and April 1995. The interview tapes were transcribed between September 1994 and February 1996. The transcripts were coded between March 1995 and March 1996. Sixty-one of the interviews were analyzed for this work. Four interviews were completed but not included in these analyses. Although prior to interviewing they seemed to fit selection criteria, interviews revealed that in one way or another they did not.[1] Four of the businesses (two black- and two white-owned) were operated by partners who were both present at the interview. Because of this, the study includes 61 interviews with 65 women. A few respondents had business partners who did not take part in the interview.

DATA COLLECTION

The study was an interview/survey study. Data were collected using a semi-structured qualitative interview questionnaire, administered face-to-face, and a mail-back survey questionnaire. This allowed collection of a broad range of information in a short period of time, yet also allowed personal contact with, and observation of, respondents. Study participants were African American and European American women business owners in three types of communities in the Southeast: rural, small city, and a large metropolitan area. The respondents were chosen from lists generated from sources listed below and from participant referrals as the study progressed.

The first five interviews were used as a pilot study to test the interview and survey questionnaires. Adjustments were made to the questionnaires, and several questions were added or changed. The interview questionnaire included questions concerning start-up, women's motivations and business goals, their education, training and work histories, help and barriers in start-up, business and financing strategies, and family influences. The survey questionnaire included additional questions on the business and business owner, financing, personnel, business strategies, and financial information. Copies of the interview and survey questionnaires are included in Appendix B. Data were coded and analyzed for emergent categories according to women's motivations for business. Groupings were then examined to understand women's resource mobilization processes and how these were linked to race, business locale, and type of enterprise (see Data Analysis, below).

Sampling

I employed a purposive sample and make no claims that it is a statistically representative one. In qualitative research, theoretically driven sampling allows comparisons of selected groups in order to better understand processes and contexts for decision making and action (Glaser and Strauss 1967; Huberman and Miles 1994). A snowball method of sampling was employed in combination with maximum variety sampling (Morse, 1994:229) across many types of businesses. Several sources were used to identify potential study participants. They included Bell-South Yellow Pages for selected cities and towns; Women's Yellow Pages and Black Pages for selected cities; businesses identified as woman-owned by Chambers of Commerce in selected counties; businesses identified as woman-owned from a list provided by the Small Business Development Center at the University of Georgia; and participants of business trade shows for women and African American business owners. Other sources included newspapers and other documentary material; formal and informal business women's organizations; referrals from prominent members of the African American community; and referrals from personal contacts in the study areas.

Selecting Businesses and Respondents. To protect the privacy of those participating in the study, all place and person names are pseudonyms. To distinguish urban, small city, and rural communities, I chose the following names: Stanley for the large metropolitan area; Grafton for the small city; and Bingham, Ludlow, and Acorn for the rural communities. Bingham was the largest town, numbering around 15,000 with about 70 percent white and 30 percent black residents. Ludlow was slightly smaller with a 70-80 percent black population. Acorn was a tiny rural hamlet consisting mostly of African Americans residents.

The first 15 interviews were conducted in the small city of Grafton. I started with hair salons, selecting randomly from a list of black Grafton hair stylists. This was the most common type of business for black women in Grafton to own. In the rural areas, it was one of only a few business types black women owned.[2] I then found black women attor-

neys and other black owners, and also interviewed white women business owners in Grafton.

To locate women business owners in Grafton, I used a directory of
women-owned businesses in the area. I also sought the aid of insiders.
While not precisely informants in the ethnographic sense (Fontana and
Frey 1994:367; Spradley 1979: Ch. 3), these women were active members in their cultural group. The first was a female coworker from the
Grafton African American community. Although not a participant in the
study, she gave me a list of black women she knew who owned businesses in Grafton. Along with the Yellow Pages of the local telephone
book, these sources provided the start of my small city sample. As I interviewed Grafton women, I gained more help. One of the European American owners had founded a women's business organization in town. She
provided a long list of women business owners in Grafton, both black
and white. I interviewed many of these women.[3]

Early in the study, I solicited interviews from rural respondents to
identify the types of businesses owned by black and white women in the
rural sample areas. This allowed me to target similar types of businesses
in the small city and metropolitan areas for comparison purposes. Again,
I sought the aid of an insider. An African American colleague who had
lived in one of the rural communities, and whose husband owned a business with locations in both communities, supplied the names and addresses of several women business owners, both black and white, in two
of the rural communities sampled here.[4]

I began by interviewing African American women. I thought I
would later be able to persuade the more numerous and perhaps more
willing white owners of similar businesses to participate once I had attained the cooperation of black owners in specific businesses. Thus,
much of the early sample was based on the availability of African American respondents, and the subsequent selection (random where possible)
of corresponding European American respondents in similar businesses.
In the rural areas, this meant that I was limited to sampling from a) those
businesses that existed and b) those owners who were willing to participate in the study. I called all the black women on my list of rural owners
and interviewed as many as I could reach who agreed to participate. The
same was true for the white owners in Ludlow.

Bingham provided a larger field from which to choose. Once I had
matched as many rural black owners as possible with similar white businesses, I then began trying to match rural business types with similar
urban businesses. The more populated cities had a broader base of busi-

nesses, allowing limited random sampling. Here, women owned a greater number and variety of businesses, and I was able to interview women with larger and more non-traditional businesses.

Where possible, I chose individuals randomly within groupings. It soon became clear, however, that most of the women in certain businesses had little time to participate. This was true of African American dentists, and most other medical professionals. I had luck with psychologists, and was able to interview two, one black and one white, both from Stanley.

In order to reflect the types of businesses women owned, and their business experiences in the more populated areas, I interviewed a set of owners in Grafton and Stanley not comparable to those in the rural areas. I found a much wider variety of businesses owned by black women in Stanley than in the smaller sample communities. Because many of these business types were not represented among African American owners in the smaller locations, I over-sampled black owners in Stanley. I found both a greater number and a wider variety of businesses owned by white women than black women in Grafton, so I interviewed more whites than blacks in that smaller city. In the rural towns, white women owned businesses that were more non-traditional than those owned by black women, so I interviewed several white, non-traditional business owners. Here, I was able to interview the same number of rural African American as European American women.

Because I specifically wanted to include women in non-traditional businesses, I explicitly chose businesses with the most non-traditional sounding names and called them. This resulted in interviews with women who owned residential contracting, commercial mailing, chemical manufacturing, wholesale petroleum, architectural, laser recycling, security alarm, and tavern businesses.

I also included businesses in fields where women and minorities have been numerous in recent years. I therefore sampled women realtors, travel agents, and proprietors of business service firms. The real estate and travel fields have become dominated by women, while increasingly well-educated urban blacks have moved into business related occupations (see Bates 1993b: 49). In choosing realtors, I included only those who individually owned firms.[5] Where possible, I chose white and black subjects in similar businesses in similar types of communities. A complete list of owners and owner/business characteristics is listed in Table 1 in Appendix A.

The sample included women of varying ages and class backgrounds.

Many of the women had experienced class mobility in the course of their working lives. Although not specifically targeted, this history enhanced assessment of the impact of social class on work options. Although the study primarily compares black and white women, two Hispanic women were interviewed. I knew the ethnicity of one prior to the interview, but the Hispanic origins of the other became apparent only during the interview. Both were in non-traditional businesses.

Experiences in Attaining Comparable Cases. In trying to match similar types of businesses across race and community size I had variable success. Limited occupational opportunities in the rural communities (particularly for African American women) influenced the types of businesses from which to sample. Many women had a limited amount of time to devote to the study. I sometimes had trouble scheduling interviews, and occasionally had to reschedule meeting times that were missed. I had particular difficulty reaching some of the rural African American respondents who had jobs in addition to their businesses. Several rural black owners refused to participate, stating that they did not have time (see below).

Partners. Partnerships hold important implications for theory in that they potentially provide an opportunity for entrepreneurs to augment skills they lack in starting businesses. One partner might have more business-related skills while the other might provide expertise in the product or services they sell. In addition, partners may split the cost of start-up, reducing the amount of financing either one would have needed alone. Each partner can draw upon social networks that may not overlap, or may only partially overlap. Thus, partnerships potentially increase entrepreneurs' access to human, financial, and social resources for their businesses.

Several of the women in the study had business partners, many of whom were other women. However, some were in business either with their husbands or with other males. I chose to include these women for various reasons. In eight cases I didn't know until part way through the interview that the women had male business partners. In all but two or three cases, the women were either totally responsible for the daily operations of the business or were a dominant partner who carried the title "president" or "CEO." Male partners were predominantly silent partners by virtue of having contributed financially, or they played a lesser role in the business than the woman. In a few cases, the male partner explicitly owned a smaller share of the business than female partner, fitting the definition herein of a woman-owned business as being 51 percent or more female owned.[6]

Contacting Respondents

Using names chosen from the sampling lists, I made initial contact with potential respondents (PRs) via telephone. For those persons not immediately available, I called at least three times and left messages asking the PR to return my call. Upon contact with a PR, I introduced myself as a graduate student working on a study of women-owned businesses and asked for their participation.

If the PR remained interested, I described the study in some detail. I explained that the study would require a face-to-face interview of about an hour and a half in length, plus a written survey taking about 10 to 15 minutes to complete. I explained that the interview would be confidential, that I would not reveal the name of the PR or the name of her company, and that in writing up the results, I would do so in a way that would not identify the respondent. I told each PR that I would send all participants a summary of my findings.

If a PR agreed to take part in the study, I set up an interview at a time convenient for her. The interview usually took place at the respondent's business, or, if the business was home-based, at the respondent's home. A few people asked to meet me at a local library, where we found a quiet room in which to conduct the interview.

While I found many sources helpful in providing suggestions for how to conduct myself and communicate during the interview (for example, Berg 1989:26-27; Fontana and Frey 1994: 367; Spradley 1979:55-68), I found little guidance on making first contact with potential respondents. Over the course of time, I refined my initial presentation of self. I always tried to be polite, but I had to learn how to balance the timing of my initial explanation with the amount of information I presented. Usually, I learned more about how to present myself from the questions the PRs asked during my presentation. Most notably, I soon realized that I had to give some description, but not too much, of why I was calling before asking for their participation. I found that if I couched my subsequent request with a qualifier (asking if they might be willing to participate if I described the study further) I received a better response.

Refusals and Non-Response. Making first contact with a potential respondent was not always easy. Many women expressed interest in the study but said they had no time for it. Response rates varied both by race and by location. Counting only those contacted who either agreed or declined to participate, about 55 percent of the rural sample, about 83 percent of the small city sample, and about 72 percent of the metropolitan sample agreed to take part in the study. These figures do not include the women I was not able to reach by telephone, nor those I found who did not meet selection criteria for the study. A full listing of these response rates by race and locale is reported in Table 4.1 in Appendix A.

Conducting the Interview

At the beginning of the interview, I explained the consent form and procedures of the interview. Explanations of all forms and questionnaires were carried out according to procedures outlined by the Institutional Review Board Human Subjects Office at the University of Georgia. Interviews were taped with the respondent's consent. Only one respondent did not want the interview taped, so I took extensive notes in that session. A copy of the consent form is included in Appendix B.

The Interview and Survey Questionnaires. I constructed a verbal interview questionnaire to use as a guide in interviewing the respondents. The interview questions were designed to gain information on several aspects of the owner's experiences, her business, and business operations. By and large, I read the questions directly, now and then probing with additional related questions. In a few cases, I asked an additional sub-set of probing questions about a particular type of business, or a particular aspect of operations, that I felt were relevant to the study and would provide additional valuable information (see Berg 1989). This strategy resulted in collection of particularly rich data in several cases.

Individuals were screened to determine 1) if the business was woman-owned; 2) if the respondent was sole owner or if she had a partner; 3) if she started the business herself;[7] 4) if the business provided the respondent with her main source of income; 5) if the business was a franchise; 6) if the respondent had employees; 7) and, if so, how many employees she had. Information was also recorded on whether the business was home-based; minority/non-minority status of the respondent; and whether the respondent had a disability. A mail-back survey was left with the respondent at the time of the interview, along with a self-addressed stamped envelope. The respondent was asked to fill out and mail the survey. The purpose of the survey was to supplement and expand information generated in the interviews. Presenting certain questions in a written survey format allowed more time for open-ended questions during the interview.

The Interview Format. I began by asking general questions about the business: what it was, what it did, who were its clients and competitors. I asked about the owner's reasons for choosing the type of business she did, and her reasons for starting a business in general. These questions were designed in part to establish rapport with the respondent, to allow her to display her knowledge of her business, to allow her to feel confident in her ability to provide meaningful information to the study, and to establish trust (see Fontana and Frey 1994:367; Spradley 1979:57-68). It also gave me an overview of the business and a foundation upon which to identify motivation-based groupings of women owners.

Next, I asked the respondent about her educational background, training, and work history. These questions were designed to determine human capital resources available to the new business owner and additional training she sought during and after start-up. I then gathered information on the respondent's social resources and networks by asking who helped in starting the business. Then I asked about limitations and opportunities the respondent faced in financing her business.

The next questions were designed to elicit information on the respondent's business strategies and structured networks. They included questions on business organization memberships, trade show attendance, referrals, suppliers, trading and bartering, and advertising. These provided information on social capital, business networks, and formally structured learning opportunities. The following questions were about the respondent's goals, visions, and expectations for the business. These questions provided more depth for analysis of women's motives and circumstances in starting their businesses. The last questions were about the respondent's family and personal life.

At the end of the interview, I asked the respondent if she had anything to add and received permission to contact her to clarify anything that might remain unclear. I also asked for referrals of other women business owners who might participate in the study.

The Survey Form and Response Rate. The survey was based in part on a questionnaire from a 1992 rural economic development study conducted by researchers at the Small Business Development Center in Athens, Georgia (see University of Georgia 1992). The survey included questions on the characteristics of the businesses and the owners; sources of financial capital (personal, commercial, alternative); sources of social capital and networking (help with the business, help with financing, help with training and information); and questions for further research (personnel issues, business strategies, sales and expenditures for the year 1993, and other family background information.)

The response rate for the written survey was 91.4 percent for the European American women and 53.3 percent for the African American women. The rural women responded the least, with 25 percent black and 89 percent white survey returns. Highest response was in Grafton, where 75 percent of blacks and 93.3 percent of whites responded. The survey data are therefore more reliable for the white sample than the black. To enhance the response rates, I made several calls to non-respondents, but this strategy resulted in only two or three surveys being returned. Because of low response rates, the survey data were not analyzed for this study. I occasionally referred to them to confirm details such as respondent's age but have otherwise left them for future analysis.

The Interview Experience. Every woman I interviewed had a unique contribution to make to the study, and most were very friendly and willing to talk. Thus, I collected very rich data, including detailed and fascinating life stories. Interviews averaged one and one-half hours, with a range from 1 to 3 hours. Some African American women were guarded at first, but most of these women seemed to relax and become friendlier throughout the interview. As the number of interviews I had completed grew, I, too, was able to relax more as I gained experience in asking questions and in explaining the purpose of the questions and the study. All women who agreed to participate completed the entire interview.

DATA ANALYSIS

The transcriptions of the taped interviews were first coded by major thematic topics (see Berg 1989:43). These included, but were not limited to, 1) circumstances surrounding business start-up, including situational factors, motives, goals, and influences; 2) the respondent's human capital resources, including education, training, and work experience; 3) financial capital resources, including commercial, non-commercial, personal, and alternative cost-reduction and cost-saving strategies; and 4) social capital resources, including help networks, business contacts, family networks, and other contacts. Other coding included such topics as business strategies, family information, technology information, and employee information. I then used a system of filing cards to index details under each topic with reference to page numbers in transcripts (see Berg 1989:43). Using this file card system, I then analyzed the data, comparing motives, human capital, financial capital, and social capital across cases.

Following analytical strategies outlined by Strauss and Corbin (1990), I identified two general emergent categories, based on the circumstances of business start-up. Some women were internally motivated and had planned their businesses, while some were externally motivated, and had embarked on business ventures that had not been planned for many years or in some cases envisioned at all. Consistent with Gerson's (1985) theory of choice within a larger structure of opportunities and barriers, the women in the present study varied in their experiences and, therefore, in their paths to business. Some had planned their working lives to include the likelihood of business ownership, while others had had no intention of owning a business. For the latter women, circumstances outside their control propelled each of them into making the choice to own a business.

As coding proceeded, I was able to identify seven sub-groups and explored the ways in which these were linked to race, business locale, age (in some cases), and type of enterprise (traditional or non-traditional). In the next step of the analysis, I examined within these categories women's experiences related to 1) resources used in starting businesses; 2) skill and funding each group had; 3) mobilization of skills and financing in business start-up; and 4) social resources used in resource mobilization processes. I also compared the two general categories and their sub-groups to determine differences across groups in human, financial, and social capital resources and resource mobilization.

These lines of analysis became the foundation upon which I examined how rational choice, social capital and social embeddedness, and feminist and black feminist theories of economic behavior fit women entrepreneur's economic activities. By gaining an understanding of women's motives and the circumstances surrounding business start-up, we can begin to understand environments in which women make choices for business. In examining how women mobilize resources for businesses within those environments, we can refine our understanding of women's access to resources, and how they use social contacts to build human and financial capital for business.

NOTES

[1] I left out four interviews with women who either did not start their businesses themselves, or who were not business owners. (One of the women interviewed was the manager of a branch of a large corporation.)

[2] Others included restaurants, daycare centers, florists, dry cleaners, and nursing homes, all personal services traditionally provided by black women. The two rural and small city black women I found in business service industries, one in Ludlow and one in Grafton, both refused to participate in the study.

[3] Likewise, one respondent in Stanley gave me a list of members of a minority business owners' organization. I called several black women owners on this list.

[4] I heard about the single black woman in Acorn from the first respondent I interviewed.

[5] Although I tried to avoid interviewing women in direct marketing, two women, both metropolitan blacks, reported during the interview that their businesses were franchises. Neither woman was in a pyramid-style franchise such as Mary Kay Cosmetics. Both women had personal start-up costs, training concerns, employees, and client bases that could have occurred in any business. The women's reasons for choosing franchises rather than starting their own companies revealed an important aspect of African American's entrepreneurial experiences and motivations that may have been overlooked had I not included them in the study. Franchises offered legitimacy and name recognition of a large company that could reduce potential client discrimination against them as African American owners. It also provided training.

[6] Five women started businesses with male partners who no longer took part in the business by the time they were interviewed.

[7] Because I wanted to examine what skills and knowledge women bring to businesses they start themselves, I purposely left out those women who inherited existing businesses. For instance, I interviewed two women who had inherited their businesses from family members. One had inherited her father's heating and air conditioning business; the other had inherited a horticulture research business from her late husband. While both had valuable insights regarding ownership of very non-traditional businesses for women, their reasons for taking over the businesses, their training, and their loan experiences were significantly different from the other women in this study. On the other hand, I included three women who bought existing businesses because they faced similar training and financing challenges as women who started their own businesses.

CHAPTER 5

Motives, Goals, and Strategies in Start-Up
Situation-Based Decisions and Actions

A detailed analysis of women's situations, motives, and goals for business is essential in determining how applicable traditional rational choice, social embeddedness, and feminist theories are to black and white women's business experiences. Entrepreneurs start businesses for many reasons, some of which they control and some they don't. Women's non-economic motives and choices made in response to macro-structural constraints contradict neoclassical economic theories of atomized actors pursuing profit and call for broader perspectives provided by social embeddedness and feminist theories in which to frame women's entrepreneurial experiences.

Women's motives and goals for starting businesses affect and are affected by the resources with which they approach ownership. Operating a business is, in itself, a two-fold occupation. The owner must know not only business operations and procedures, but also the service or product she is selling. Because of the dual nature of entrepreneurship, and the sometimes unpredictable circumstances surrounding start-up, women's reasons for starting and owning a business are frequently more complex than for choosing an occupation. Resources available at the moment of choice and other resources owners know will become available are intrinsic in their decisions to start businesses. Those who plan to own a business can prepare for it with relevant education and training, and by saving or investing money and building good credit. Those who start businesses unexpectedly may be unprepared with formal skills. However, they may bring skills gained through paid employment and funding saved from regular paychecks. Depending on the types of jobs they've had, some may be more prepared with business related skills than women who have trained for a specific trade or profession. Availability of these resources again come into play in making decisions to start businesses.

In addition to human and financial capital, the social resources women bring to business ownership may differ according to their motivations, goals and intentions for the business. Circumstances surrounding business start-up may determine the types of social contacts women have that are relevant in starting a business. Those who plan for business by training in a trade or profession might have contacts with other professionals. The unexpected entrepreneur might have contacts from prior jobs. These different social contacts could provide substantially different types of help to the business owner.

Women's social resources may also differ by race and locale. White women may have informal social ties to white male business leaders who can provide information and references to a fledgling business. Black women may have strong extended family ties and social ties to an African American community that may provide unpaid services to business owners. Rural areas lack organizational resources available in larger urban centers. Thus, women starting businesses in rural areas have less access to advocacy aid or help with loan packages.

Little work has examined links between entrepreneurs' decisions to start businesses (and the circumstances surrounding start-up) and their resource mobilization processes. Below, and in the following chapters, I examine these linkages. First, in this chapter I introduce the women entrepreneurs and examine the circumstances surrounding their decisions to start a business. I identify types of women entrepreneurs and describe women's motives, goals, and intentions for business ownership within each type.

In Chapter 6, I examine how women's business motives and intentions affect their access to and mobilization of human capital resources for their businesses. In Chapter 7, I explore how women's business motives and intentions affect their access to and mobilization of financial capital resources. In Chapter 8, I examine how women use social ties to build human capital for their businesses, and how these interactions differ by motivational group. In Chapter 9, I analyze how women use social ties to build financial capital for their businesses. Again, I examine interactions of social and financial capital by type. Chapter 10 discusses theoretical and practical implications of this study.

INTERNALLY AND EXTERNALLY
MOTIVATED PATHS TO OWNERSHIP

In this study, women came to business ownership on different paths. As with Gerson's (1985) study, some of the women intended to own businesses and some were unintentional owners. For the former, owning a business was frequently the fulfillment of a dream. For the latter, changing circumstances in their lives led them to consider entrepreneurship later in life as an alternative to continued employment. For this reason, I identified two groups among my subjects based on women's motivations and goals for their businesses and the circumstances they encountered in start-up. Women in the first group, Business Planners, were internally motivated to start their businesses. Although many had not explicitly mapped out paths toward business ownership, they all chose trades or professions or had pursued business training with the intent of starting a business. They frequently had held occupational and entrepreneurial goals since childhood.

The second group consisted of owners who had not intended to own businesses from the beginning of their labor market involvement or who were motivated by external forces to start their businesses. I call these women Serendipitous Owners. They chose business ownership as a reaction to external events. When confronted with situations that barred or discouraged continued employment, or in response to social problems or life circumstances, they chose to start businesses rather than continue to seek paid employment.

Within the two main groups, women reported many factors affecting their decisions to start their businesses. Because of this, I divided the two major types into seven subgroups. These subgroups reflect different motivations for business ownership that expose variations in women's decision-making processes. Examination of how these variations fit rational choice, social embeddedness, and feminist theories of women's labor market activities allows an evaluation of how well these theories fit women's entrepreneurial decisions. Business Planners fell into four subgroups: 1) Trades women; 2) Professionals; 3) Natural Entrepreneurs; and 4) Retirement Planners. Serendipitous Owners fell into three subgroups: 5) Work Skill Owners; 6) Career Problem Solvers; and 7) Community Service Providers. (Table 1 in Appendix A provides a full list of owners and owner/business characteristics.)

Women in each of these seven subgroups approached business ownership differently. Race, locale, or age affected women's placement in subgroups, but not in a deterministic manner. The most notable racial differences occurred in the Trades, Professionals, Retirement Planners and Career Problem Solver groups. The Trades and Professions were split largely by race, with black women dominating the Trades group and white women making up a majority of the Professionals. Retirement Planners included black and white owners, but their business goals differed by race. The Career Problem Solver group was made up of urban black women who held corporate positions affected by restructuring and downsizing. It also included white women from all locales who had experienced layoffs, restructuring, or other sudden career changes. Below, I describe each of the sub-groups and introduce the women and businesses that typify each group.

INTERNALLY MOTIVATED BUSINESS OWNERS

The following four groups consist of women who were internally motivated to start businesses. In general, I call them "Business Planners," and they include Trades Women, Professionals, Natural Entrepreneurs, and Retirement Planners.

Group 1: Business Planners—Trades Women

With few exceptions, the Trade and Professional women differed by race. All but two of the Trades women were black, while two thirds of the Professional women were white. The Trades women lived in rural or small city areas, and almost all followed desires to practice a skill or talent they had "always done" or "always wanted to do." This was often coupled with a desire to own a business. Most trades were based on services traditionally provided by African American women in the South. All but one of the Trades women sought training in technical schools to gain greater skill and licensing.

Seven of the ten women in this group were hair stylists. Others were a rural seamstress and two Grafton women, a restaurant owner and an alterations shop owner. The salon owners generally served clients of their own race, although the African American owners reported serving "a few whites." The white stylists said they were willing to serve blacks but were not adequately trained and had little practice in styling African American hair. As Kathy, the young Ludlow beautician explained,

> I would kill their hair. I would set it afire. I mean, no doubt about it. I can't deny them if they come in here, but I can just say "Please, if you don't want your hair messed up . . ."

A black stylist from Grafton corroborated Kathy's observation:

> Even today, you see more blacks cutting white hair, simply because
> your hair is straight, and it's easy to cut a straight line, where our hair is
> not straight, you see. So there's a technique in cutting it, in perming it,
> in combing it. In managing it.

Linda, the white Grafton hair stylist, served men and women in her combination hair salon/barber shop, as did Sabrina, a young black stylist from Ludlow. In contrast, black sewing and alterations shop owners and the black restaurant owner served more whites than blacks.

Decisions to Start. Women in this group started their businesses as natural outgrowths of the pursuit of their trades. For some, owning a business was something they had always wanted, while for others friends and relatives had pointed out the benefits of ownership. All were in business doing something they had trained for and enjoyed. Several commented that they had "always done" their trade. A restaurant owner, Corinne's dream was to take care of people, and part of taking care of them was feeding them. She explained, "Two things I always wanted to do, and that was take care of older people and cook. I used to take my dolls and play as though I was taking care of them. And then I would always cook for 'em and set 'em at the table."

Independence and the Chance to Practice a Talent. For the Trades women, business ownership provided a living and an opportunity to be independent. Business ownership also became an opportunity to escape menial work and practice a skill. Carol, a seamstress, said she found little challenge in the factory and secretarial jobs available to her in Bingham but knew she had the talent to succeed in her alterations business.

Ivy, with partner Diane (see Entrepreneurial women), easily progressed from paid employment to business ownership. She had worked in several salons before finally realizing she could operate her own shop. After Ivy trained Diane, the two worked long hours for their boss until they realized that they could reap more benefits from their hard work if they opened their own salon.

Family Influences. The road to business ownership for Cynthia (black) and Linda (white) was influenced by others. Cynthia worked in a series of shops and department store salons before her cousin convinced her to open a shop in Grafton. Her last paid position was in a rented booth at a shopping mall. This was a step towards ownership, but the booth owner still controlled her hours and the sign advertising her services. Renting her own space allowed her more autonomy and cost her little more.

After high school, Linda's parents encouraged her to seek training to gain an employable skill. She chose hair styling because she enjoyed it. After working in a salon for the experience, she then worked in a meat packing plant because her husband thought she couldn't make enough money doing hair. She hated the plant and quit within months, returning to work in a salon. When the opportunity arose to buy the salon/barber shop, she jumped at the chance, knowing it was a stable shop in a good location with a good reputation.

Fulfillment of a Dream: "Deeply Anchored Businesses." While the other Trades women reached out for freedom and independence early in life, two older black women from Grafton, Hazel and Corinne, became owners only after years of working for others. Whether they were products of their time or were in occupations that afforded more opportunity in paid employment, they moved through formal training, then remained in paid employment for years before starting their own businesses. Yet their late entry into business was not due to earlier lack of desire. Both had always wanted to own a business, but neither had the means until late in life to fulfill their life-long dream.

This theme of early childhood training and experience appeared in the lives of many of the women in the study, especially the older black women. Those who described such childhood experiences had often gone on to complete formal training in the same skill they had learned as children. Some pursued paid employment in the same occupation, but some, like Corinne and Hazel, had waited years to fulfill a dream of using their talent in a business.

Elly had trained early to "do hair" and had practiced her trade in her backyard for years. Her dream was fulfilled when her younger sister, Lenore, came home to open a downtown salon with her. Elly explained,

> [I had a] beauty center for 30 years in my backyard. And when Lenore
> was in high school, *I* decided that she was gonna be in business with
> me, and I didn't give her no opportunity to say yes or no. I just made
> the plans. And while she was in high school, she trained and helped me
> out a lot, and when she graduated, she decided that there was some-
> thing *she* wanted to do. And she went on to school, and she was gone
> 27 years. And then she said, "Yeah, I believe I *do* wanta be with you."
> So she came back and put everything she had learned and earned into

the business. I kept in my backyard until she got back. Kep' holdin' on
and holdin' on, and knowin' that this is what's gonna happen. I didn't
know when, but I knew it would.

This ability to create, maintain, and fulfill long range plans based on
skills and talents learned in childhood was not unique to the African
American women in the study, but was manifested most strongly in their
experiences. I identify women with these experiences and abilities as
having "deeply anchored careers." Almost all of the hair salon owners,
young and old, reported "always doing hair" or "always wanting" to do
hair. Some of the European American salon owners expressed the same
desires. All of these younger women, now salon owners, may be on their
way to developing such deeply anchored careers.

Group 2: Business Planners—Professionals

Fifteen women pursued professional careers as the primary focus on
their journey to business ownership. All but two pursued college and
graduate degrees to gain skills and credentials with which to practice.
While the Trades women were fairly uniform in their motivations, the
professional women's motives included secondary goals such as filling
market niches, making money, and forming business partnerships. Two
of the women had not wanted to own businesses, but they were forced to
open businesses because employment was not open to them in their occupations. All but five women in this group were white. One of the white
Stanley women was Hispanic. Except for one Grafton woman, the black
Professional women were also from Stanley. The white women came
from all the areas sampled.

All but three metropolitan women served corporate clients. Marsha,
a white real estate agent, served primarily white families; Olive, a black
lawyer, served a majority black clientele; and Barbara, a black psychologist, served black and white clients. In Grafton, blacks served primarily
blacks and whites served a majority of whites. Bonnie, the only rural
professional and the only dentist in her area who accepted Medicaid,
served both black and white clients. She herself was white.

Decisions to Start. The Professional women fit traditional rational
choice models of business ownership better than did many other women
in the study. They started businesses as natural outgrowths of pursuit of
their careers. Skills learned through schooling and work experiences related directly to their businesses. Yet these women also reported varying

reasons for starting a business. Several were drawn by a desire for independence. Some sought escape from employed positions they did not like and looked to self-employment as an alternative. Others wanted to set their hours to spend time with children. Marsha said that entrepreneurship was a "family ideal," that to "have your own situation" was considered the best way to earn a living.

Differing Perspectives on Opportunity. Several women reported recognizing an opportunity to start their businesses. Two black women, Fern and Gina, saw a market niche in their particular occupations when they realized there were few black females in corporate law or graphic design. Their decision to capitalize on their minority and female status was critical to their entry into business. Similarly, Marsha, a white realtor, recognized a market niche, but it was for a particular type of real estate sales. She bought property, developed it, and sold units in planned communities.

Olive had a different perspective on choosing her profession. As an African American undergraduate in the late 1970s, she and her friends were influenced by a speech of Jesse Jackson's in which he noted that less than 4 percent of lawyers were black. In response, Olive decided to go to law school. Because so many other young African Americans were doing the same thing, she said it seemed like "the thing to do" at the time. Olive described her experience not as stepping into an unfulfilled market opportunity as Fern and Gina had. Rather, she was fighting to provide equal opportunities for her community at a time when few blacks were earning law degrees.

Desire for Greater Income. Only two women entered business to increase their financial income. Isabelle, with a life-long career in architecture, decided she knew as much as her boss and wanted to make the kind of money he did. Similarly, Marsha had changed careers, from a dental assistant to real estate developer, specifically to increase her income.

That so few women chose business ownership specifically for financial reasons, even among the professions, is consistent with theories advanced by Folbre (1994) who argues that non-economic motives are central in women's labor market decisions. Clearly, women choose business ownership primarily for reasons other than increased income. To try to fit women's experiences into a male business mold where financial motivations are of paramount importance does an injustice to these women. Other factors shape women's business decisions. Any theory claiming to reflect women's business experiences will not faithfully do so unless it contains a definition of motivation that includes non-monetary goals.

Reluctant Entrepreneurs. Two women, Meg and Marge, reported that, if given the chance to be employed, they would not have chosen to start a business. Both would have preferred to remain in employed positions, but could not. Marge reported that she would have preferred to work in an established chiropractor's office. Because of the way chiropractors structure their offices, however, no paid positions were available to her in the city where she lived, and she did not want to move. She was forced to open her own practice. In contrast, Meg realized soon after graduating with a film degree that if she wanted to be a film director, she would have to own her own business because at the time no one was hiring women directors. Discriminatory practices kept her from pursuing paid employment as a film director.

Barbara opened her private psychological practice for similar reasons, although she seemed to enjoy her practice and maintained it after its initial purpose was no longer so pressing. Barbara started her business in response to the structure of academic tenure traditions. As a black woman in the university tenure system, she did not trust that her employment as a university professor would last. To insure continued income, she founded a private practice.[1]

Accidental Entrepreneurs. Two women started businesses somewhat haphazardly. Originally, Bonnie had arranged to work in an existing practice in Bingham after graduating from dental school. By the time she passed her Boards, however, that dentist had closed his office. She moved to Bingham as planned because her husband attended school nearby and only one other dentist still practiced in Bingham. She opened her own practice and now enjoys the independence and money she makes on her own.

Kay hated her job with a large architectural firm in Stanley. She decided to leave it and go to medical school. While taking courses to fulfill pre-med. requirements, she began moonlighting with her architectural skills to support herself and found that she liked it. She explained, "It was not architecture I didn't like, it was working for this firm that I didn't like. As I got busier, I decided not to do the medical school and concentrated on building a practice."

Partnerships. Two businesses in the Professional group were partnerships, one of the Stanley architecture firms and the Grafton interior design firm. Kay had started her architectural business alone and later invited Jackie to join her in partnership. The nature of the firm changed from a home-based enterprise to a firm with a business location and employees. For Frieda, the partnership was an integral part of her decision to start an interior design business. She met the woman who would become her business partner, her advisor in interior design, when she returned to school for a Master's degree. By graduation, they decided to start a business together. While her partner continued to teach, Frieda worked for two years in an established firm to gain experience, then the two started a business. These partnerships point out the importance of social relationships in women's decisions to start or expand businesses and suggest additional avenues through which women might gain resources for start-up.

Deeply Anchored Careers. For the Professional women, recognition in childhood of what would become a deeply anchored career was more difficult than it was for women in Trades. For a woman to have a profession at all was unusual at the time some of the older respondents were children. To become an architect, a non-traditional career for women today, was extremely rare. In this study, all of the women in architectural and building-related fields reported knowing, at least in retrospect, that they had a deep interest, going back to childhood, in designing or building structures. However, all received little if any encouragement from the adults around them to become architects or designers. Because they were females considering non-traditional careers, most were discouraged by their parents, laughed at, and ridiculed.

Isabelle was 12 when she decided to become an architect. She said, "Everybody laughed at me. You're supposed to go through two or three changes in your life. I haven't gone through one yet." She learned skills in childhood that became the base of her career. She sketched and designed doll houses, *making* houses rather than playing with dolls. She said, "If we had to do a physics project I would do a village." A love of the craft led her to a life-long career anchored deeply in childhood. She explained,

> I just like it. I like the idea, the creativity, the problem solving about it; the technical aspects of it, the people aspects. You feel like a god. You're creating space. You're informing people, making them do things that they never thought they had to do. Totally unconsciously because you put the bathroom where you did, or you put the kitchen where you did, or you put the public space this way. Then the visual perception of that public space is what you created. So that makes you feel good.

Her love was not for business itself, but for her craft. Of the business end of her work, she said, "Entrepreneurship—it takes a breed of people. I don't think I'm an entrepreneur. I think I'm a dreamer and I have a direction to go and I found that this is the best way to achieve what I want to do."

Retrospective Recognition. Some women could see connections between their professional choices and their childhood interests only in retrospect. Because they were discouraged from their early interests, they lost sight of their original career aspirations and only stumbled on them later as something interesting to do. Kay explained,

> I didn't have any really pre-conceived notions about being an architect. I did things when I was young that would indicate that I would want to be an architect. I'd collect little materials from the neighbor's house when they were building a new house, and make a model of that house. But I think at that time, being a female, my parents never encouraged me to be an architect. My father said I was crazy when I said I was going to architecture school. [He said,] "Be a teacher, that's what you should do.". . . There were architects in my family, but again, it was never connected with me. But I remember going downtown and I loved watching these new buildings being built. I'd just stand there for hours and watch construction. There were so many things about it that are so obvious now, but at the time, it just never came together.

When it did come together, it came seemingly out of the blue. Kay said, "I was thinking about it one day and I thought, 'Well, architecture. That sounds sort of interesting, maybe I'll try that.' And went and enrolled and followed through. That's how it happened."

Family Support. Kay's partner, Jackie, was the only architect who reported having any support for her career choices. Unlike the black Trades women, who experienced broad kin support for their careers, Jackie's support was from a single advocate in an environment otherwise void of encouragement. Her sister, older by a year, took engineering courses in college that Jackie found interesting. Combining this with her interest in art, she went to a junior college and "took all of their art courses and all their engineering courses." She was in school during the early 1980s, a time when women were beginning to enter non-traditional careers in larger numbers than in the past. Still, she felt a lack of direction from her school guidance counselors. She explained, "I remember my counselor from junior college said, 'I don't know what you're doing, but your grades are fine, so just keep doing it.' And I thought back about that, and I thought, 'Why didn't he say something?' Engineering? Figure it out."

Again, it was her sister who put her on the right track. "My sister came up to Tech and studied civil engineering. And after her first year, she said, 'Jackie, you've gotta come up here. I've got the perfect major for you.' And it was industrial design." She transferred to Tech and began an industrial design major, taking the same courses required for the first year of an architecture degree. At the end of a year, the industrial design department "seemed like [it] was falling apart." Her professors asked her to stay in architecture, so she did.

In retrospect, Jackie, too, could see the connections between her childhood interests and her chosen career. She said,

> I look back on when I was growing up and I was building models and drawing maps and designing houses and building things, and so it's a very similar kind of activity when you're young. And I baby-sat for an architect who I thought was—I loved going to his house. But I can't say that there was anyone, other than my sister, that got me into architecture. . . . I was really heavy in an art direction. I almost went to an art school in Florida until [my sister] came up to Tech, and that was really what changed it. My parents did not want me to go major in art 'cause they said, "You'll never get a job" and that sort of thing.

Group 3: Business Planners—Natural Entrepreneurs

The Entrepreneurial women were largely motivated by a love of business. Entrepreneurship was more central to them than practicing a specific trade or profession. Bitten by the "entrepreneurial bug," they found fulfillment in many different economic situations, and most had owned businesses in the past, or owned one concurrently with the business described in this study. The Entrepreneurs started their ventures with business skills learned in prior job and entrepreneurial positions. They sometimes had to learn new occupational skills in order to start their businesses.

Most of the Entrepreneurial women were from rural and small city areas. All but Trish, a black Stanley woman, lived in Grafton or one of the rural towns. Five of the nine women were African Americans and four were European Americans. Two white Grafton women, Pam and Donna, were partners who owned a second business in another state.

Charlene, Eleanor, and Diane provided services traditionally performed by black women. Rachel and Trish, the two remaining African Americans, operated businesses closely related to traditional black service occupations. Rachel operated a T-shirt business in the back room of a commercial building she owned in downtown Bingham.[2] Trish operated a monogrammed clothing service. As clothing services, Trish and Rachel's businesses were similar to the traditional sewing and alteration services of the Trades women. However, Trish and Rachel relied on greater technology. Rachel bought specialized silk screen machinery, and Trish computerized her sewing patterns. This allowed her to produce large quantities of highly stylized, professional work for her corporate clients.

Three of the four European American women owned food service businesses, a traditional occupation for women. Pam and Donna built a street vending cart and served Italian-style espresso to passers-by. They operated the business during the warm Southern winter months and moved West for the remainder of the year to operate a river rafting business. Melissa started a taxi service for children. A mother herself, she based her innovative business on skills learned while raising her children.

Of the five black owners, two (Charlene and Diane) reported serving primarily black clients, two (Rachel and Eleanor) served a mixed clientele, and one (Trish) served corporations. Of the four white business owners, three reported serving "everyone." Melissa had not been operating long enough to be able to estimate her clientele. She is likely to serve primarily white working mothers.

Decisions to Start. The Entrepreneurial women's reasons for starting businesses grew not so much out of prior careers, as had the Trade and Professional women. Rather, they pursued business for its own sake, combined with economic need. Several women had always wanted to own a business, and some wanted a particular type of business. Some were dissatisfied with paid employment and sought autonomy. All of the women in this group, both black and white, had a propensity to move through business-related experiences where they learned skills to operate their businesses. Many operated more than one business at once. This process of repeated ownership and skill building epitomized women in the Entrepreneurial group. Although three younger women, Pam, Donna, and Melissa, had not experienced as many situations as the others, each had operated another business and seemed to have caught the "entrepreneurial spirit."

The Entrepreneurial Spirit. In one of the best examples of the "entrepreneurial spirit," Charlene's love of business went back to her childhood. She remembered family members doing "little things" to provide a livelihood. She explained,

> My mother, she was like the head of the household. She did it all. She made sure we had everything she could provide for us. 'Cause when we were comin' up, she'd sell stuff. Like on Fridays at the house, they'd go kill a hog or something and they would [do] a barbecue. She was raising money to get us stuff we needed.

Other family members contributed to Charlene's business experiences in ways directly relevant to owning a restaurant/lounge, or "club" as she called it.

> My brother used to DJ. And so I used to go do all his bookin' for him, and then I used to go round with him to some of his shows. So that's how I got involved with DJing. And my daddy had built me a little house outside, and then I used to fix it up like a little music store and I'd get out there like I'm on the microphone, play the music.

Entrepreneurial Succession and the Deeply Anchored Business. Even though Charlene was one of the youngest women in the group, she exhibited a tremendous ability to seek out and move through a succession of business-related money-earning situations. These included working as a radio station DJ; doing booking for her brother's DJ job; selling hot dogs at her brother's stand; operating an ice cream truck; washing cars, pumping gas, and selling fast food at her brother's service station; selling clothes door-to-door; and operating her own cleaning service. This last enterprise included contract maintenance in a factory and was a business that she still worked full time along with operating her restaurant. As she said, "I love business. Always. Like I say, I started my cleaning business about seven years ago. And I still have some of my clients from the day I started. I just love business." Charlene's early childhood experiences, both in play and in family work, formed the basis of another "deeply anchored business." Unlike women in Trades and Professions, however, Charlene was anchored by a love for business rather than for a particular trade or occupation.

A Multi-Dimensionally Anchored Business. One woman more than all the others in the study personified the self-made entrepreneur. Learning both her occupational and business skills informally, Trish embarked on a business venture that was deeply anchored in both a love of her craft and a love for business. Trish had learned embroidery from her mother in childhood, but to start a business, she modernized and commercialized it to fit the technological '90s. She said she had taken "a few days" training to learn the basics of computerized embroidery, but reported learning the bulk of her computer skills by networking with other women in her industry and "tearing her hair out" figuring it out for herself.

Not only was Trish basing her business on skills learned in childhood; she was also putting to use knowledge learned in a succession of entrepreneurial ventures. Like Eleanor and Charlene, she had moved through a series of employed sales positions and business ventures that gave her business and sales experience. Her love for business and embroidery combined to produce another variation of a deeply anchored business, one that was multi-dimensionally based. In addition, though she was only in her mid-40s, Trish, like the older African American Trades women, demonstrated a tenacious capacity for long-term planning. She had looked into monogramming fifteen years before actually starting her business. She said she was waiting for costs to go down, but they never did.

Filling a Market Niche. Some women recognized a market niche and took advantage of an opportunity. This was the case for Eleanor. As a tour guide, she heard visitors express a desire to rent overnight accommodations in her area. Noticing an ad selling used trailers, she decided to buy two and start a small, overnight rental business. Rachel and Melissa each expressed a desire for a particular kind of business. Rachel's T-shirt business was the result of a dream to start a sporting goods store in Bingham. Melissa read an article describing a taxi service for kids and couldn't stop thinking about it. Finally, she started a kid taxi service in Grafton where none existed.

Acting out of Economic Need. Trish, Karen, Pam, and Donna started their businesses out of economic need. Pam and Donna started a business about which they knew nothing to have an income during the winter months when their rafting business lay dormant. In contrast, Trish and Karen started businesses related to their prior job and business experiences. Trish had always had some enterprise going. After quitting a sales job with limited advancement potential and undesirable work hours, she decided to start a business based on something she knew, embroidery. She opened a clothing monogram service and sought corporate clients who could afford large orders. Karen recognized a decline in her industry and wanted a business that would provide a good income through retirement. Her years as a waitress and manager in the food service industry helped her step into restaurant ownership with little difficulty. She bought an existing cafe in downtown Bingham with her husband and began renovating and up-grading it to serve better food and more customers.

Helping Others. Eleanor and Trish started businesses in part as a means to address the economic needs of others. Living in a small community, Eleanor sought ways to develop the local economy and provide jobs for the community's youth. Trish, living in a large city, provided jobs for unwed mothers who might otherwise have to rely on welfare. This theme of helping others was expressed by many of the women in the study, especially the African Americans. For these women, helping others through their businesses was a way to "uplift the race" or give back to their communities (see Collins 1991:147-151; Higginbotham and Weber 1992). Although community service was not a primary motive for these Entrepreneurial women, it played a significant part in their business choices.

Drifter. Diane, the only woman who did not clearly choose either her occupation or her business, learned her occupational skills from her partner. She had taught physical education for several years before quitting to work in retail sales. After years of job changes, her current business partner, Ivy (also her hair stylist), convinced her to "do hair" and trained her. Initially talked into her trade, Diane did not quite fit into the Trades group. She seemed more of a drifter, yet followed the entrepreneurial process of moving through different business opportunities. She found fulfillment, finally, as an entrepreneur in a new trade with Ivy.

Group 4: Business Planners—Retirement Planners

Nine of the women in the study planned their businesses to provide for retirement, but they did so for different reasons. Black women wanted to stay busy in retirement; white women sought to build retirement income. The Retirement Planners were from all locations. Most were in their 50s and 60s, but two Grafton African American women were in their late 40s. Their businesses ranged from small, one-person enterprises in the rural areas to larger firms with several employees in Stanley. The African American women owned traditional businesses in the rural areas and more non-traditional businesses in Stanley. In contrast, the European American women's businesses were evenly mixed with both traditional and non-traditional occupations occurring in all locales.

The African American women served mostly an African American clientele in the rural and small city areas, but in the metro area served corporations. The white women served a mixed clientele, some serving primarily whites (Amanda and Emily) and others serving both black and white clients. Deborah was trying to attract more blacks and Hispanic clients to her practice by hiring black and Hispanic psychologists, but reported little success. Maggie, a Ludlow realtor, served primarily blacks. She said a large part of her work involved educating her rural clients about the legal aspects of buying and selling property.

Decisions to Start. The Retirement Planners started businesses for reasons that differed distinctly by race. The African American women, after retiring from full-time careers in paid employment, planned their businesses as activities to keep them busy during their retirement. Earning an income was a consideration, but not necessarily their prime motivation. In contrast, almost all of the European American women started their businesses specifically to provide income in later years. All of the white women had spent time raising children. Although some had worked during that time, none had held full time jobs for their entire adult lives as the black women had, and none had followed a "career" as such. All of the white women had little retirement income of their own, and all expressed interest in building more.

Three out of five African American women had raised children, but all of them had held full time jobs during that time. This is consistent with the literature, which suggests that white women are more likely than black women to take time off to raise children (see Murrell et al. 1991).

Racially Linked Motives. Two of the African American Retirement Planners, Rosalind and Betty, chose businesses that would provide services to their race. Rosalind started a much needed daycare center in the county for children of working mothers who did not qualify for the new Head Start program. Betty opened a beauty supply store to provide a link between black salon owners and distributors. As she put it,

There are more Koreans selling black products than blacks. And that kind of bothered me, looking at the Korean population getting into the product line that's a black product line. I thought it was senseless [and inappropriate] for me to be going to them to buy products for myself. It's something we should be doing ourselves. You can't *know* about the hair or the skin of a black person if you're a Korean. As well as someone from that race.

In addition, she saw the business as a means to provide herself, her friends, and her family with products they use frequently.

Building Equity for Retirement. In contrast to the African American Retirement Planners, the European American women viewed their businesses not as something to do, but as an important source of retirement income. Some feared they would be left without an income after the death or desertion of their husbands. Others, such as Deborah, started businesses in response to actual separations. Emily, the financial planner, said that, even with continued support from her husband, rising inflation would soon make his retirement income insufficient for their needs.

Another Deeply Anchored Career. Amanda's life and work are an example of how a career anchored in childhood experiences may be forgotten or mislaid, used as a distraction during a husband's career, and finally rediscovered and developed late in life. Amanda had pursued art as a hobby throughout her married life. Once her kids were in college, she worked in retail jobs to help out with their college expenses. She soon realized that if she lived alone and had to support herself, retail would not provide an adequate income. She explained,

> My experience going into work in retailing scared me. Because I saw that they took terrible advantage of divorced and widowed women and gave them the worst hours, the worst pay. I thought, "If I ever need it . . ." or even wanted a career, I wanted to have that opportunity. So that was my main reason for really getting in there and going back.

She returned to school to earn a BFA, but soon realized she wanted to pursue more than art. She explained,

> While I was in the process of getting my degree, I came to know myself a lot better. I just started evaluating the things that I enjoyed doing. I remember often telling my children when they were trying to decide on a career, to think of the things that you most *enjoy* doing and see if there's a field related to that.

She found her enjoyment in something related to art but more practical in terms of a career. Anchored in her experience as a military wife, she chose a career in residential design because it was "fun." She explained,

> Throughout my husband's military career, we were assigned government quarters in all these different locations all over the world and by

and large, it was pretty frustrating living in those quarters. So I escaped on paper. I would do a mock plan of each quarter that we were in, and then I would completely renovate it with enough closet space, with a nice laundry room, everything that I wanted in that structure within the boundaries. And then I would fantasize that I'd get a government contract to just do them all right.... And so that was my play. And I realized I spent more time actually doing *that* than I did the fine arts. But I kept thinking that it was because it was just easier to pick up a pencil and a paper than to set up and get the oil paints out and do all that. But I think not. I think it was what I had most fun doing.

Like the architects, Isabelle, Kay, and Jackie, Amanda traced her earliest interest in housing design back to her childhood. She said she played house by dragging lumber from where it was stacked behind the garage to lay it out in the yard as the rooms in a house. In this "house" she and her friends would play dolls from room to room. Like the architects, she received no encouragement for her interests. She said, "It goes way back. I have male cousins on both sides of my family that are architects. If I had been born a man, I probably would have been encouraged to pursue that."[3] These women's career goals and processes of human capital development were affected by traditional societal norms, situational contingencies, and structures of opportunity and constraint detailed by Gerson (1985) and Folbre (1994). These intricately interlocking factors influenced these women in their resource mobilization processes, allowing greater choice as societal norms changed over time.

EXTERNALLY MOTIVATED BUSINESS OWNERS

The next set of business owners consists of women who were externally motivated to start businesses. These women either fell or were "pushed" serendipitously into ownership. They include Work Skill Owners, Career Problem Solvers, and Community Service Providers.

Group 5: Serendipitous Owners—Work Skill Owners

Six women were drawn into business ownership as a natural outcome of their paid employment. None had planned or intended to own businesses. Yet all of these women, whether encouraged by friends or drawn into business as a result of other circumstances, entered businesses that followed naturally from their prior work. With occupational skills built in prior employment, most entered business with few financial or business management skills.

Half of these owners were from Grafton, two were from Stanley, and one was from Bingham. Only one African American woman fell into this group, and she was from Stanley. Most were in their 40s and 50s with one younger rural woman and an older Stanley woman. The businesses ranged in age from two to 14 years. The oldest businesses were owned by the small city women and the metropolitan white woman.

Nell and Camilla, two of the white women, owned insurance agencies, one in Bingham and one in the metro area. The other three white women owned businesses in Grafton. Irene owned a restaurant, Sally owned a tavern, and Becky sold office equipment. Dee, the single African American woman in this group, owned a large temporary employment agency with headquarters in Stanley and satellite offices in two other cities.

Most of the businesses served a racially diverse clientele. Becky's office equipment business, however, served public and private sector businesses. Sally's tavern catered to neighborhood residents, primarily working class whites. The insurance agents served different groups. Camilla, the younger rural agent, represented many different insurance companies and served clients of widely different ages and incomes and an evenly balanced racial mix. She also reported serving clients with no violations and those with "terrible violations." Nell, the older Stanley agent, catered to an older clientele who "had already gotten there"—individuals and firms with money to spend on the carefully planned insurance packages she crafted for them.

Decisions to Start. The Work Skill Owners started their businesses for different reasons. Sally and Dee were persuaded by individuals who wanted to partner with them, and Becky accepted an offer made by an agent of a large company to sell office equipment. Irene and her partner started their restaurant on a "whim" after serving as waitresses for years.

Camilla and Nell started their insurance agencies because of factors related to their paid employment at the time of start-up. Nell worked for a large insurance firm and wanted to provide services not available through her employer. Legally, starting a business also helped her separate her personal funds from her business income.

Camilla admitted always wanting to own a business. Her second job was with an insurance agency that was "too big," and her third job required a long commute. She knew she had to make a change. She asked her third employer to consider opening a branch office in Camilla's hometown so she could work for the company without commuting. Industry regulations wouldn't allow that arrangement, and, with a nudge from her husband, Camilla opened her own agency.

Group 6: Serendipitous Owners—Career Problem Solvers

Thirteen women experienced unplanned changes in their employed careers, resulting in opportunities to start businesses.[4] These women were fired from jobs, nudged or forced out of jobs when their companies restructured, or burnt out in careers no longer suited to their needs. Faced with starting a new job, the Career Problem Solvers used significant equity from prior employment to start businesses rather than search for new jobs. Many carried business and occupational skills with them from prior employment, but some started with few relevant skills.

Most of these women were from the metropolitan area, although three (all white) came from the rural and small city areas. Six of the women were African American and seven were European American. Most were in their 40s. The exceptions were three women from the metro area, two younger and one older woman. The businesses ranged in age from little more than one year to 15 years.

Four of the white woman and four black women started businesses that were occupationally different than the employed positions they had left. The majority of businesses were non-traditional for women. They ranged from white-owned security alarm and residential contracting businesses, to black-owned specialty advertising and chemical manufacturing companies. Two of the women, one black and one white, had started travel agencies, an industry increasingly dominated by women. Businesses more traditional for women included a hair salon and a book and antique store.

The African American women largely operated non-traditional businesses. However, these firms remained tied to traditionally black industries or were in business services, an industry that has increasingly attracted more highly educated black workers (see Bates 1983 and 1987; Suggs 1986). Geneva, the chemical manufacturer, produced beauty and personal products designed for African American skin and hair. Sonia, the environmental cleaning products owner, sold her products to janitorial services, an industry dominated in the South by blacks. Sheila, the temporary employment agent, started a business that aided African Americans in finding work. The video producer and the specialty advertising agent catered to mainstream, white-owned businesses as well as African American-owned enterprises.

The businesses ranged from small, one person companies to larger firms employing 10 or more workers and operating on million dollar budgets. All of the rural and Grafton businesses were relatively small, employing few workers in addition to the owners. The Stanley businesses varied in size from Sonia's home-based sole proprietorship and Jill's one-woman hair salon to Geneva's manufacturing facility that employed a dozen or more workers. The businesses served a mix of clients, with the rural whites serving more whites and the metro area businesses serving primarily corporate businesses and government agencies.

Decisions to Start. All of the Career Problem Solvers chose to start businesses rather than look for other work as a result of leaving their jobs. Half the women (Gail, Julie, Sheila, Jill, Valerie, and Libby) were forced to leave their jobs due to cutbacks, lay-offs, or restructuring. The rest (Judy, Heather, Geneva, Candice, Sonia, Nora, and Sigrid) chose to leave in response, either directly or indirectly, to circumstances beyond their control. These circumstances ranged from macro-structural factors, such as a changing economy, to micro-level factors involving job dissatisfaction and perceived discrimination.

Forced Unemployment. Those who were forced to leave their jobs did so for different reasons. Gail and Valerie were fired from their jobs. Julie and Sheila worked for firms that restructured, offering them jobs in other cities, which they both declined. The construction company where Libby worked was sold to another firm, restructured, and broken up, shutting down the division where she worked. Not wanting to work for another company, Libby started her own residential contracting business. Sigrid recognized the impact a recession would have on real estate sales. Though not forced to leave her job, she chose to start a business in another industry (laser recycling) to avoid displacement.

Company Restructuring. Several women left jobs in response to actual or potential restructuring of their firms. Although they were not forced to leave, they were dissatisfied with the outcome of restructuring. Some were not assigned positions they wanted; others feared they would not be happy after their companies were restructured. Placed in a position she didn't like when her company reorganized, Sonia admitted, "I think the people who were males were pretty much taken care of, or they had what they really wanted to do in any structure." Unwilling to label her treatment discrimination, she was not given what she wanted. As a result, she quit.

Maternity Leave. Two women left paid employment because of job dissatisfaction, but they left under somewhat different circumstances. Taking a maternity leave at the same time the company was restructured,

Heather chose not to return to work and face the stress of "crazy changes." Having also experienced subtle forms of discrimination, she found it easier not to go back. Candice, too, left her position with a national airline when she became pregnant. Never having really liked her job, she was encouraged by her husband to pursue her own business through a franchise. She and her husband, along with another couple, started their own travel agency, choosing the franchise in order to have immediate name recognition and financial backing. Thus, like the women in Gerson's (1985) study, these women made decisions based on personal factors in conjunction with structured constraints. Circumstances leaned in favor of family relationships at the same time that economic climates raised barriers diminishing work options.

Health Problems. One woman left her job for health reasons. While working for a prestigious hair salon, Jill became pregnant. Her doctor said she was in a high-risk occupation for her unborn child. The chemicals she worked with every day could be harmful both to the baby and to her own health. She developed allergies to the chemicals at the same time her husband started importing natural hair care products from Europe. She quit her job and started working for him without pay. After the birth of her child, her husband left her, unemployed and a single mother. Rather than apply for welfare, she bought a small existing shop and started her own natural hair salon.

Burnout and Changing Societal Values. Two women left their jobs in response to personal issues. Nora had experienced burnout working in the mental health profession. She was introduced to specialty advertising by the relative of a friend who was in the business. After initially representing his company, she decided to start a business of her own with his encouragement and help. She "fell in love" with the business, describing it as "not a hard sell" and saying, "most companies buy something."[5] Judy left a career as coach and high school teacher to start a business. She explained,

> As far back as I can remember I always wanted to be a school teacher. My mother spent lots of money to send me to college so I could be a physical education teacher and a coach, and I did that for twelve years [until] I decided I was gonna smack one of them kids one of these days. And they weren't near as bad as they are today. That was back in '85.

In response to generational changes in how children were being raised, Judy decided to leave teaching rather than "smack" a kid. After trying out a few jobs, she learned the security alarm business from her brother and opened her own establishment in Bingham.

Two Deeply Anchored Businesses. Judy's choice of business occupation may have been based on something more than interest. In a business involving carpentry and electrical work as well as sales, she had no problem picking up the skills. Judy reported,

> My mom says that I was always mechanically inclined, that even when I was growing up when I took the tests, and all my tests came back real high in mechanical stuff, and that if there was ever one of her kids who could change the oil it was me. The boys can't do it at all, but Judy could. So if something had to be fixed, I had to do it.

Libby's construction experience began long before she held her first job. Her family background introduced her to it, and may have provided a blueprint for her career, just as the sewing and cooking skills learned by Trades women Hazel and Corinne anchored their careers in early childhood. Libby explained,

> I was actually born inside a lumber yard. You don't think about things like this until you're already grown. And it's very simple things that you did when you're a kid that later on in life, here you are back doing it again. And you love it, and you don't understand why you love it, but you do. . . . My Dad was in saw millin'. And then he worked for this guy who had a lumber company. And he was kind of like the overseer of the place. And we had a little house inside that lumber yard, where I was born. [I] would go with him out into the yard and stay with him when he stacked lumber and did all this stuff.

This early experience may have contributed to her lifelong ability to intuitively solve construction problems. In describing her life in the lumber yard, she added an analysis of her own, saying,

> And I've never really thought about it that much. [But] there's things, I swear to God, I know I've learned from somewhere, but I can be on a job and something can come up, and I can't even figure out how I know how to do that. It just comes to me, the answer to do it. It's an instinct or something. I don't know where I've gotten it from or anything, 'cause I had no formal education in construction. I didn't finish the tenth grade in high school.

Group 7: Serendipitous Owners—Community Service Providers

Three women in the study started businesses to provide needed services to their communities. Each perceived her community as lacking something she felt compelled to provide. They started businesses in response to cracks in existing social safety nets, gender-biased social networks, and the spiritual need for contemplation in a low-income neighborhood. Deficits in these macro-structural social constructs caused the Community Service Providers to start businesses to help fill the gap.

The Businesses. The Service Providers came from each of the different locales. Two white women, both in their mid-40s, were from Grafton and Stanley. The sole African American, a woman in her 60s, came from Bingham. This woman operated her business for 8 to 10 years before closing it due to ill health. The two white women had been operating their businesses for three years (Jeannette in Grafton) and 21 years (Laura in Stanley) at the time they were interviewed.

Personal Care Home. Bernice started a personal care home for elderly blacks in Bingham. Though she had no experience in such work, she sought training and, with the financial support of her husband and help from other relatives, started the business. At first, she operated the care facility out of a rented house to see if the business was what she wanted to do. She kept her job in case the experiment failed. Meeting with success, she hired workers to renovate her home to accommodate six to eight clients. She quit her job and was operating the facility full time when she went blind during a series of medical tests. For a short while, her mother and cousin kept the care home operating, but eventually Bernice closed the business.

Women's Network. Jeannette, a white Grafton woman, started a business to support and provide exposure for women's art and culture. Her main efforts included production of a member-supported newsletter and a yearly directory listing women in the arts, health services, and professions, as well as organizations supporting women. She also worked as an educational consultant, focusing on women's empowerment through information and education. Jeannette co-sponsored a yearly women's trade show to further introduce women business owners to the community, and continued to develop curricula, hold workshops, and sponsor poetry readings and girls' confidence building sessions. She was dedicated to a vision of promoting women as capable members in society, and to making the existence of women's art, culture, and business ventures known to the public.

Bookstore. Laura opened a bookstore in Stanley to provide a sanctuary of quiet beauty and respite in the midst of inner city poverty. She had never owned a business or worked in a bookstore before deciding to start one of her own, but she had a vision and financial backing, so she started the business. After more than ten years in a rented building, Laura applied for and received a loan to buy a building in the same neighborhood. With overwhelming community support, the move was made easily and quickly, and her dream of providing a permanent home for the bookstore came to pass.

Decisions to Start. Bernice, Jeannette, and Laura started their businesses with high ideals to address unmet needs of their communities. Bernice founded her business in response to the survival and physical care needs of an older, rural black population she encountered through her work as director of Head Start.[6] In contrast, Laura started her metropolitan bookstore to provide a spiritual and intellectual refuge in a low-income community surrounded by a complex and bustling world. Jeannette, too, saw a spiritual need in her community, a need for the sensibilities of women's art and women's perspectives. But she also saw the financial need of women artists and professionals to support themselves and their work. Focusing on both economic and spiritual needs, Jeannette came closest to bridging the gap between these two views of service.

Physical Need. During the course of her Head Start work, Bernice visited families with children in the community. While on these visits, she encountered conditions of neglect and abuse in the care of elderly family members. She explained,

> I went one time and I saw a man that had all this medicine poured in a bowl *together*. He would pick a blue pill and a yellow pill and a red pill. And see, he'd take some sometime, and he'd take some of the others [another time]. And I saw this and I said, "My god!" You know, people are dying, their hospital bills are going up because of lack of preventive type things; if you get them where they take this right, then you don't have to go to the hospital. . . . And seeing things like that happening out in the county. Some of 'em just suffering. There was holes—and that wasn't my *business*, the holes in the floor. But you see ants coming up through the floor, you see everything else coming up through the floor, and yes, they are still living there. There's nothing wrong with living there, but I felt that maybe if we had something to

help them get out of their situation. And that's really what made me interested in it.

Bernice's business was deeply anchored in a desire to help others. Growing up in the South, she moved North to attend college where her service orientation blossomed. She explained, "In my second year in college, I went to work as a live-in maid in New York, and I saw situations that were deplorable. I changed my major. I wanted to be a social worker and just to save the world. I wanted to start *something* to help some*body*." Her business became one of the ways in which that desire was fulfilled.

Spiritual Need. Laura and a partner opened a bookstore under the auspices of an inner city educational organization. As young idealists, they felt called to fulfill their vision of creating a quiet, welcoming space. Both were Christians,

> So there was a sense in which this was a mission for us, but it wasn't a mission about witnessing to people, it was a mission about encouraging people in their own spirituality. The theology that we had on the shelves was never evangelical Christianity, it was more Thomas Merton and that kind of encouragement of spirituality.

Her direction was "always about service." With her father in the army and her mother a "stay-at-home mom," Laura's business was deeply anchored in childhood examples of service. She explained, "We chose to do the store in this area because it was a very impoverished area with nothing in it to offer to people that was beautiful and encouraging. That comes directly from my background of having been raised in the church, but in the church in a sense of being always looking for ways to serve."

Economic Need. Jeannette's initial goal was to publish a women's directory. Growing up in the South, she felt disadvantaged as a woman. She wanted to provide support and a structure of network contacts for women that only existed for men in the culture in which she was raised. As a working woman, she faced discrimination in every job she held. She said:

> I think networking is of primary importance. In one of the women's studies texts that I've used, their analysis was that networking was the most important [way] women—[especially] women in non-traditional jobs—solved some of their problems, which were sexual harassment,

etc. [They did it] through coalitions of networking and participation in
unions. It's the old "organize" is what it is. And support. Because men
have those. Young men whose fathers are in business know what it
means. "OK, sonny, so-and-so's got a store over here. He's got a place
for you 'soon as you get your degree done." They know what it means.

Jeannette took this philosophy and began building a support network to serve the needs of women. Her desire to provide a network for
women came from a deeply felt absence of connection, a connection
made by men but missing between women.

SUMMARY

The motivational groupings provide an opportunity to compare planned
and unplanned paths to business ownership. Some women followed career paths that remained relatively unchanged from preferences formed
early in life, while others followed unpredictable paths that developed
over time in response to external circumstances. This is consistent with
Gerson's (1985) theories of personal preference mixed with situational
opportunities and constraints. Women's experiences included situation-
based, circumstantial decisions about business ownership. Those who
knew what they wanted and had clear career paths in mind acted positively to achieve their goals. Even so, structural changes in markets and
the economy sometimes dictated changes in occupations. How a profession was structured and race- and gender-based discriminatory attitudes
affected women's decisions to start businesses.

Externally motivated owners were affected even more by outside
circumstances. Women moved by societal problems opted to start businesses to contribute solutions. This service orientation broadens Collins'
(1990) theory of African American women's "othermother" activism to
include white women, and it expands application from volunteer activities to business ownership. Those whose jobs were restructured felt the
most immediate effects of economic recession. When not fired outright
they were given choices that they found unacceptable. Their subsequent
decisions to start businesses and their methods of garnering resources to
do so reflected desires for greater control over their lives and efforts to
minimize future lay-off risks. These responses to stratified, inequitable
career options are consistent with Folbre's (1994) theories of structured
constraint and women's multiple, sometimes non-economic motives in
making labor market decisions. Application to women business owners

further broadens Folbre's theories to include entrepreneurial decision-making processes.

Women are likely to start businesses with different skill sets and financial resources depending on the circumstances surrounding start-up. Those who plan their businesses might have time to build occupational and/or business-related skills, save financial resources, and plan cost-saving strategies to avoid dependence on commercial loans. Those who focus on trades and professions are likely to have occupational skills learned in formal educational settings, while those who pursue entrepreneurship for its own sake are more likely have business-related skills. Women who found businesses as a result of unexpected career changes are likely to have less time to plan businesses. Coming from paid employment, many are likely to bring significant personal funding to business start-up. Depending on their work experiences, many will also bring significant business and occupational skills.

Most groups identified here consisted of a mix of black and white owners. However, race and locale clearly affected the types of businesses women entered and, for some, their reasons for entering business. Rural African Americans founded primarily personal service and retail businesses, while rural European American women founded a wider range of businesses. Only in the large metropolitan area did black owners enter a wide variety of industries similar to those occupied by white women. These differences portend different needs for human and financial capital, and different abilities to access these resources.

NOTES

[1] At the time of the interview, Barbara had received tenure and remained employed full time at the university while operating her practice. She was also working on a major research grant with funding channeled through her business, and she spoke of expanding the business to include at least one new location in another part of the city.

[2] Much of her interview centered on ownership of the building, unusual for an African American in this rural town, and her other entrepreneurial pursuits. These included renovation and rental of the building, other housing restoration projects, and a tax preparation service. At the time of the interview, she and her husband were beginning plans for a chicken farm.

[3] I asked if she ever got to renovate any military housing. She responded by saying, "I want you to know that with all the bases closing, my historic renovation magazines are showing me all these beautiful Army quarters that have been converted to condos. No kidding. So had I just stayed around there. . . ."

[4] Women who left their jobs on pregnancy leave might have planned their pregnancies, but they did not always plan to quit their jobs. Once children were born, they decided not to return to work. Instead, they started businesses they hadn't foreseen before becoming pregnant.

[5] Specialty advertising is, in Nora's words, "a distributorship of imprinted merchandise, like pens, mugs, T-shirts, caps, [and] jackets, that small businesses and corporations use to market and sell. We also do corporate gifts, executive gifts, award programs, recognition programs and things like that. We are distributors; we buy directly from manufacturers, and usually the merchandise is drop-shipped from the manufacturer directly to the customer. And we in turn invoice the customer. That's it in a nutshell."

[6] Although not included in this group, two other rural black women expressed similar commitments to serving the physical and economic needs of low-income blacks in their areas. Rosalind served working mothers by providing pre-school care for their children. Eleanor became a role model for members of her community to create jobs for themselves in a limited rural economy. She might have also helped to create jobs for the area's youth.

CHAPTER 6

Human Capital

Women who had entered businesses via different pathways (Chapter 5) varied in the types of education and training they received. Women who planned their businesses had more formal education, especially those in the Trades and Professions groups. The women who had not planned their business relied much more on job experience for skills needed in start-up. Most women in the study had education, training and work experiences that helped them in starting and operating their businesses, but some had no relevant experience. When starting their businesses, most women sought additional training and/or sources of information, outside help, and skill building beyond the formal educational process.

Traditional rational choice theories of buildup of human capital for economic gain only partially fit the experiences of women in these groupings. While women in some groups pursued education and job training as means to greater economic opportunity and business ownership, others made do with what skills they had and learned as they went. Consistent with Gerson's (1985) theories, situational contingencies frequently affected women's decisions and actions in building human capital, and their levels of already-accumulated skills relevant to business ownership. Responding to changing situational factors meant improvising with available skills. Social capital and social ties played an important role in allowing women to gain additional skills (see Chapter 8). Becker's (1964, 1975, 1993 editions) theories of human capital as an investment in self are most applicable to women in the planned groupings. Even so, structural constraints (Folbre 1994) and disadvantages based on racial discrimination (Folbre 1994; Collins 1990) limited levels of education some women could achieve. Thus, feminist and social embeddedness theories become equally if not more important than neoclassical rational choice theories in explaining women's accumulation of human capital for entrepreneurship.

Below, I examine each of the groups identified in Chapter 5. I describe how the women in each group gained skills through formal education, training, and job experiences that aided them in their businesses. I define formal education as training received in high school, a technical school, two or four year college, or graduate/professional degree programs beyond college. Formal training can occur on-the-job, in a return to school to update information, or in certificate programs. Job training and experience occurs on-the-job and includes formal training seminars and workshops as well as less formal, hands-on learning that takes place while doing a job. Informal learning can take place on-the-job or can be information or skills gained from social contacts (see Chapter 8) or learned independently.

INTERNALLY MOTIVATED BUSINESS OWNERS

In preparing for business ownership, the internally motivated planners moved through two basic skill-building processes. Women in the first two groups pursued a particular trade or profession. They learned occupational skills in formal educational settings and honed them with job experience related to their business occupations. As to be expected, the greater investment in higher education for the Professional group resulted in higher income levels and more technically advanced businesses than for women in the Trades group. Theories of human capital as investment in self have some relevance to these women.

Only one of the Professional women reported having significant business skills at the time of start-up. Perhaps because they spent so much time in school learning their professions, or perhaps because they were going into professions that would pay well enough to hire business professionals, almost none of the Professional women had business skills going into business ownership. In contrast, the Trades women as a whole (almost all African American) had more training in business-related skills than did the Professional women. Across all groups, the African American women more frequently had *both* occupational *and* business skills. These findings run counter to other writers, such as Wendy Luttrell (1997), who argue that white rather than black women value formal credentials more highly. However, Collins' (1990) theories of African

American women's valuation of education and teaching as a means of uplifting their communities supports these findings.

Unlike the Trades and Professional women, the Entrepreneurial women had little formal training in their occupations. Instead, almost all had gained occupational skills from previous jobs and/or in non-formal work and training settings. They reported having somewhat more training in business operations than the first two groups, and they relied on their experiences in other entrepreneurial pursuits, or in sales, business, or management positions, to help them with the operational side of their businesses.

The Retirement Planners, split between African American entrepreneurs and late-blooming European American professionals, were also split in their skills preparation. The black women followed the Entrepreneurial group's path of gaining business training and experience. They put to use both business and occupational skills learned in paid employment settings over the course of their working lives. In contrast, the white women followed the Professional group educational process, learning occupational skills in school and in applied work settings. Two of these women brought few business skills to ownership, while two had significant earlier business training.

Group 1: Business Planners—Trades Women

Women in Trades relied heavily on formal occupational training, primarily from technical or trade schools, and on prior employment in their trades to gain skills needed for their businesses. Few of the women who pursued trades had any school-based business training. Some gained these skills in prior jobs, but most learned them on-the-job, or had a friend or relative help them with business tasks such as accounting. Of the women who reported no formal training in business and management skills, half were black women age 40 or over. Few of the Trades women who lacked accounting, management, or other business-related skills sought training to gain these skills.

Formal Education. All women who pursued a trade had completed high school, and most had attended a trade or technical school. All hair stylists had completed cosmetology training. Elly, one of the older African Americans from Grafton, completed her cosmetology degree in 1952. Her course included classes in business management, accounting, and taxes. Mabel, too, had completed "beauty school" in the early 1950s but had no business training. Although Ivy, in partnership with Diane, had taken a salon management course in school, she found it unhelpful. The book from her class, however, worked "as a guide that told us all the permits and different things that we had to get [to] set up."

One of the few to train professionally in business, Corinne had majored in business management with additional courses in nutrition at a local technical school. Hazel graduated from high school and went to tailoring school, an unusual move for a woman in the early 1960s. Tailoring, or sewing on men's clothing, was considered a man's job, while seamstress work, or sewing on women's clothing, was considered a woman's profession.

Job Experience. Almost all the Business Planner-Trades women had worked in jobs within their trades to gain experience before starting their businesses. Not all their experiences were alike. This was particularly true of the older black owners. Hazel had perhaps the longest career as a paid employee in several department store alterations shops and men's clothing stores before starting her business. Elly had operated a business in her backyard[1] for 30 years before opening a beauty shop in downtown Grafton with her sister.

Mabel, a 72-year-older black hair stylist in Bingham, worked in another shop to gain experience after graduating from beauty school and later was hired to operate a shop in her home town. The owner established the shop to bring jobs and income to the community. He wasn't interested in profiting from the business, so Mabel operated the salon as her own for 10 years, reinvesting any profit. When the owner of the shop passed away, Mabel moved to Bingham and opened a salon. Her experiences working first for another hair stylist, then operating a salon for an absent owner, gave her the business skills and hair styling experience she needed for her salon.

Learning Business Skills On-the-Job. The very youngest salon owners, Sabrina (black) and Kathy (white) from Ludlow, started their businesses with very little prior salon experience. They were both in hair styling and their shops were situated in the same block on the main street in town, but their stories illustrate similarities and differences by race. Sabrina had worked in a salon for only six months before opening her own shop. She reported,

> I was scared to just jump out and get my own business. But the other
> work showed me that it wasn't really hard. All it really took was for me
> to get a business license, and all the other stuff come along with it. The

water turned on and the electricity. The basic stuff. So when I saw that, then that made me really wanta go on and do it.

Sabrina's fear of business ownership came from her inexperience with business skills. In contrast, Kathy started her own shop right out of cosmetology school with the help of her father. She had worked in his furniture store for more than six years. She said, "I could pretty much run the store." She had learned sales, bookkeeping, and other business-related skills that helped her in starting her own business. Her job experience gave her confidence to start a business straight out of school.

Other Important Job Experiences. Corinne, the older black restaurant owner in Grafton, reported gaining experience in supervision and management in her position as youth recreation leader for the city. She found these skills to be useful in directing her restaurant help and operating the business. In addition, while working in recreation, she also catered weddings and decorated churches, activities more closely related to the restaurant business.

Shared Skills in Partnerships. Two women in trades are examples of how teamwork in a partnership can provide more skills for a business than a single owner. Elly's sister and partner, Lenore, had supported herself through business school and followed a 27-year-long career in two different fields, including one as manager of a fast food franchise, before entering business with Elly. Lenore's business and management training and Elly's long years of experience in hair styling combined to provide all the skills needed to operate their business successfully from the start.

Gaining Needed Skills and Knowledge. The Trades women found diverse ways to gain skills they needed for their businesses. From workshops at industry trade shows to formal training and independent study, the Trades women sought ways to expand and update their occupational and business-related skills and knowledge. These were rational decisions made by these women to invest in self as a means to stay current and competitive in their businesses. However, the larger contexts in which they made choices for additional training reflected dependence on social capital provided by the structures of their occupations. This extends Gerson's (1985) notion of women's situational opportunities and Folbre's (1994) structures of opportunity and constraint to include occupational structures as they are linked to business ownership. Below, I examine some of the formal and self-taught strategies used by the Trades women to increase their skills and knowledge.

Industry-Structured Learning. A major source of on-going training for Trades Women was hair shows. These industry shows taught them about new styling techniques, new products, and business operations. Most salon owners went to hair shows at some time while they were business owners, although one older beautician complained that the shows today focus too much on product information and not enough on styling skills.

Formal Training to Update and Expand Knowledge. Elly returned to school to update her skills. She explained, "The chemicals come in way down the line, so I had to go to classes to learn how to give relaxers *and* perms;[2] learn how to do the extended braids, learn how to do everything. And I still, to keep with the ladies, have to go to workshops."

Women also sought additional training to add a new product line or service. Kathy, the white salon owner in Ludlow, had taken a home correspondence course in nutrition to be able to give clients nutritional counseling. She was also planned to take courses in hair chemistry and accounting. Linda had taken three computer classes since starting the business and hoped to buy a computer for her shop. She also had taken business management training at hair shows.

Self-Taught Skills. The sewing and alterations shop owners were self-taught. Carol, the younger of the two, learned by watching her mother sew. Eventually, she picked up new skills on her own. No one ever showed Hazel how to sew. Her mother didn't sew, and no one else taught her. But Hazel recalled:

> When I was small, playing with dolls, my mother would give me her old clothing and I would tear them apart and make doll clothes. And I had about the best dressed doll because I made clothes for my dolls. I just could always *sew*. And as I got older, the better I would sew and make things. And when I was in high school, I could make basically anything that I wanted. So finally, I think I was about 13 when I got my first sewing machine, and it just kinda boomed from there. When I went to tailoring school, it was pretty boring, because whatever the instructor had for us to do, I could just do it. So that's why I take it as a gift.

Thus, Hazel's career as a tailor was deeply anchored in skills learned in childhood and carried into adulthood.

Group 2: Business Planners—Professionals

Whether owning a business represented independence, increased financial income, or an escape from an uncomfortable employment situation, all Professional women were in occupations they had trained for and enjoyed doing. As a result, they were well prepared to operate the occupational side of their businesses. Like the Trades women most of the Professionals were unprepared with business skills. Few had received business training. Some reported gaining business skills through continuing education courses. Others found alternative means to gain needed business skills.

Formal Education. All of the Professional women had trained in their occupations, and all but one had a four year college degree or higher. Marge, the exception, reported having an AB in physical therapy and a two-year chiropractic degree. Several had advanced degrees appropriate to their professions.[3]

Dual-Career Training. About one third of the women reported that their business occupations were not their first careers. Some who had started working in other careers received formal training in fields related to their business occupations. For instance, Carla, the black attorney from Grafton, had started her career as a parole officer. She returned to law school to start her own practice. Marge, the white chiropractor from Grafton, had first trained as a physical therapist before entering chiropractic school.

Others also had formal training in their first occupations, but their degrees were unrelated to their later business occupations. For example, Frieda, the Grafton interior designer, originally majored in education and taught bi-lingual education for six years before returning to school for a graduate degree in interior design. Frances, a white attorney from Grafton, had trained and worked as a social worker for ten years before entering law school. Fern, one of the black metro area attorneys, had started a career in dance. After an injury, she drifted through school first in psychology, then in architecture, before finally deciding on law school. Marsha, a white, metro-area real estate agent, had earned a BA in elementary education to please her parents. She then trained and worked for 10 years as a dental assistant. Desiring a higher income, she attended real estate school at night before opening her realty firm.

Business Training. Several women took accounting or other business-related courses in school while pursuing their professional degrees, but most agreed that these courses did little to prepare them for business ownership. As Marge put it,

> Until you get your own practice, you don't realize how much you're spending on having an employee. You don't think about it when you're

in school. You're thinking about being a chiropractor, you're not thinking about being a business person. Taxes were just astronomical in my
life when I first got out.

Carla had taken one course in how to operate a law firm while in
school, but found that it helped little in starting her practice. Like Trades
woman Ivy, the book from Carla's class continues to aid her in business
operations.

Job Experiences. Almost all of the women had worked as professionals in their occupations prior to opening their businesses. The exception was Bonnie, the rural dentist. Bonnie worked in another dental
office *after* starting her own business to see if she might want to form a
partnership. She said,

> I went for three months, one day a week because I wanted to see what
> it was like to get into another office because I never had experienced it
> before. And I hated it. I would never want to be an associate or work
> for somebody else.

Informal Apprenticeships. Some of the Professional women had
jobs in their fields before they graduated. These served as informal "apprenticeships." For instance, Kirstin worked in a friend's dental office
during the summer while in college. She used the experience to see if
dentistry was really what she wanted to do. She reported, "I loved it."
Similarly, Marge worked in a chiropractor's office during her senior year
of high school. She helped with physical therapy, paperwork, insurance,
and scheduling, all skills she later used in her office.

After completing her AB, Marge worked as a physical therapist in
an industrial clinic. Her physical therapy experience bolstered her chiropractic skills. She noted: "I think I do a lot more tissue work than a lot of
chiropractors." Her only other chiropractic experience before opening
her Grafton practice came from operating a similar practice elsewhere.

Learning Business Skills On-the-Job. Marge worked as a financial
director at a private school between her two chiropractic practices, learning about financial management and business operations. She reported,
"I was actually dealing with everything I didn't learn in chiropractic
school, and that has helped me the most when I opened this office." This
reliance on skills learned across widely disparate settings is somewhat
similar to Gerson's (1985) arguments of situational opportunities and de-

cision-making. Skills learned in settings not looked for in the progression of a career come in handy when applied to the other skill sets (business and financial management) needed in business ownership.

Small Scale Freelancing. Gina experienced a microcosmic view of business ownership while freelancing prior to opening her business. After leaving her second job with a graphic design firm, she worked on her own for two years. She explained, "I was doing the production, the managing—'cause I had other designers helping me—I did all of the invoicing. I did the presentation. I was doing a lot of those things necessary for business, just on a smaller scale. So I got to play lots of different roles doing that, that I'm now managing as an owner." She translated skills from this early, small-scale experience to the operation of a larger business.

Gaining Needed Skills and Knowledge. The Professional women found many ways to gain the management and financial skills they lacked. Many attended trainings and seminars on business related topics. Because of the requirements of their professions, many took continuing education classes. They read professional and business journals. Below I examine these formal avenues through which Professional women gained skills and knowledge for their businesses.

Structured Learning. The Professional women used a variety of resources available to them through the structures of their occupations. Almost all were required to take continuing education courses to maintain licenses. Most of the training available to them was oriented toward updating their occupational skills. However, several women took business and financial management training through continuing education.

Another form of structured learning came in the course of doing business, rather than as a legal requirement. Meg, the white metro video producer, learned how to operate a business by making videos about business procedures for her corporate clients. She said,

> Much of my work is about what other companies do to make their businesses run right. I've done training pieces on every aspect of business development and human resource development and fair employment practice and finance and creative strategic planning. And I've filmed or sat in on dozens of seminars. You do have to learn a tremendous amount in order to turn it into another product.

Creative Learning, Self-Taught Skills, and Training Gaps. Several women had no formal training in business management but had learned business skills "hit or miss." A typical case was Meg, who said, "No, I didn't have any official [business] training. I've done seminars and I've read a lot." Frances was continually trying out and teaching herself new computer programs. Olive's membership in a national organization for women business executives gave her access to conferences, classes, and networking opportunities. She also received a helpful trade journal.

Isabelle read books on accounting and operating architectural offices and taught herself a computer accounting program. She did so to close the training gap between those, like herself, trained in manual drafting techniques and more recent students who had learned computerized drafting. She recently had purchased a computerized system, and she had also hired younger architects who knew these techniques.

Group 3: Business Planners—Entrepreneurs

The Entrepreneurial women had more training and job experience in business, but little formal occupational training. Most of the African American and one European American woman made up for this lack of occupational training with extensive job experience. Several women, both black and white, learned their occupations through informal means, however, from friends, from someone in the same type of business, or through trade seminars and self-taught methods.

Formal Education. There were racial differences in the levels of education attained by the Entrepreneurial women. Three of five African American women had graduated from high school and attended college or a technical school but not received a college degree. Charlene took business courses at a technical school. Rachel, the only women with formal training in her occupation, dropped out of college. She returned to an art institute for silk screen courses but did not complete a degree. Her extensive business training in high school, her paralegal training, and her experience in tax preparation gave her business skills for her business. Trish majored in music during her two years of college but dropped out before finishing a degree.

Of the two remaining African American women, Diane earned a Bachelor's degree in physical education, a field unrelated to her business. Eleanor dropped out of high school to work to support her ailing mother. Years later, she took night classes to earn her GED.

In contrast to the African American women, all of the European American Entrepreneurial women had completed four-year college degrees. Karen majored in Information Systems. She learned bookkeeping, accounting, marketing, management, and personnel in school but claimed to have forgotten much of the course content by the time she bought her business. None of the other white women had any formal training in business or their business occupations.

Job Experience. All of the Entrepreneurial women had prior job experience in their occupations or in sales or business management. Trish held many retail positions, always keeping an entrepreneurial activity going on the side. Karen had the most experience in her line of work: 11 years in all facets of restaurant work. In addition, the previous owners of the restaurant trained her for two weeks.

Eleanor's experiences in paid positions constituted the best example of how the typical Entrepreneur learned skills on-the-job. Eleanor had held many paid positions, though she claimed to have no experience that helped her in operating her business. An examination of her work experiences and the culture in which she grew up, however, tells a different story. Eleanor's family took part in the constant barter and sale of things needed for life within a small African American community in the rural South. They also pursued more formal entrepreneurial enterprises, providing a model for income generation. She said,

My [grand]father on my mother's side was like a walking salesman. Because he sold Ernest Blair products. And they sell vanilla flavoring and the first powdered cool-aid I ever drink. Grandpa also sold suits, so he ran around and measured the men for suits. So I guess I kind of grew up with it, and I sold Blair products for awhile also.

A Patchwork Method of Learning. Eleanor's work history provides a fine example of how the motivation behind a true entrepreneur led her through multiple money making activities. She explained,

I did a little of everything. Volunteer work at the schools, the Chamber of Commerce, I tour guided, I was a maid, I was a cook, I was a laundry person, a baby sitter. I never was a person that wanted to stay doing one thing all of my life. So if I was a baby sitter when I first started in the work field, then I became a dishwasher in a restaurant, then I became a maid for someone and I just kept going. And every step generated me further up to be something else, because I never wanted to settle and say I wanta be a baby sitter all of my life. I get bored easy or something. I have to involve myself into more than one thing at a time.

And so I just went from one step to the other. And besides selling—
over at the gift shop, we sell somebody something, or doing the trailers
or going over to tell stories or lectures. That's what I do.

Eleanor's work experiences provided her, bit by bit, with the patchwork of skills she now uses in her trailer rental business. Not wanting to
"settle" eventually led her to use the bits and pieces from all her past jobs
in operating her business. No longer a laundress or a maid, she still
cleaned the trailers and laundered linens after guests departed. No longer
a cook for hourly pay, she occasionally served home-cooked meals to her
guests. She sometimes worked as a tour guide, both as an employee of a
local organization and for her guests. No longer selling for Blair, she operated a small gift shop next to the trailers, selling hand crafted souvenirs
made by community members. And, no longer a school volunteer, she
told stories to visitors and children who vacationed in her trailers.

Charlene, too, reported holding numerous jobs, many in small businesses owned by herself or her brother. All of these positions contributed
to her sales abilities. Her food service, DJ work, and cleaning experiences built skills she used in operating her restaurant/lounge.

Self-Generated Skills and Knowledge. Several Entrepreneurial
women taught themselves skills needed for operation of their business.
Trish taught herself computerized embroidery. Pam and Donna taught
themselves carpentry in preparing to operate their business. They saw an
espresso cart advertised for sale and wanted to buy it to start a business.
When the owner didn't sell, they decided to build their own. As Pam said,
"It was neat because we weren't carpenters before we started, and now
we are."

Group 4: Business Planners—Retirement Planners

Several of the Retirement Planners started businesses that capitalized on
skills learned during their working lives. These skills differed by race.
The African American women followed the entrepreneurial group's educational process and sought more business training than occupational
training. Only Lenore and Rosalind had training or experience in their
occupations. In contrast, the white women followed the professional
group's educational process. All had either trained or gained job experience in their occupations. Only Maggie and Emily had both business and
occupational training. Two rural women, Rosalind (black) and Maggie

(white), had the most formal training and job experience, and both had extensive occupational and business skills.

Formal Education. This group was one of the few in which more African Americans (four out of five) than European Americans held college degrees. Of the four, all but one earned a degree early in life and all majored in business-related fields. Betty earned her degree later while in the armed services. Trudy was the only African American woman in the group to drop out of college.

Three of the four white women held college degrees, but two had completed degrees after their children were grown. Amanda finished a BFA and took graduate courses in residential design after moving closer to her daughter and grandchildren. Deborah returned to school at age 50, earning both her undergraduate and Master's degrees in psychology and counseling within five years.

Emily earned a Bachelor's degree in business with a minor in English before raising a family. Maggie, the only white woman in the group who dropped out of college, took two years of college business courses that provided her with means to earn a living. After her children had grown, she returned to real estate school, commuting and taking night classes to complete license requirements.

Job Training and Experience. The Retirement Planners sought opportunities for structured learning in addition to their prior work experience. One woman integrated her entire work history into a deeply anchored business.

Structured Learning. Two of the white women, Maggie and Deborah, started businesses in fields that required internship training for licensing. This meant that their training included job experience in their occupational fields but not business or management training. Maggie gained valuable experience for her realty business when she worked in the Clerk of Courts office researching land titles. Emily received occupational training from the companies whose financial planning products she sold.

Business Experiences. All five African American Retirement Planners gained business and management skills in prior employment. Only two of the European American women had done so. Helen used administrative skills learned from a life-long career in corporate administration. Lenore, Trudy, and Betty had also learned business management skills in past jobs. Maggie and Emily, both white, had each worked in bookkeeping. Maggie had prepared the family's taxes and taxes for her son's business. Emily worked as legal secretary and operated a small business prior to starting her financial planning enterprise.

A Deeply Anchored Career. Rosalind provides a striking example of how well the African Americans Retirement Planners integrated their businesses with their lifelong careers. The only African American in the group with both business and occupational experience, Rosalind had spent her entire working life in the Ludlow public school system. During this time, she performed many functions in the operation of the schools, describing her work as "like operating a business." She helped set up the County's first Head Start program and took training seminars and workshops in how to start and operate the program. Although she worked full time for the Board of Education, she

> ran [Head Start] during one summer. That was when I really had my first experience with working with [an] early childhood program. Even though I worked in the office full time, during that summer I was able to really be in the set-up of the Head Start program for [the] County. And I kinda worked my way on into it from there.

Rosalind's on-the-job financial and personnel management experiences, plus her experience implementing a Head Start program, prepared her to start an early childhood daycare center.

Gaining Needed Skills and Knowledge. The Retirement Planners used formal training sources to gain information and skills for their businesses. They taught themselves using library references, trade journals, and magazines. Network contacts were important training resources. Below, I examine formal and self-taught means of gaining knowledge used by members of this group. In Chapter 8, I examine how social capital in the form of network contacts provided information, skills and knowledge.

Structured Learning. Three of the African American women sought training to aid them in business formation. Trudy took accounting and tax law courses while working for the Internal Revenue Service and attended business classes at a technical school. She went to training seminars sponsored by the Chamber of Commerce and the Post Office. Helen enrolled in private training seminars to learn how to recycle new cartridges as they come on the market. Betty gained knowledge of bookkeeping through class work sponsored by a local minority business organization.

Self-Taught Skills. Four women, three white and one black, used skills they learned through independent study. Emily taught herself the basics of financial planning, her business occupation. She was the only woman in the group to report doing so, although Trudy may have also learned a good part of her mailing service on her own. Amanda, Helen, and Deborah said that they read books and trade journals. They did so not only to find out what was new on the market, but also to gain needed business and occupational information.

EXTERNALLY MOTIVATED BUSINESS OWNERS

Women in the unplanned groups relied largely on prior employment for skills used in their businesses. The Work Skill Owners brought occupational skills and, in some cases, business management skills to business start-up. A few of the Career Problem Solvers had formal training in their business occupations or in business and financial management, but most relied on prior employment for business and occupational skills. The Community Service Providers were least prepared with formal training and job experience.

To gain skills, women in the unplanned groups sought training and information from a variety of sources. The Work Skill Owners generally learned on their own or sought help from friends in similar businesses. The Career Problem Solvers and Community Service Providers sought needed skills through more structured programs available from professional trade associations, Small Business Development Centers, and correspondence courses. In addition, when hiring outsider knowledge, the Work Skill Owners tended to hire skilled accountants on contract, while the Career Problem Solvers hired full time employees, service providers, and consultants. The Community Service Providers hired employees, some part time, but also relied on donated labor. Women in all the unplanned groups used social contacts to garner information and knowledge for their businesses (see Chapter 8).

Group 5: Serendipitous Owners—Work Skill Owners

The Work Skill Owners relied primarily on training and experiences gained while working for pay to start businesses. All had worked in jobs related to their businesses. Two-thirds of the women also had training or experience in business-related skills. Only two started businesses with little or no prior business training or experience. Much of this informal learning doesn't "count" as human capital in paid employment, but can be maximized in business ownership. Experiences honed in daily practice on-the-job translate into sure knowledge when ownership requires management decisions and financial commitments based on knowledge of a service or trade.

Formal Education. Only one of the European American women, Irene, had a college degree, and it was unrelated to her business occupation. Of the other white women, Sally and Becky dropped out of college. Camilla started working for an insurance agency directly out of high school. Nell did not specify her level of formal education. Dee, the only African American in the group, finished a BA in Sociology and did some work toward an MBA. She was the only woman to have any formal training useful for operating her business.

Job Training and Experience. The women in this group had all held jobs directly related to their business occupations. Job experience was the only training they reported having in their occupations. In addition, Camilla, Nell, and Dee reported learning business-related skills while working for pay.

Dee had the most training and the most extensive knowledge base in the group. With formal training in business (a year of MBA classes), Dee had solid business training. She gained financial and management skills while working for a large, business service corporation, as well as knowledge of customer service, human resource policy and procedures, sales, banking, and government service. She recalled that her employer was big on training, and she continued to take seminars and workshops while working for the firm. Her work as Vice President with a second company, a large temporary employment agency, gave her experience directly relevant for operating her own temporary agency.

Camilla learned all of her occupational and business skills through work with three different insurance agencies and continuing education classes taken while working. She became licensed in auto insurance and learned computer skills at her first job. She became licensed in homeowner's, boat, and motorcycle insurance while at her second job and also learned office management, management training, and financial management. Since all of the software that now serves the insurance industry was developed during her working career, she learned all of her computer skills on-the-job.

Irene and Sally were the least well trained to own businesses. Both had worked for years, Irene as a waitress and Sally as a bartender, and each knew the daily routines in taverns and restaurants, but neither had management, financial, or other business-related skills. The need for business training was brought home to Sally in a particularly dramatic way. After eight months of operation, she discovered that her partner had "ripped off a good $15,000 to $20,000 because I didn't know what I was doing with the books." After parting company with him, she combined his bank loan with hers and eventually paid it off.

Gaining Needed Skills and Knowledge. The Work Skill Owners sought very little training. With occupational and some business skills learned in prior jobs, most reported learning any additional skills either on their own or from others around them. Below I examine the experiences of a self-taught owner. In Chapter 8, I examine how women learned from others in networks around them.

Self-Taught Skills. Becky had no training or experience in bookkeeping, accounting, or taxes that prepared her to operate a business. She proclaimed, "Nothing can prepare you for owning your own business!" She figured out how to do "moderate bookkeeping just 'cause I had to." She claimed, "I learn better that way." She took a financial management course when she first started the business and said it was helpful, but claimed, "It was more helpful to network than it was to learn [in a class]. To me it's all common sense. If your numbers don't balance, it's like keeping your checkbook at home. [If] you don't have it, don't spend it!" Transferring skills learned and used in household activities to the business arena is an example of Daniels' (1988) notion of the "seamless" quality of everyday life.

Group 6: Serendipitous Owners—Career Problem Solvers

Because the Career Problem Solvers had not planned to have businesses, they illustrated how women sometimes make situational decisions about business ownership and gain needed skills through less formal means. Many of these women, especially those who had worked in large corporations, had business management, marketing, and finance skills learned on these jobs. Some sought further training, usually in specific occupations, to help them open their businesses. Only one woman, Geneva, had formal training in business as well as job experience in the occupational field in which she started a business. Four others had worked in jobs similar to their businesses. The rest opened businesses in occupations in which they had little if any experience.

Formal Education. More African American women (four of six) earned college degrees than had the European American women. However, Geneva was the only African American to earn a degree in a field helpful to her business operation. She held a BA in accounting with a minor in education. Heather, Candice, and Nora all held degrees unrelated to their business occupations or to business in general. Sonia and Sheila did not provide specific information about their educational backgrounds. Of the white women, only Judy and Gail in Bingham and Sigrid in Stanley had college degrees. Judy and Sigrid's degrees were unrelated to their businesses or to business in general. Gail held a degree in business administration, including general accounting.

The four remaining white women, one from Grafton and three from Stanley, had varying levels of education. Jill, the only one with formal training in her business occupation, had graduated from two technical school programs, interior design and hair styling. The latter helped her establish her natural hair salon. Valerie had no schooling beyond high school, and Libby dropped out of high school in the tenth grade to work so her brother could graduate.[4] She later obtained her GED. Both women founded highly successful businesses with very deep knowledge of their business fields and had fascinating stories of how they learned to make their businesses work for them (see below and Chapter 8).

Julie, a travel agent, had taken business classes at a technical school for a year after high school without earning a degree. She then went to night school at two area colleges for two years without completing a degree, however, the courses she took helped her get a job working for H&R Block. While there, she learned more and eventually taught in their tax school. Julie's training shows how women can gain knowledge and skills in formal settings without necessarily obtaining formal credentials. With only a high school degree, Julie gained the skills necessary to successfully operate two businesses.

Job Training and Experience. Women in this group gained most of their knowledge from prior work experiences. Skills most frequently learned in work settings were business management and marketing skills. Five women (Geneva, Candice, Valerie, Jill, and Libby) had prior work experience in their current business occupations. Nine women (Geneva, Sonia, Heather, Sheila, Gail, Julie, Valerie, Libby, and Sigrid) had learned sales, management, or financial skills that helped them operate their businesses.

Geneva, Valerie, and Libby were the only women in the group with prior work experience in *both* their occupations *and* in business skills. With her degree in accounting, Geneva worked as a financial director for a chemical manufacturing company for eight years before starting her own manufacturing firm with the same product line. Valerie was a manager in a company that sold wholesale petroleum products. When fired, she took revenge by starting her own petroleum firm in competition with her former employer. Libby worked her way up from an apartment manager to a project manager for a construction firm, learning personnel and budget management along the way.

All of the other women had work experience in *either* business *or* their occupations. Gail and Sigrid had both worked in sales. Sonia gained administrative skills in her corporate positions. Heather used technical skills, gained during prior work, in her video production business. Sheila used her banking experience in operating her temporary employment agency. Julie's experience with H&R Block is an example of business skills learned most thoroughly through job training and experience. She later worked for a CPA, then operated her own tax service part time. Her training in accounting and tax preparation helped her to operate the business side of her travel agency.

A Career Based on Job Skills. Libby's experience building her contracting career from scratch illustrates how on-the-job experience can provide virtually all skills necessary for a career and for business ownership. From a job as an apartment manager, she began acquiring maintenance, renovation, and building skills as well as management and financial skills that eventually led to her own residential contracting business. She described her first learning experiences this way:

> In order to rent an apartment you have to make sure that it is ready to be rented, i.e., gettin' carpet put in, walls painted, things repaired, and the heating and air systems, and maintaining the grounds. All of the things involved in managing an apartment complex, I also learned how to do them. I cut the grass with a tractor. I have painted units myself. I have shampooed carpets. And I followed my maintenance man around like a little puppy dog, and he had the patience just to hang in there with me. And I would physically stand there and watch him repair something.

As she continued to manage apartments, her skills grew. She became more involved in larger management issues such as marketing properties, advertising, and development and construction of new properties. Eventually, she moved entirely into construction, becoming a liaison between management and construction. She traveled throughout the Southeast to hire and train staff and check new units being built. She said of the experience,

> I had become a really good asset to them because of my knowledge of
> construction and knowledge of management. It really evolved to a
> point where I could get along with the construction men so well, and
> also to take it over into management, which I knew their side real well,
> too.

She next worked full time doing quality control for construction,
handling several jobs in several states and negotiating bids. Then she
spent a year as a site manager, responsible for the entire job of renovating
400 units, with a budget of $2.5 million. With a promotion, she started
traveling again, overseeing renovation of units in several states. She explained,

> It was my job to make sure that the whole big picture was taking place.
> Once a month I would sit down and audit everybody's draws. 'Cause
> they would be sending in draws for a hundred, two hundred, three hun-
> dred thousand dollars at a time. I had to make sure that everybody was
> staying in the budget. And so when I would go to that property once a
> week or every other week, I'd go over things with them on the site, any
> kind of problems they were running into, and then I'd fix it and get 'em
> going again.

From a position as a low-paid apartment manager, Libby built a
high-profile career in construction management, a competitive, non-traditional industry for women. She became well respected for her skills by
the men with whom she worked, although only after a long fight for
recognition of her abilities.

Gaining Needed Skills and Knowledge. The women who felt they
lacked adequate skills with which to start their businesses found numerous ways to build the skills they needed. Some sought training in similar
businesses, in franchise settings, or in other occupational settings. Others
networked with business contacts, mentors, and employees. Some
women hired skilled workers or consultants. Still others taught themselves, learned from relatives, or developed what they saw as a "natural"
talent or ability. Many employed multiple strategies to gain needed
skills.

Informal Apprenticeships. Two women volunteered in work settings
to learn an occupation. Julie worked for a few months in a travel agency
to learn the business. Judy, after "dabbling" in one of her brothers' land-

scaping businesses, trained with her other brother in his security alarm business. Being mechanically inclined, she picked up skills quickly. She then went to fire alarm school and attended a seminar on central station monitoring.

Structured Learning: Franchise Training. Both Sheila and Candice opened franchise businesses and were trained by parent companies. Sheila, who already had business skills, used the training to learn the temporary employment business. Candice, who knew the airline industry from her previous job, used her franchise training to gain business-related skills. Both women chose franchises at least in part because of the training opportunities they provided. Each felt that a franchise would give them more solid information and skills needed to start their businesses than hit-or-miss informal learning.

Structured Learning: SBDC Training. With little business training and no previous experience with their business occupations, Nora and Sigrid both received help from a university-affiliated Small Business Development Center. Sigrid felt that the sessions she attended were not specific enough to her industry to be of help, but Nora learned how to better organize her business. She said,

> I was really pleasantly surprised because initially, my reaction was "These are students. What can they tell me?" But they really showed me how to do my record keeping so that things flowed more smoothly. Because I had stuff here and stuff there, and they helped me to get the office really organized and running a lot more smoothly.

Other Training. Sigrid and Nora attended other industry-sponsored training sessions relevant to their businesses. Nora's industry trainings provided not only skills, but also an atmosphere conducive to networking. Nora took advantage of network opportunities at training sessions (described more fully in Chapter 8). Although Nora took a course on how to start a business at a nearby university, she insisted that most of her skills came from on-the-job learning. Sigrid and her partner sought training for the technical side of their laser cartridge recycling enterprise wherever they could find it.

Group 7: Serendipitous Owners—Community Service Providers

The women in this group provide another opportunity to examine women's choices and strategies in gaining skills they hadn't planned on needing. All the Service Providers had college degrees, but their formal education afforded them little help in their businesses. They had few business skills, and only Jeannette had prior experience in her business occupation. Laura and Bernice sought the bulk of their training either just before starting or during the time they were operating their businesses.

Formal Education and Job Experience. Jeannette, with a Ph.D. in English, was the only woman whose degree helped her with her business. She used her language and writing skills to produce her directory and newsletter and her teaching skills to develop seminar and workshop curricula. Her experience in her early 20s of owning a small boutique and helping her ex-husband operate a business for six years contributed to her knowledge of bookkeeping and business management. Yet she still felt she needed business skills.

Laura had a BA unrelated to her business interests when she opened the bookstore. Only after starting the business did she complete a graduate program in theology and literature. Her graduate work helped her with knowledge of books and literature, but it contributed nothing to her knowledge of how to operate a business. Laura had worked in a Christian organization for a few years and had been in charge of training volunteers. She thought this work had given her "personal skills" that helped her relate to customers and co-workers.

Bernice left home to attend college in the North, where she received a BA in early childhood education. After returning to the South, she got a job with Head Start, eventually becoming County director. She took correspondence courses in accounting and business management, but did not finish a business-related degree. The responsibilities of her job as Director of Head Start and her business knowledge from correspondence courses gave her the skills, direction, and self discipline to start her business.

Gaining Needed Skills and Knowledge. In gaining skills for their businesses, the Community Service Providers sought structured training opportunities. In addition, one woman gained knowledge on her own.

Structured Training. As a result of her observations while on home visits for Head Start, Bernice took workshops at a personal care organization in a nearby city and learned how to operate a family model care home. She received support and referrals from her contacts in the organization when operating her business.

Jeannette attended Small Business Development Center workshops and seminars on business management. One of the SBDC representatives helped her achieve a more business-like demeanor. The first year Jeannette produced a women's directory, she had given most of them away. She explained, "N. has been patient with me because I've had no profit motive. [She said,] 'If you're gonna be in business, you have to think profit!'"

Self-Taught Skills. At the time of the interview, Jeannette was teaching herself about computers, but she explained,

> I'm studying what all they can do and the different programs [that are] available. And that in itself changes so much that I don't really anticipate myself being a computer wizard. I've found [that] some people just do that better. I think I'd like to learn to delegate some work.

SUMMARY

Women's motives for founding business and the circumstances surrounding business start-up affected the types and levels of human capital they accumulated. Those who planned to own businesses frequently sought formal training, either in a specific trade or profession or in business and financial management. To gain additional skills, they sought structured training opportunities through continuing education, trade associations, or employed situations, and other less formal training opportunities, including learning from social contacts (see Chapter 8).

Women who did not expect to own businesses were not necessarily less prepared, but they accumulated human capital resources differently than women who planned businesses. They more frequently learned relevant skills on-the-job, both in their business occupations and in business management. They frequently had a mix of business and occupational skills and relied on social contacts and self-taught methods to learn needed skills. This strategy of combining skills learned in disparate locations does not suggest planned investment in self as a means to further business goals, as would be consistent with Becker's (1964, 1975, 1993 editions) theories of human capital. Rather, it indicates a hodge-podge of circumstantially based opportunities realized by women who unexpectedly found ways to focus and use skills in business ownership. Gerson's (1985) theories of situational career development and Daniel's (1988) seamless quality of women's lives provide better frames than traditional rational choice theories in which to understand these women's skill-building strategies.

Some racial differences were apparent by group, locale, and age. African American women who sought occupational training more frequently learned a trade rather than a profession. For European American women, the opposite was true. While this is not a statistically representative sample, it illustrates the experiences of women in different locales. Educational opportunities were more limited for rural black women than for urban black women and white women in all locales. Limited education influenced the types of businesses women founded and the levels of commercial funding they needed and were able to obtain. Despite these limitations, black women more frequently had both occupational *and* business skills, while white women had either occupational *or* business skills. In addition, older African American women had more job experience from life-long careers than did older European American women, who had worked less while raising children.

These patterns are consistent with the literature on African American educational and work expectations. Drawing from both an emphasis on formal education and an expectation to work all their lives, black women sought more varied and relevant skills for their businesses than white women. They also fit Folbre's (1994), Gerson's (1985), and Collins' (1990) analyses of limitations based on structural constraints, societal norms, and race- and gender-based discrimination. Decisions made and actions taken within these contexts were rationally based on existing opportunities at the time. They might also have been profit maximizing given the situations in which women found themselves, however, they were not all economically motivated.

Clearly, women gain human capital from more sources than formal educational settings. Skills learned in jobs are often crucial to formation of businesses. In addition, industry-structured learning opportunities, informal training, and self-taught skills are important. All too frequently, women learn as they go. One of the most important findings in this study was the extent to which women relied on social contacts for information and to gain skills. In Chapter 8, I examine in detail how women made these contacts, what information they gained from them, and the range of social resources used in building human capital.

Human capital also affects access to financial capital. The ability to demonstrate real skills with which to operate businesses provides proof to bankers of a woman entrepreneur's potential for success. Without skills, the business venture becomes too risky and lending unlikely. The more skills and abilities women have, the more likely they are to secure commercial funding. In Chapter 7, I examine further how women's education and job histories affect their experiences with the commercial funding process.

NOTES

[1] "Backyard" was a term used by many of the black hair stylists to indicate business operations out of the home. Many made clear that this term had a negative connotation, saying they had never worked in their backyard, but had always had a "real" shop.

[2] Elly explained that a "perm" for African American hair is different than a perm on white hair. For blacks, a perm straightens the hair, while perms curl white hair.

[3] The attorneys had JDs; the dentists had DDSs; the interior designer had a Master's degree in interior design; the video producer had a graduate degree in film; the counselor had a PhD in psychological counseling; and two of the architects had Master's degrees in architecture. Jackie, one of the partners in architecture, had a Bachelor's degree in architecture.

[4] According to her family tradition, "women don't need a high school education."

CHAPTER 7
Financial Capital

Another component essential to success of small business ownership is financial capital. Prior research suggests that women are disadvantaged in seeking commercial financing and more frequently start businesses with personal savings and investments. Many of the women in this study did use commercial financing, however, but almost always combined commercial sources with personal and alternative sources of funding. One woman secured a grant, and two received SBA guaranteed loans. None used venture capital to start their businesses, not even those in Stanley who started high-growth firms.

Most women, both black and white, reported that they either had difficulty getting a commercial loan, were refused a loan, or did not even try to get a loan because they anticipated rejection. In a few cases, white women perceived today's lending climate as favoring minorities, saying, "You have to be black to get a loan." Black women's experiences in applying for commercial loans frequently belied this perception. Although some black women obtained credit relatively easily, they did so with prior credit histories, collateral, co-signers, and franchise or SBA backing. Many had established relationships with bank representatives that were similar to relationships established by the white women who received loans. Most black women who applied for larger loans experienced the same difficulties white women did in their applications.

Women's financial resources were intricately entwined with their social resources, even more than their human capital resources were. Individuals' relationships provided avenues to wealth, trust in lending, and collateral backup. Women obtained finance capital in three ways: bank loans and credit; personal or family resources (savings, investments, etc.); and cost reduction strategies. Social relationships were deeply implicated in all of these.

Below, I examine how women financed their businesses. I look at how women's intentions, motivations, and goals for their businesses affected financing by examining each motivational group separately, as identified in Chapter 5. First, I look at the Internally Motivated owners and discuss their pathways to funding businesses. Then I examine the Externally Motivated owners' business funding processes. I examine the link between women's social ties and their financial capital in greater detail in Chapter 9.

INTERNALLY MOTIVATED BUSINESS OWNERS

The women who were internally motivated for business ownership used several methods to finance their businesses. Nearly two thirds (24 out of 38) obtained commercial loans or second mortgages to finance start-up. They often combined loans with other non-commercial funding sources. These included personal savings, continued employment earnings, and family loans and gifts.

Both the Trades women and the Professional women used commercial sources as their main method of financing. While some relied solely on savings or continued employment for financing, others combined these with bank or credit union loans. Several of the Entrepreneurs relied on continued employment earnings to fund their businesses. In addition to commercial loans, the Retirement Planners relied on assets earned during careers and family investments to finance their businesses.

The white women in the Trade and Entrepreneur groups reported having more financial resources than the black women, including some from social contacts (see Chapter 9). These women reported receiving help from family and friends who contributed rent-free buildings or personal financing. They also used credit cards for financing and, for one rural white entrepreneur, SBA loan backing. The Grafton black Trades women received help with loan packages from a local organization created to help disadvantaged women and minorities prepare paperwork for loans.

Each group used different combinations of cost reduction strategies, related to the resources and knowledge available to them. The most common cost reduction methods were opening home-based businesses or relying on husbands to pay the bills at home. Less common methods were barter, cost analysis, and expense tracking. One cost reduction strategy not previously identified in research on small businesses was stockpiling. This allowed owners to buy equipment on sale or at used prices, sometimes over a long time period, to minimize costs. Donated family labor also reduced costs. This strategy was used primarily by rural black owners, but was also employed by some white owners (see Chapter 9).

Group 1: Business Planners—Trades Women

The Trades women relied largely on commercial sources of finance, although two white women relied on family aid, one exclusively so. Most African American women took out bank loans, but they combined commercial financing with personal and alternative funding sources. As the group with the lowest personal wealth in the study and least ability to finance businesses, the Trades women reported an innovative method to minimize start-up costs: stockpiling equipment. This strategy allowed African American women with little access to financial capital to extend their initial costs over time, reducing the amount of borrowed money needed for start-up. It was also an indication of long-term planning on the part of the owners.

Commercial Loans and Loan Experiences. Of the ten women who pursued trades, six (Mabel, Cynthia, Ivy, Corinne, Hazel, and Linda) received commercial loans to start businesses. Five of the six businesses were located in Grafton and one was in Bingham. Lenore and Elly had tried to obtain a loan with the help of the minority loan organization in Grafton, but their application was rejected because they started their business with their own money while waiting for their request to be processed. Other than these two, none of the women had any difficulty obtaining commercial loans. Most had built good credit ratings with previous loans, had established positive relationships with local bankers, and most had co-signers.

Personal Sources of Financing. The Trades women used personal capital to support and fund their businesses. They also used family and other sources of funding, as reported in Chapter 9. Four of the African American women (Sabrina, Carol, Elly and Corinne) used savings as their primary funding source. Carol and Corinne also relied on continued employment earnings. Elly's sister and business partner, Lenore, contributed $50,000 from profit shares and stocks, funds derived from her management career.

Cost Reduction Strategies. One of the most innovative strategies to reduce initial start-up costs was stockpiling. Cynthia and Corinne bought equipment over time prior to business start-up and stored it for future use. Cynthia bought used salon equipment from her cousin. When she opened her salon, she had most of the equipment she needed. Over several years Corinne bought pots and pans at department store sales, planning to one day open a restaurant.

Mabel operated her business out of a trailer located next to her house, eliminating rent. She explained that while her daughter was young, having her business next to her house allowed her to take the child to work with her, reducing childcare costs she might otherwise have to pay. Women often establish home-based businesses to combine household and employment responsibilities.

Group 2: Business Planners—Professionals

The Professional women, largely white and metropolitan black women, usually combined several sources of funding into a strategic mix of commercial, personal, and alternative funding. African American women and European American women were equally likely to use this strategy, and it appeared in all three types of communities. This strategy was a reflection both of the group's greater access to personal resources and the larger capital needs of the types of businesses they founded. Twelve of the sixteen had access to savings, earnings, pensions, and/or family loans and gifts for use in starting their businesses. The white Professionals were able to obtain larger loans than most women in the other groups because of stronger educational credentials and earning potentials.[1]

The Professional women used some of the common cost reduction methods discussed above, such as starting home based businesses and relying on husbands to pay home bills. Yet, with a greater knowledge base and more technology available to them, they also relied on more sophisticated methods such as tracking expenses and performing cost analyses to reduce expenses. Some bartered professional services for resources such as office space.

Commercial Funding Sources. Ten black and white Professional women received commercial loans for their businesses. While most of the women borrowed money for start-up, two borrowed to expand after their businesses were established. Fern reported needing money only later, after operating her firm for more than a year. Similarly, Gina used savings to start, and operated off of receipts for several years. She only applied for a loan later, and did so merely to build good credit.

Bonnie, Kirstin, and Isabelle each took out loans of $100,000 or more. Bonnie and Kirstin, starting dental offices, needed significant financing to purchase equipment. Isabelle used her loan to purchase and renovate a house for use as an office and residence. Although Marge said that most chiropractors start out with large loans, she opened her practice with a $2,000 loan from her aunt and "a wing and a prayer." Most other Professional women borrowed smaller amounts to buy buildings or purchase equipment.

Commercial Loan Experiences. A few of the women had significant trouble getting their loans, and a few had no trouble at all, but the experiences of most who applied for loans fell somewhere in between. All but one of the women needed collateral or a co-signer in order to get their loans. Carla was the only one who needed neither a co-signer nor collateral for a start-up loan. She reported having a previous loan co-signed by her husband. With one exception, those who had trouble getting their loans had applied for the largest amounts of money. Despite having significant educational credentials, these women had to provide voluminous proof of credit-worthiness.

For her first $7,500 loan, Isabelle was required to have her husband co-sign the loan, and she had to submit letters from her clients confirming the work she would be doing for them for the next few years. She continued to borrow money to build good credit. By the time she borrowed $180,000 for her residential office, she had "too much" credit and had to pursue the loan with the help of the SBA. Eventually she received the amount she needed but was required to take out a $150,000 life insurance policy to cover the loan in the event of her death. She was also required to put a lien on the house, stipulating that any profits she made would go to house payments.

Operating Strategies. Gina owned a small operation requiring little start-up financing. She was able to build the business with what money she and her business partner had, paying the bills as they went. She felt this strategy made a difference in how the bank viewed their applications when they finally applied for credit. She explained, "The things we've asked for have been in a realm of control and what we can manage. A lot of firms have probably gotten in trouble because they have cash, but they have not learned how to manage it, so they get in all this debt. We've operated our business fairly debt-free."

Personal and Other Non-Commercial Funding Sources. Eight Professional women used personal sources of financing to fund their businesses. Four white women (Frieda, Frances, Marsha, and Kay) and three black women (Carla, Barbara, and Gina) used personal savings. Barbara reported using credit cards to start her psychological counseling practice. In addition, Barbara, Olive, and Frieda used continued employment earnings, while Fern reported starting with pension money from a previous job. Jackie entered the partnership with Kay after the business had started and did not mention contributing money to the business.

Cost Reduction Strategies. The Professional women used various cost-cutting strategies, most commonly starting home based businesses (Frieda, Isabelle). They also reported using fiscally conservative practices such as tracking expenses and analyzing projects financially (Kay and Jackie). They used social resources to reduce costs, a strategy discussed more fully in Chapter 9.

Group 3: Business Planners—Natural Entrepreneurs

The Entrepreneurial group relied on fewer commercial sources than did other groups. Instead, they started businesses using continued employment earnings, personal savings, and/or family loans, as well as some bank loans. Almost all African Americans, but only one European American, relied on commercial sources of funding. The rural black women more frequently relied on continued earnings (both personal and family) because of limited economic opportunities in their communities. Two white Grafton women worked part time to support very new businesses. The black women also reported using cost reduction strategies such as donated kin labor (Chapter 9).

Commercial Loans and Loan Experiences. Five of the nine women in the Entrepreneurial group sought commercial funding for their businesses. All of the African Americans from the rural areas and from Grafton took out bank loans and/or second mortgages. Rachel (black) and Karen (white) were the only women to report having difficulty with loans, and these were the biggest loans in the group. The rest had no problem, although most had a co-signer or used collateral.

SBA Guaranteed Loan Experience. In Grafton, Karen applied for a $180,000 Small Business Administration guaranteed loan to buy an established restaurant with her husband. They had been turned down by local banks and told to go to the regional Small Business Development Center. According to Karen, "No bank will loan money on restaurants. All these small banks are under such stringent government regulations now, because of all the bad loans that have gone through, that they're watching them very carefully." They had good credit at the outset, but needed to be patient, persistent, accurate, and willing to jump through many hoops to get their first loan. Karen was convinced that she could have gotten the loan by herself based on her restaurant experience. At the same time, she reported that, "[Banks] don't lend money on buildings. We had to prove our renovation was going to happen and we were going to expand the existing business."

Experiences with Credit Discrimination. Because of Rachel's loan experience in buying a commercial building, she and her husband had to severely limit the business they had planned to operate in it. Rachel had perfect credit when they bought the building. The couple put a second mortgage on their home to finance renovation of the building into office suites upstairs and a storefront downstairs. When they received the funds, the bank promised them additional money to finance inventory for a sporting goods store in the storefront. The store was the inspiration behind both their T-shirt business and the purchase and renovation of the building. Before they were finished renovating, however, the bank backed out and did not lend them money to stock the store. Lacking funds, they were stranded with only partial means to repay their debt.

Rachel's husband quit his full time job to complete the renovation, saving money they would have paid to builders. They rented out the offices upstairs and finally rented the downstairs storefront to a retail owner. They began operating the T-shirt business in a back room. They managed to survive financially, depending on Rachel's husband's income and rental income from the storefront. However, Rachel filed for bankruptcy with her credit ruined.

Rachel believed her problem was with one particular bank that held the building note. She felt that the white male business establishment frowned upon a black woman owning a major commercial building on one of the main streets in town. She said,

> I really thought that I was discriminated against, being a black female. It was like somebody was out to get me. And they really tried to take this building from me, but I filed [for bankruptcy] and stayed in it two years. I didn't do it on the business, but I did it personally because we were going under fast. And I came back out, and really, what one bank wouldn't do, the next bank [would]. I have credit in the Credit Bureau, I have a lot of pull. If I sold all the land I had, I could walk away and *buy* chicken houses [another enterprise they were planning], but I gotta

> prove to them that a woman can do it. I'm gonna somehow manage to
> do what I wanta do just by working and not giving up.

Rachel continued to operate her T-shirt business and regained her
line of credit. She was convinced that bankers in general favor women
when they dispense loans, saying,

> My husband will tell you, he has always put me out front to go to the
> bank. It's because the same banker that told him "no" told me "yes."
> He went one day and they say "no." I go back the next day, don't tell
> 'em who I am, they say "yes." It's sad. His credit is better than mine.
> Men look favorable to women when it comes to lending. Women[-
> owned] businesses, minority[-owned]—you fall into all kind of cate-
> gories with bankers.

Non-Commercial Finance Strategies. The women receiving loans
combined their commercial financing with personal and other sources.
Those who did not apply for loans used personal resources and other
means to finance their businesses. Below, I examine women's personal
financing. In Chapter 9, I examine how women mobilized social resources to help finance their businesses.

Personal Sources of Financing. Most of the women had personal
sources of income to use in their businesses. Eleanor, Trish, and Pam
used personal savings. Five of the women (Charlene, Rachel, Eleanor,
Pam, and Melissa) remained employed full or part time, using earnings
to support their businesses. Pam and Donna used credit cards and profits
from their rafting business to partially finance their espresso stand. Trish
and Karen each reinvested profits from the business back into the enterprise.

Group 4: Business Planners—Retirement Planners

The Retirement Planners used a greater variety of funding sources than
women in any of the other internally motivated groups. Less than half applied for bank loans, and one did so only after 5 years of operation. These
women started businesses largely with savings, investments, and retirement money. Because they were older, they had more access to personal
funding sources. This was especially true for the African American
women with businesses in Stanley. Having worked for pay all their lives,
these women had earned significant assets. Still, more than half (three
blacks and one white woman) relied on commercial loans in addition to

their own funds. Trudy, in a non-traditional mail processing business, applied for the largest loan in the group, but did so only after she had been operating the business for five years. The European American women relied more frequently on family investments than commercial financing. Most also chose businesses requiring minimal start-up funding.

In keeping with their assets, these women used few cost reduction strategies. They received aid from their families and communities. In the rural areas, labor and supplies were donated; in the metro area, labor was paid.

Commercial Loan Experiences. Deborah, the white Stanley psychologist, had no trouble obtaining a personal loan for the business, having a recent student loan history. However, the African American women's loan experiences varied. They experienced more difficulty negotiating loans when 1) they sought large loans; 2) they owned non-traditional businesses; and 3) they were in urban areas. In Ludlow, Rosalind applied for a loan to buy and renovate a small building for her daycare center. With a prior loan history and relationships with both bankers in town, she had no problem getting the loan without a co-signer or collateral. Both Betty, in Grafton, and Trudy, in Stanley, had trouble obtaining commercial funding. Both were turned down repeatedly and were not able to secure loans until they sought aid from minority advocacy organizations.

Non-Commercial Sources of Financing. Most of the women in the group also reported using resources derived from personal and family sources, cost reduction strategies, and solicitation of family labor. I examine personal funding and cost reduction strategies below and discuss use of social resources in Chapter 9.

Personal Funding Sources. Because they had spent their lives working for pay, the African American women had more savings (Rosalind and Helen) and retirement income (Trudy, Helen, and Lenore) than the European American women. Nevertheless, Maggie, the white Ludlow realtor, also used savings exclusively to start her home-based business. Although she had taken time off to raise her family, she had worked more than the other white women in the group at a number of jobs. Lenore and Amanda reported using money from stocks and investments in starting their businesses. Maggie reinvested early profits into her business.

Cost Reduction Strategies. The Retirement Planners reported several cost reduction strategies that directly or indirectly reduced the capital they needed for their businesses. After a trial period, Betty obtained credit from her suppliers, paying them as she sold her products. Maggie operated her business out of her home, eliminating rent. Emily started her business in a small business incubator where her rent was low for the first year and increased to the market price of office space as her business grew.

EXTERNALLY MOTIVATED BUSINESS OWNERS

The women who were externally motivated for business ownership used several methods to finance their businesses. Despite having significant personal funding sources from prior jobs, all but three obtained commercial loans or lines of credit. Not all commercial funding, however, was for start-up. Many women relied first on personal savings, retirement accounts, and investments, later seeking commercial loans for business growth. The Community Service Providers, and to a lesser extent the Work Skill Owners, relied heavily on family and volunteer labor to reduce costs. The Service Providers also relied on personal gifts and family loans as sources of revenue. Two of the metro area women limited their salaries in the early months of operation.

The level of skill learned in prior business service positions allowed some of the metropolitan African American women in the Work Skill and Career Solver groups to obtain commercial funding relatively easily, and banks competed for their business. This high level of experience was no help, however, for a black Stanley woman opening a non-traditional manufacturing firm. Geneva faced difficulties with financing her business, despite her depth of experience, preparation, and personal funding.

Group 5: Serendipitous Owners—Work Skill Owners

Almost all of the Work Skill Owners used commercial loans to start their businesses. Because all had worked previously, several had significant savings to use in start-up. Perhaps because of the loans, few reported using cost-reduction strategies, but several of the Work Skill Owners reported that family members worked in their businesses.

Commercial Loan Experiences. All women in this group except one relied on commercial financing to start their businesses. Since Nell's business was created as a legal mechanism to separate her personal and business finances, she did not need money for start-up. Her business was also home-based, eliminating office rental costs. Camilla and Dee were the only women in this group to receive loans without co-signers or collateral. Camilla applied for a small equipment loan and received it based on her past loan history. Although her father-in-law was on the Board of Directors at the bank, she said she had always done her own banking and she did not believe this relationship affected her loan application.

Use of Human Capital in Financing. Dee did not apply for commercial funding until after start-up. With the largest business and the most need for start-up capital, Dee stood out within this group of women entrepreneurs. Not only was she the best prepared for her business with relevant skills; she was also one of the most successful in obtaining capital. After leaving an eight-and-one-half year career in a large temporary employment agency where she rose to Vice President, she used her savings to operate her own agency for the first four months. When she applied for a $250,000 line of credit, six of seven banks were interested. Dee's experience shows the importance of human capital to the business funding process. Had Dee not been as well prepared to operate her business, she would probably have had difficulty obtaining the credit she needed.

Use of Collateral. One woman encountered some difficulty in getting a loan. Irene used her house as collateral on an $8,000 loan. She reported encountering some initial discrimination based on her appearance (T-shirt and jeans) and her apparent youthful age. She took this with humor and was able to convince the banker she was serious because she already owned property.

Group 6: Serendipitous Owners—Career Problem Solvers

The financing experiences of the Career Problem Solvers provide an opportunity to examine women's strategies to mobilize financial resources in difficult situations. Because they started businesses without previous planning, these women were forced to use resources at hand on relatively short notice. Having worked in successful employed careers, however, all had ample resources from their personal and professional lives. The Career Solvers started businesses ranging in size from major manufacturing and wholesale establishments to small, home-based sole proprietorships. Thus, level of funds needed was variable. Most businesses were between these extremes, however. The mid-range businesses required sizable financing but often were founded by women who left high-paying jobs in the corporate sector. These women commanded significant savings, severance pay, or retirement funds. This was as true for the African American women as for the European American women in this category.

Commercial Funding Sources. Nine out of the 13 Career Solver women received commercial funding for their businesses. Four were African American and five were European American. Three of four African American women used these funds as their primary sources of financing. In contrast, all five white women applied for commercial funding only *after* their businesses were established, and two said they did not really need the loans to start their businesses. Gail did not take out a loan to start the business and probably would not have applied for any loans if her banker had not offered them to her. One of the loans was guaranteed with inventory, and both were co-signed by her husband, the other stockholder in the business. Judy put a second mortgage on her home at the time she re-opened her business in order to have money to pay her personal bills. Nora, the fourth African American to apply for commercial credit, did so only after her specialty advertising business was established.

Commercial Loan and Credit Experiences. The nine women in the group who received commercial financing appeared to have adequate funding to start businesses. Yet their experiences lend credibility to literature on the difficulties many women have encountered in applying for loans. Half the African American and half the European American women who applied for commercial loans or credit had difficulty getting them. Geneva and Valerie, with excellent credit and past experience but with the largest, most non-traditional companies, had trouble, but so did Nora and Sigrid, with much smaller firms. The black women who easily obtained loans were experienced either in business or in their business occupations, opened franchise operations, and used a SBA guaranteed loan or a private co-signer. Black women who had trouble getting loans had either little experience or little backing. Most of the white women who applied for loans encountered almost no difficulty when they had co-signers.

Personal Funding Sources. Ten of the Career Solvers had personal sources of financing to start their businesses. The African American women relied primarily on savings from previous jobs. Nora's specialty advertising business didn't cost much to start. She stated, "You don't need a lot of capital to *start* [this business] because you're not warehousing a lot of merchandise and inventory. And you're not buying it until it is actually sold. I had about $2,500 in savings and that's pretty much what I used." Heather used a credit card to start her business. Geneva used income from selling personal property in addition to her loan, and she lived on savings for a few months.

More of the white women relied on retirement accounts from prior jobs. Judy used teacher's retirement, Gail had money from a 401K fund, and Libby used money from an IRA account along with her last paycheck. Jill used credit cards, and Sigrid relied on savings. Julie used severance pay from her last job and money from the sale of her house.

Alternative Funding Sources. Many of the Career Solvers used alternative means to partially fund their businesses. These ranged from family loans to innovative strategies to reduce costs and the extreme income fluctuations that occur as a result of cash flow problems. One woman paid much of her business expenses with credit cards and barter, while another didn't take a salary for the first 18 months. As Chapter 9 shows, women in this group combined social and financial resources to fund their businesses.

Group 7: Serendipitous Owners—Community Service Providers

All of the women in the service provider group relied on volunteer labor to help support the business and reduce costs. This was truer of Bernice and Laura and somewhat less true of Jeannette. Bernice and Laura used commercial loans to start or expand their businesses, while Jeannette used continued employment and savings. Jeannette and Laura also received personal gifts.

Commercial Loans and Loan Experiences. Both Bernice and Laura obtained commercial loans for their businesses, but at different times for different needs. Bernice started her personal care home as an experiment while still working as Director of Head Start. When she "saw it [was] workable and it was *needed*," she got a bank loan to renovate her house to meet State regulations for live-in elderly clients. Bernice paid her cousin to renovate her house. She had no problem getting the bank loan, having good credit, a previous loan history, and her husband as co-signer. Once the renovation was complete and standards for a group home met, she began receiving a stipend from the state for each client.

Laura opened a bookstore with the financial help from a woman friend and benefactor, Annie. She did not apply for commercial financing until the bookstore had been in business 10 years and she needed to expand. To buy a new building she applied for a credit union loan, but needed Annie's co-signature to get it.

Because of her recent student loans, Jeannette did not want to incur more debt for her business. To expand, she knew she would have to seek commercial funding in the near future. Based at home, she was considering renting office space at the time of the interview.

Alternative Funding and Cost Saving Measures. All three Service Providers found alternative means to finance their businesses. All stayed employed and used earnings at first to support their businesses. Laura used income from rented office space located behind her bookstore for monthly loan payments. She also took very little salary from proceeds. Jeannette received a small technical assistance grant within the first few years of operation that allowed her to hire a woman to help her with production of the women's directory. Both Bernice's and Jeannette's businesses were home-based and rent-free. In addition to these measures, the Community Service Providers relied extensively on social contacts to reduce costs, raise money, and help operate their businesses (see Chapter 9).

SUMMARY

Women in this study used widely varied sources of financing and often combined sources to start businesses. Sources came in three broad categories: commercial, personal/alternative, and cost reduction strategies. These financing strategies reflect diversity in women's personal and career circumstances at business start-up. Dependence on commercial funding indicates an acceptance of traditional economic relationships and the necessity of pursuing profits to repay debt. This strategy is therefore consistent with conventional rational choice theories of profit motivations. The difficulties women encounter in obtaining commercial loans reflect disadvantages women face as members of gender- and race-based groups in lending environments. Discrimination and structural constraints in the lending process reflect the relevance of Folbre's (1994) and Collins' (1990) theories to women entrepreneurs' financial resource mobilization process.

Many women in the study borrowed commercially, but most of these women combined commercial debt with personal financing and cost reduction strategies. Others did not borrow commercially at all. Because of perceived and experienced "hassles" obtaining credit, these women sought private funding sources and ways to reduce costs. Those who had planned their businesses had more time to plan cost saving strategies than those who had not. Personal resources varied by group and depended largely on family wealth and prior earnings. Reliance on contin-

ued earnings by rural black Entrepreneurs indicated limited opportunities and client bases in smaller settings.

These strategies of combining sources of financing or using only
personal and cost-saving resources indicate women's abilities to mobilize resources outside of conventional economic relationships. Drawing
upon social ties for help with funding and cost savings (Chapter 9), and
on personal incomes and savings to avoid debt dependence, women dis-
played how social networks within which they were embedded provided
resources and created situational settings in which alternative financing
contingencies worked. Social capital and social embeddedness theories
are therefore important frameworks within which to begin understanding
women entrepreneurs' financing processes.

All the women in the study who sought external funding sought
commercial debt financing, primarily in the form of bank loans or lines
of credit. None used venture capital and only one received a small grant.
Many women were able to obtain loans despite obstacles in the application process. Education and prior work experience improved women's
chances of receiving commercial funding. Thus, Becker's (1964, 1975,
1993 editions) theory of human capital as investment in self hold some
relevance for understanding women business owner's commercial financing processes and supports Bates' (1993a) findings tying more education with greater access to commercial loans for African Americans.
Black women who most easily gained commercial financing were older
rural owners who had planned their businesses, trained in a trade, built
good credit records, and sought relatively small loans. Urban owners
who easily gained commercial loans had worked in large corporations,
had honed business or occupational skills in their work, and who presented professional packages (often created with franchise or advocate
help) with clear, achievable goals. White women who most easily obtained loans had credit histories, collateral, a co-signer, and/or were professionals with high earning potentials. Many women, both black and
white, applied for growth loans after starting businesses.

Some of these patterns of loan success are counter-intuitive to current assumptions about women's access to commercial loans. Older rural
black women, thought to have difficulty borrowing commercially, especially in the past, were among the most successful in obtaining loans. By
focusing on loan assurances that were within their control (personal
characteristics such as training, traditional skills, planning, and good
credit records); asking for small, do-able loans; and using them in businesses that did not compete with white-owned businesses, these women

had little trouble obtaining loans. Asking for larger loans, urban black women relied on even more assurances (including personal characteristics with organizational advocacy backing) to create public images of good character that got them loans. White women more frequently relied on relationships with white men (co-signatures) and personal wealth (collateral) to obtain loans.

Difficulties obtaining commercial financing generally increased with size of loan, size of locale, and business type. In all groups, white women were no more likely than black women to receive large loans, or to avoid difficulties in applying for and guaranteeing them. Several strategies became increasingly important to successfully obtain loans as loan size increased. These were: (1) to establish good credit; (2) to provide multiple assurances of ability to repay loans (collateral, co-signer, life insurance, etc.); (3) present a professional loan package; (4) to ask for funding within the bounds of what is possible or do-able.

An important study finding was the extent to which women innovated to fund their businesses. As one of the biggest challenges women face in starting businesses, financing is a natural focal point for innovation, especially for those with little personal funding resources and limited backing. This focus on survival is an outcome of starting businesses with disadvantages associated with race and gender (Collins 1990; Folbre 1994). Unlike those who innovate to create more value for higher profits (Schumpeter 1934, 1943), women with few assets must focus instead on ways to get started and keep businesses afloat, and it is here that their innovations are most evident. This stretches theories of entrepreneurial innovation to better reflect women's experiences in disadvantaged lending atmospheres. Innovative finance strategies may also be resources created out of women's financial need, much the way ethnic resources are created by minority groups in theories of minority response to disadvantages in labor markets (Light and Rosenstein 1995). Women as members of a disadvantaged group tap innovative energies to gain financial resources for business in response to gender bias in lending.

The literature on small business lending suggests that in order for businesses to grow significantly, owners need loans to invest in their businesses. Where does this leave women who do not want debt? Several women in this study did not borrow money, but instead built their businesses slowly, suggesting an organic model of business growth that fits Daniels' (1988) concept of the "seamless" quality of women's lives. This model emphasizes continuity across the personal and public aspects of women's lives. Others wanted to operate at a certain level immediately and sought large loans, sometimes with franchise backing, to achieve their goals. These women's goals more closely fit conventional rational choice theories of labor market decisions and activities. Clearly, women entrepreneurs do not fit one "ideal type," nor do they have the same business needs. Varying contexts in which women make business decisions (educational opportunities, available work experiences, business types, and personal funding sources) shape their needs and preferences for financing. Feminist theories of women's labor market activities are relevant in understanding contexts and contingencies surrounding women's decisions in financing businesses.

NOTES

[1] One rural white woman in the Entrepreneurial group and one urban black woman in the Retirement group obtained large loans also, though not based on educational credentials. Instead, they received loans based on their prior occupational experience (Karen) and the longevity of their business operations (Trudy). Both reasons reflected increased collateral because of potential earning power.

CHAPTER 8

Social Ties and Human Capital

One of the most important discoveries of this study was the extent to which women business owners relied on social contacts in garnering resources to start businesses. These women sought help from both "strong" ties (family, friendship, and community contacts) and "weak" business ties. They sought information, skills, and knowledge. They also sought financial resources, both in monetary funding and in help through cost reduction (see Chapter 9). From close role models or even strangers, women sought information, donations, labor, services, and financing from their social contacts.

The quality of women's experiences in formal education and training settings provides insight on the importance of social capital in the process of creating human capital. While some gain little from their experiences in formal educational processes and structures, others gain high-quality skills essential to their trades in informal, work-related apprenticeships. Work experiences do not necessarily provide better human capital than educational experiences. The opposite could be just as true. More importantly, the social relationships women establish, whether in educational or work settings, can greatly increase their knowledge and skills and provide them with greater human capital with which to start businesses.

GAINING NEEDED SKILLS AND KNOWLEDGE

In many cases, women gained aid from individuals who were friends or kin *and* business contacts. Sometimes business contacts became friends.

In other cases, friends and family were skilled in business operations or could pass on valuable occupational skills. Both black and white women drew upon kin and friendship networks as learning sources, in childhood and later as adults, when forming their businesses. Family members and strong community figures provided role models. African American women, particularly in the rural and small city areas, often based their businesses upon skills learned as children within their families. Whether focused on a trade, such as cooking, sewing, or embroidery, or on the multiple business pursuits of the general entrepreneur, these women practiced skills built over a lifetime from a base of family tradition.

Women derived multiple forms of business aid from different social contexts. Regulatory structures provided contact with those imparting information about mandatory business compliance. Continuing education provided not only required professional training for licensing, but also seminars in business operations. Industry-sponsored shows and conferences provided opportunities for business owners to update skills, discover new products, and network with others in their industries. Other firms provided business services for hire. Some women who hired outsiders to perform accounting and other tasks also used service providers as a personalized learning source to increase their knowledge. In some cases, women substituted family knowledge for hired expertise.

In Grafton and Stanley, minority advocacy organizations were an important resource for African American owners. These women received aid in preparing loan packages and presenting business proposals. Minority advocacy organizations provided opportunities to network and learn informally. One woman said she "learned her business" by selling to members of one minority development organization.

Social contacts were important as sources of informal learning and in self-teaching. For some African American women contact with whites provided opportunities to learn occupational skills and practice dealing with whites that would become important in customer/client relationships. For several women, contacts made within formal educational or employment settings made the difference between receiving high quality training or training that was virtually useless. Below, I examine how women in each group used social capital to build human capital resources.

INTERNALLY MOTIVATED BUSINESS OWNERS

The internally motivated owners used both family/friendship "strong" ties and weaker business contacts to gain skill and knowledge for their businesses. Each group used different relationships for different information. Race influenced use of social networks. Black women in all internally motivated groups learned occupational skills from family members, often as children learning a family tradition such as cooking or sewing. Some learned occupational skills for their businesses from relatives later on. White women, particularly the Professionals, more often used kin relationships to network for business advice and business-related skills, however, one white woman (the child taxi owner) used her experience as a mother to help her with the occupational side of her business.

The Trade and Professional women, who had trained in their occupations, used persons encountered through regulatory, sales, and continuing education contacts to learn business skills. They also hired outsiders on contract (mostly Trades women), as full time employees (most Professionals), and as service providers, (Professionals) to manage taxes or other business-related matters. In some cases, Professionals' employees were responsible for occupational aspects of the business. In some cases, Trades women's family members provided knowledge. One rural black woman used business contacts to learn about white culture, information she used to build a predominantly white client base.

In contrast, the Entrepreneurial women and the African American Retirement Planners used business contacts to learn occupational skills. Having more training and/or experience in business, they sought skills they lacked in business occupations. The European American Retirement Planners, having followed a training process similar to the Professionals, used business contacts to learn business-related skills.

Group 1: Business Planners—Trades Women

The Trades women found many informal ways to gain skills. Families and communities became sources of information and skills development. Women received guidance from those in the business networks around them. When necessary, they called on outsiders for help with specific tasks such as accounting.

Kin Networks as Learning Sources. Kin networks provided a rich source of family tradition as well as numerous role models to follow.

Family Tradition. Learning from others sometimes took the form of following a family tradition. Corinne learned to cook at an early age from her grandfather and her mother. She said,

My grandfather taught me how to cook. I was *very* young. And I just
like cookin.' I *love* it. We had a big family, and we ate good. And most
people think with a big family you don't, but we didn't go hungry. My
mother *cooked*. And we had all kind of fruit trees, and we had every pie
in the book. And that's where I guess I learned how to cook a lot, it's
because I was always at home with her.

Role Models. Several of the women learned from others, either in
prior jobs or while operating their businesses. Linda's uncle owned a
meat business while she was growing up. Although she didn't work for
him, she said, "He was a big role model for me. I respect a lot of things
he said to me. And then when I turned 16, I had a good friend that was in
the construction business, and he let me help him in that business. Then I
realized that the only way you make money is to work for yourself."

Linda worked for seven years in a hair salon/barber shop before finally buying it. Though she had little formal training in business, Mr. B.,
the previous owner, taught Linda about operating the shop, acting as her
mentor in the business. He had stayed on to work in the shop after selling
it to her. She reported, "We worked side-by-side for twenty years. I could
walk back here and say, 'Mr. B., I've got a problem.' He says, 'Sit down.'
We talk about it. He sometimes would give me advice. He'd just listen.
And then he'd tell me his opinions. So he was a father role." The things
Linda learned from kin, friends, and her business mentor (also a member
of her church) illustrate how women apply privately learned skills and
experiences to their public lives as business owners.

"Weak" Business Ties as Knowledge Sources. The Trades Women
drew upon a variety of "weak" business ties to gain information for their
businesses. One woman found contacts within the structures regulating
business practices and learned from service providers. Others hired outsiders to perform specific tasks, thereby importing knowledge into the
business. Two women received help from minority advocacy organizations. One woman drew upon information learned in the context of employment to overcome limiting concepts.

Regulatory Structures as Conduits for Business Information. Sometimes a lack of formal training proved advantageous in opening a business. Corinne credited her ignorance with helping her to open a business.
She explained,

I don't think I woulda got the support that I got from the community—
like [from] the building inspector—if I had known all this. If I had

known the things that I had to go through and the things that I had to pay, there's no way I would have been in business. *Not* knowin'—and a lot of things I had gone ahead and had done that I didn't know you had to get a permit for. I never paid so many permits in my life! I didn't know you had to have a permit to cut a do' [door]! If you take one sign down and put another one in the same [place], I didn't know you had to have a permit.

She voiced what many in this study had experienced. Knowing little about business, they started without full knowledge of what it took to set up and operate a business.

Service Providers as Sources of Training. After opening her restaurant, Corinne learned from sales people and suppliers about wholesale pricing and delivery options that allowed her to reduce time spent buying and transporting groceries. She explained,

Since I opened it up, talkin' to different sales people [about] stuff that I bought, I have been able to pick up a lot of insight, training, suggestions. You find out a lot of things that you actually have to have that you didn't know you have to have. So talkin' to them, they have really trained me.

Hiring Outsider Knowledge. Several Trades women relied on the knowledge of outsiders hired for specific tasks, most commonly, accounting, bookkeeping, and tax preparation. However, in place of hiring an established accountant, some women relied on kin. Corinne noted,

The things I don't know which I need help with, I have a sister that has a degree in accounting. I have two sisters [that help out], one that works at the Courthouse as a clerk. Then I have another one who [does] information accounts, and then I have a niece that works at [a nearby university]. So they know it. All I [have to do is] reach [for the] phone.

Minority Advocacy Organizations. Two women received help from a minority loan organization operated by an African American-owned law firm in Grafton. Its aim was to help disadvantaged people, particularly women and minorities, in applying for loans. Both Cynthia and Hazel received help from this organization.

Overcoming Race-Based Limits. Overcoming limits based on race was not always a straightforward fight against discrimination for some black owners. Carol was another owner who started her business without full knowledge of what it took to make it on her own. She explained the process of overcoming race-based limits this way:

> I just wanted to be independent and secure. [If] somebody told me, "Would you ever thought you would have a business on Main Street? A black woman?" I really didn't give it much thought. And if I had considered that, I probably would have been scared and not done it. But having worked around white people in the office, and getting to know them, I found out that I relate with those types people more than I could with my own people, simply because their thoughts wasn't as high as mine. I would put myself on this level, thinking, "Well, you can't do this," and you draw yourself limits. But once I got into that (white) world and I learned how things worked, it was like [I had] imagined it being more complicated. "Oh, this is simple. This is so *simple*, I can do this." So I said, "We might as well try."

Carol's opportunity to work with whites, and the freedom she acquired via her business ownership, became a source of social capital not available to many blacks in her community. A white male reporter from the town's weekly newspaper interviewed her, and the resulting story helped her gain customers.

Group 2: Business Planners—Professionals

The Professional women found many informal ways to gain skills and information they lacked, particularly in business management and finance. They networked with family, friends, and acquaintances in their fields. They hired service providers not only to perform services, but also to teach them business skills. More often than the Trades women, they hired full time employees to handle office functions and specialized aspects of their businesses.

Kin Networks as Learning Sources. Friends and family members provided information and teaching. Barbara, the black psychologist, first learned about helping people from her grandmother, who aided many people with their problems. Meg had "good advisors," including her father, who helped her when she first started her business. Frances, a lawyer, learned about time management from a friend who owned a dental practice. She also learned from her husband. She explained,

> My ex-husband was a *fanatical* person about budgets. We had a budget and we balanced our checkbooks, and we did the little things that you

have to do in a business. It was just the two of us, but he majored in accounting when he was in undergraduate school, so he was into that type of mentality. Law school did *not* prepare me for running a business at all.

"Weak" Business Ties as Knowledge Sources. The Professional women learned both business and occupational skills from service providers. They also learned some very specific skill sets from those they hired.

Service Providers as Sources of Training. Gina learned a great deal from her service providers. She said,

> I have an accountant, a lawyer, a systems programmer. I use a number of different consultants and they're *all* teaching me more and more about my own business. So it's an *enormous* learning curve, and it never stops. Every time you learn one thing, you elevate yourself to another level of learning and another level of interest, and you try and manage your business on a level that's more sophisticated than you did the year before.

Not wishing to simply hire individuals on contract to perform services, Gina took a more interactive approach. In her words,

> They're training you, based on some very specific needs that *you* have as opposed to a lot of general things as though you were in a classroom. And you're paying for it one way or the other. You pay to go to school or you pay your service provider. But this way you can have some very private and some very direct attention.

A central theme in Gina's account is an absence of hierarchy in learning. Women learn from anyone who has the skills they need without regard to formal rank within an organization.

Hiring Outsider Knowledge: Business Skills. The Professional women had the means to hire specialists on a contract basis. They also frequently brought specialized knowledge into their businesses by hiring employees, from secretarial to full time professional staff. This strategy distinguished them from the other women in the study, who less consistently hired permanent employees.

Frances gained a great deal of knowledge from her secretaries. In searching for information on business operations, Frances discovered a program for legal secretaries at a nearby technical institute that included extensive training in computer packages and operations. Her previous secretary came out of this program and was able to help her organize her office and books. Her current secretary had worked for another law firm and contributed useful ideas for office management.

Hiring Outsider Knowledge: Occupational Skills. In contrast, Fern reported hiring a range of personnel to complete her corporate law firm. She hired not only an accountant on contract and a secretary/office manager in-house, but also brought seven highly skilled corporate lawyers onto her staff. These were contract attorneys, not partners in the firm. Besides handling a caseload, each contract attorney was a specialist. At the time of her interview, Fern was moving into a new service line and had sent two newly hired staff attorneys out for training. She explained,

> We are getting ready to start doing immigration law, and the Hispanic women in the office are really interested in doing that. So I sent them to a seminar to get them some education and some materials to read, and they're in a self-taught mode right now of being sure that they're familiar with [immigration law and] knowing how to talk the language.

Not only did Fern hire outsiders to cover an area she was not familiar with herself, but she also required *them* to take additional training. She thereby moved further into business management, hiring out the occupational side of the business.

Group 3: Business Planners—Natural Entrepreneurs

The Entrepreneurial women used informal social contacts to gain information and skills for their businesses. Family members provided occupational training for the black women, while informal business contacts provided information and apprenticeships for the white women. Some women taught themselves much of what they needed to know to operate their businesses.

Kin Networks and Experiential Knowledge as Learning Sources. Three of the women in the Entrepreneurial group, Rachel, Trish, and Melissa, did not have prior work experience in some aspects of their businesses. As noted previously, Rachel sought formal training in T-shirt design and silk screening. She and her husband learned real estate ownership and sales from Rachel's brother. They learned building renovation skills from her uncle and used them to renovate a commercial building to house her T-shirt business and provide rental income.

Trish and Melissa started businesses with very little formal training in either their occupations or in business. Both women gained the bulk of their knowledge through informal means: Trish from her sales positions, entrepreneurial pursuits, and contacts with others in her industry; and Melissa from her dance contacts with daycare centers and her contact with the children's taxi owner in another city. In both cases, family members played key roles in the transfer of vital information. Trish learned her original occupational skill, embroidery, from her mother. Melissa learned what it means to be a mother from having her own children. She spoke of her experience as a mother and her ability to relate to other mothers' fears and concerns while transporting their children in her taxi service.

"Weak" Business Ties as Knowledge Sources. Over half the woman in the group relied on knowledge gained outside of any formal educational or work setting for both business and occupational skills. Pam and Donna worked for a few weeks in an espresso shop owned by a woman who had advertised a cart for sale. This experience gave them expertise in operating the machinery and making espresso. Melissa's main source of information for her children's taxi business came from a few telephone conversations with a woman who operated the same kind of business in another city. She also relied on her knowledge of area daycare centers and their practices, information she gained while operating a dance school with her mother. According to Melissa, "We would go and pick the kids up from the daycares and take 'em [to our studio for dance lessons.] None of the studios offer that anymore. So I knew a lot of the directors of a lot of the daycares through that." Daycare centers were the base through which Melissa advertised her business.

Group 4: Business Planners—Retirement Planners

The Retirement Planners had gained much of their knowledge from prior work experiences and recent educational programs. However, the skills and information they needed varied by race. Two African American women reported learning occupational skills from family members. Both black and white women learned from business contacts, but black women learned occupational skills, while white women learned mostly business skills. Frequently, they found what they needed in the relationships that naturally occurred around them.

Kin Networks as Learning Sources. One of the primary methods used by the Retirement Planners to gain knowledge for their businesses was to tap kin networks. Lenore learned how to "do hair" from her sister, Elly, with whom she started a business. Trudy's husband worked for the U.S. Postal Service and provided information for her bulk mailing business. Thus, kin networks provided both direct training of a skill, and less direct information transfer.

"Weak" Business Ties as Knowledge Sources. Business networks also proved valuable. Betty reported learning about hair products from her suppliers. Helen learned the occupational side of her laser recycling business from technicians she hired to do the work.[1] Deborah had to "catch up" on business skills, learning much from her partner. Amanda was inspired to enter business by the contractor who built her house. He initially encouraged her to start the business and was her mentor, helping her with technical problems. Her husband also helped with the business.

EXTERNALLY MOTIVATED BUSINESS OWNERS

The externally motivated owners used few family ties, relying instead on friendship and business contacts to gain skill and knowledge. Only two women, one Work Skill Owner and one Career Problem Solver, learned skills primarily from family members. Most of the Work Skill Owners, who owned businesses that evolved naturally from their prior employment, learned business-related skills and information primarily from friends in similar businesses.

Both the Career Problem Solvers and the Service Providers relied heavily on business contacts within industry and business organizational structures to gain skills and information for their businesses. Membership in a minority business advocacy organization provided occupational training for one Career Solver. Another learned almost all of her skills from informal business contacts in prior job settings and while operating her business. Many Career Solvers hired outsider knowledge for both business-related and occupational tasks. Some hired family members. The Service Providers learned business and occupational skills from business organizations, through networking at trade association meetings, and from informal business contacts, including employees.

Group 5: Serendipitous Owners—Work Skill Owners

Having worked in their occupations prior to business ownership, Work Skill Owners frequently had friends in similar businesses who helped with start-up and early operations. The natural progression of their work from employment to business ownership created ongoing networks of contacts in the same industries, so finding sources of information was easy. Most white women in the group were from Grafton where business networks were small, individualized, and intimate. The single black woman owned a larger business in Stanley. Rather than hire individuals, her contracts were with entire firms.

Kin and Friendship Networks as Learning Sources. Three Work Skill Owners received help from family and friends. Irene and her partner copied prices, borrowed supplies, and received advice from a friend who owned a similar restaurant. Sally received help from friends who owned similar businesses. Becky's brother, a millionaire now retired from his business, pushed her towards business ownership and served as her mentor.

"Weak" Business Ties as Knowledge Sources: Hiring Outsider Knowledge. Four of six Work Skill Owners sought alternative means to gain skills and information. Several hired outsiders to handle accounting, bookkeeping, and tax preparation tasks. Sally hired bar tenders, leaving most of the occupational work to them. Dee hired an accounting firm to help format her business plan and advise her on multi-state tax preparation and a corporate law firm to help with legal issues. She also depended on a small board of directors to help with business strategies.

Group 6: Serendipitous Owners—Career Problem Solvers

Starting businesses after sudden career changes, the Career Problem Solvers provide examples of how women gain skills and knowledge when situations arise unexpectedly. Their career goals and visions changed suddenly. Some women found learning opportunities in the situations around them. Others left positions that had prepared them with business-related skills. They sought occupational training through industry trade shows and membership in business advocacy organizations. One Career Solver in a non-traditional business learned almost all her skills, both occupational and business-related, from informal business contacts in prior jobs or while operating her business.

Human Capital: Quality of Training. Two of the Career Problem Solvers commented that their training experiences provided different skill levels than might be expected from their educational credentials. This is an example of how illusory social capital can be. Gail held a degree in business administration and had taken general accounting classes, which should have prepared her to operate a business, but they did not. She said she took the classes "a long time ago" and never understood their content. She had worked in sales positions and insisted that these jobs were her only experiences relevant to her business.

In contrast, Jill reported learning a level of skill not found in many hair salons. According to her,

> You've got two choices when you get out of cosmetology school. You can either go to work at a chop shop and get frustrated with your trade, go to their silly little seminars, get paid by the hour, never get the same clients back twice because they don't really want you to build a clientele for fear you might move it somewhere else. Or you can go humble yourself to be a shampoo assistant or a chemical assistant and work onto the floor at a really nice salon. And that's what I chose to do.

Though working for a highly skilled beautician was frustrating, the experience she gained was invaluable. It secured for her positions in several of the finer shops in Stanley and earned her a clientele. She explained her apprenticeship this way:

> My mentor was absolutely brilliant. I graduated top of my class in cosmetology school, and I was young, and I was very confident, and I thought I knew it, and she had me broke down to tears underneath the table. I swept floors and I shampooed, and I stood at attention and I watched her cut, because that's what she told me to do. And after I stood and watched and watched and watched and realized what she did was different than what I did, then she started allowing me to ask questions.
>
> So she was pretty strict, but it was what I needed, and I really believe it put me in the position I am now. Because I remember going into the bathroom *cussing* every hair on her head, swearing that if I got the chance I would flatten her tires. Because she had totally humiliated me in front of clients by making me take down half a head of rolls that I had already rolled and re-roll them because I had not sectioned them close enough, straight enough, angled enough. But she was very adamant in the way she wanted it done and there was only one way to do it and that was the right way. So we came to several head buttings. But I loved her dearly for every one of 'em because it made me grow and it made me a whole lot better than I was when I walked in thinking I was OK.

Experiences such as these provide insight into women's lives and the quality of their experiences in formal education and training settings.

Kin Networks as Learning Sources. One of the Career Problem Solvers had a source of business information in her family. Gail's husband, a business executive, commuted to work in New York City every week from their rural Southern hometown. Although frequently absent from the household, he was quite involved in purchasing and transporting antiques for the business and a personal collection. She said of him,

> He's my financial investor, [and he's] the other stockholder. He has been associated with a large [retail] corporation, and he does all the manufacturing and distribution for them, which is different from the marketing side, but he's in all the executive meetings and they *talk* marketing strategy. So he's my sole source for business advice. He's very creative so he helps me with ideas. We spend our weekends talking about this business.

"Weak" Business Ties as Knowledge Sources. Networking was a common method of skill building for the women in this study, especially for those in sales. Nora's case is particularly instructive because she learned both business skills and her business occupation outside of any formal education or job setting.

Industry-Structured Networks. When Nora started her business in 1979, white males dominated the specialty advertising industry so Nora turned to them to learn her trade. She made contacts primarily through trade organizations specific to the industry. One man, whom she met at her first industry seminar, was especially helpful. She described the meeting this way:

> I walked into this room, and there was only one seat, and it was next to [this older gentleman]. And there were just all these white people in there. And they were mostly men. And most of the women who were there were secretaries. The industry has changed considerably since then. And I was really very scared and intimidated. But this gentleman, I think he'd been in business then 20-something years. He really became a mentor to me, because this is someone that knew the inner and outer workings of the industry. And I would call this man five and six times a day, asking him some of the dumbest questions. But he was just always really excited to help me.

Another industry contact helped her with business ideas and encouraged her when things went wrong. Nora considered these two men, both white, to be mentors and felt lucky to have their help.

Minority Organizations as Social Capital. Another source of help for Nora came from two minority business advocacy organizations. One, consisting of minority business owners and corporate buyers, served as "a liaison between the two, to give minorities access to corporate business." The second group was an advocacy group made up of minority and corporate owners that worked for legislation to insure equal opportunity for minority businesses.

Although she was a member of both groups, Nora received more support from members of the second group. She explained,

> I really *learned* how to sell specialty advertising by practicing on the
> [second group's] members. And they were very, very supportive. Some
> of them were established businessmen and -women, and they gave me
> my first orders, and didn't scream and yell at me when I made a mis-
> take. They really worked with me. So I owe a *lot* to that organization.

Most of the members at the time were African American men. "Naturally," said Nora, "because at the time [1979], that's basically who owned businesses for the most part. But there were a few women also."

Hiring Outsider Knowledge. One strategy used by several women to gain skills personally and to "get the job done" was to hire outsiders with knowledge or skills they lacked. Julie, Valerie, and Nora hired employees with expertise that they lacked. Julie was required to have two years ticketing experience to open a travel agency. With only a few months' experience herself, Julie hired a couple through a newspaper ad who had the required experience and "knew exactly what they were doing," so that Julie fulfilled the licensing requirement until she could build the necessary skills.

Like Gina in the Professional group, Nora and Valerie learned from service providers and consultants. In addition to a full time secretary, Nora contracted with an accountant to keep her books and do taxes. In the process, she taught herself bookkeeping ("I read books on how to keep books") and learned from her accountant. She nevertheless described the process of learning the business as "a baptism by fire" and recommended to others that they learn by working for a company like the one they want to own.

Valerie hired full time employees with computer programming and marketing skills and consultants for specialized needs. She explained,

> Where I used to take no advice, it's amazing how dumb I've gotten through the years. [Now] I like being surrounded by experts. By people that can protect my interests and advise me on things I didn't know; people that I can learn from. I used to think consultants were such a rip-off, but I've got one consultant that went to work as CEO for another company, but it was just wonderful working with him. I *learned* so much, as far as borrowing money and things like that go. I value other peoples' advice [now], so I do seek it when I feel that it's necessary.

Social Contacts as Outsider Knowledge. When a business is small enough that the owner cannot afford to hire outside consultants, a relative or family member may supply needed advice or knowledge. This was the case for Heather in her video production business. Her husband, who owned a construction business, helped her with the "business side" of her enterprise. Valerie also hired paid family members: "My dad works for me, and my brother is doing my [computer] programming right now."

Situational Learning and Social Ties: Informal Learning and Self-Taught Skills. Several Career Problem Solvers were self-taught, learning aspects of their businesses informally. In all cases, social contacts played key roles in providing environments in which to learn. Heather used technical and sales skills in her business that she had learned in her prior job, but her video production skills were largely self-taught. She and her husband bought a video camera to record the birth and first years of their baby's life. Later, she wanted to give her husband a video for Father's Day. On discovering that a professional tape would cost $250, she decided to make one herself. The results were so good that a girlfriend encouraged her to start producing birthday and wedding videos, and she soon realized she could make money doing something she enjoyed.

Although Jill had trained to "do hair" in cosmetology school, her formal training taught her to depend heavily on chemicals. After 10 years of exposure to them on a daily basis, she became overly sensitive. When she left her salon job on maternity leave, she spent three years learning natural hair treatment methods. She explained,

> The whole time during my pregnancy, her father was starting a company importing natural body and hair care products from Germany.

They were very interested because he knew business. And he knew computers and he's fluent reading and writing German, but he didn't have a clue about make-up, about facial care, about hair—anything. So I was the product knowledge behind the business on the US market. . . . I started working, trying to earn my keep with her father. I built warehouse shelves, I did product knowledge stuff, I answered the 800 line on the hair color. While we were in Mintzdorff, I helped formulate and start revising the colors for the U.S. market, to tone them down a little so they weren't so vibrant.

Jill had never taken business classes. Upon starting her business, she sought help from the wife of a man who helped her renovate her storefront. She said, "She put together this spread sheet complete with projections with two months in business. And this projection of what the earnings would be. I learned a whole lot about books."

Creative Observation, Financial Innovation, and Product Flexibility: A Non-Traditional Case. The most non-traditional businesses in the study provide examples of how women learn things they aren't usually taught growing up. While boys often learn about cars and carpentry at an early age from older men, young girls rarely break into the male world of physical prowess and technical skill. If they want to learn how to do "male" things, they must pick them up as young women wherever they can. Valerie's experiences in learning to sell wholesale petroleum products are an excellent example of this. She learned all of her skills, both occupational and business-related, informally, in prior job settings, or while operating her business. Her story provides numerous examples of how casual and business contacts provide small yet critical pieces of information for operating a successful, high-powered business.

Learning From Casual Business Contacts. Some of Valerie's earliest lessons came in her early 20s, when she owned a small convenience store. She explained how she learned strategies important for her business:

I used to like to shoot skeet, and there was a gun store that I used to go to. And I remember the owner, he had mentioned something about always being overdrawn. And I was like, "Well, how can you do that?" And he says, "Well, it takes a couple of days for the check to clear." So when I first started my business, the little convenience store, I figured out very quickly that I could write a check for beer on Thursday, and

with the weekend and Friday sales, cover it by Monday. So just little
things like how to float money.

When asked if she had any experience or training that prepared her
for owning a business, Valerie responded,

> I may have observed other people, but I had no real experience or train-
> ing. It depends what you call training. You can sit on the bus next to
> somebody every single day, and they're going to work, and it's their
> own business, and you talk to 'em about what's happening. And if you
> observe them, that's training, so to speak. So nothing *formal.*

When she started her petroleum business, Valerie did her own taxes
and bookkeeping. She learned how to work on spreadsheets by observing others at a prior job.

Learning From Clients. After starting the business, Valerie learned
from her customers. She said,

> In '87 or '88, [a] customer didn't order fuel for heating. They'd filled
> up their tanks every winter. And when I inquired, they said, "Cause
> natural gas is cheaper." And I said, "Huh?" And they said, "We buy it
> from the well now." And I said, "Really?" And I said, "How does that
> [work]?" So I just started [questioning them] 'cause I didn't under-
> stand it. So then I said, "Well, I can do that." And that's how we
> branched into the natural gas. So it was a real natural growth, natural
> diversification. One thing just led to the other.

Valerie's experiences provide another example of non-hierarchical
learning from social contacts surrounding the business owners.

"Be Nice": Learning a Philosophy of Business. Valerie's business
philosophy became clear in her description of how she taught herself to
operate. Not only did she place emphasis on technical skills but she described the art of sales and management as a function of behavior
towards others. According to Valerie,

> There's a lot of things in business that you learn that have nothing to do
> with business. I mean, just how to treat *people* in general. There was a
> time when, if a load of gasoline was late, when I think about how *abu-
> sive* I may have been, emulating what I did know when I worked for a
> company, because that was the way people operated. "What do you

mean . . . !#@*?" It was cool to be rude and demanding, especially if you were female. . . . So as I matured in business, I think that it's much cooler to be very sweet, and for people to know you that way, and to be always understanding if there's a problem. I very seldom get upset. I just tend to be nice to the people I work with. I can be very demanding, but I can always be very nice. So I think training and skills is one thing, but training and behavior, as far as how to conduct business, is equally important.

Group 7: Serendipitous Owners—Community Service Providers

Of all the women in the study, the Community Service Providers were the least prepared to own businesses. The African American woman in this group had the most relevant training and experience. Yet, all of the women in the group had to do significant learning to open their businesses. Jeannette, the directory publisher, was prepared with writing skills and some business operations but was starting a unique business and had to invent much of it as she went along.

"Weak" Business Ties as Knowledge Sources. The Community Service Providers did not use family contacts for skills or to gain information. Instead, they relied on industry trade organizations and informal apprenticeships.

Trade Networks. The Service Providers learned both occupational and business-related skills from trade or business service organizations. Bernice learned her occupation, family model personal care homes, from a personal care organization in a nearby city. Jeannette learned business management skills through a Small Business Development Center. Laura learned bookstore management, both occupational and business skills, at yearly trade shows. Industry trade shows also provided settings in which to network. Even after 21 years of operation, Laura regularly attended yearly meetings of the American Booksellers Association (ABA) and met like-minded bookstore owners. She explained,

> We always do some kind of training during that time, whether it's about customer service or about going on the computer or whatever. We spend a day a year, probably, in some *really intense* training with each other, helping each other out. And sometimes we bring in somebody who knows something about that [subject] who really does talk to us about it. But I never took any of the ABA schools that they do for new booksellers or any of those kinds of things.

Again, here is an example of non-hierarchical, collective learning strategies in which bookstore owners taught and learned from each other. *Informal Learning.* Laura also learned management skills through an informal apprenticeship. She volunteered in a bookstore for a few weeks so she could "see how they did it." Books had always been an important part of Laura's upbringing, something her parents encouraged, yet she gained most of her bookstore knowledge after opening the business. Knowing little about business management and computers, she learned most of these skills from employees while operating her business.

SUMMARY

Women in this study used both "weak" and "strong" social ties to gain skills and information for business ownership. They frequently used multiple forms of social contacts, including family ties, contacts made in organizations and other structured settings, job contacts, apprenticeships, employee relationships, and business partnerships. They used contacts to learn specific skills and to hire skills done, both on contract and internally with employees.

Owners of small-scale businesses relied on kin and friendship ties to help with business tasks such as accounting and taxes. Some of these also hired professional business services on contract. Larger and more professional owners hired full time employees and larger service providers. Structured learning sites included technical schools, trade shows, Small Business Development Centers, continuing education facilities, and minority advocacy organizations. In addition, prior jobs sometimes provided formalized training. Many women also learned on their own.

Types of contacts and types of information gained also differed by group and partially by race. Internally motivated owners used both strong family ties and weaker business contacts to gain skills. African American women learned occupational skills, while European American women learned business skills from kin. Externally motivated owners relied primarily on friends and business acquaintances to gain needed skills.

Structured settings provided significant social capital and network opportunities, not only for the purpose they were intended, but also for different purposes unique to individual women. Continuing education settings provided formal learning opportunities to comply with occupational licensing, but also for business management training. Contacts made in regulatory structures provided information on steps to comply with licensing laws. Service providers offered business services, but also provided information on types and sources of supplies, and they taught owners business skills. Industry trade shows provided settings in which women learned about new products and techniques, but also became networking sites where women met and learned from others in similar businesses. Minority advocacy organizations provided a cultural resource by aiding African American women in learning to package loan applications. They also became a source of social capital when an African American woman learned her business by selling to organization members.

All these forms of social capital aided women in learning skills, performing business operations, and informing them about opportunities and requirements for their businesses. What is not so obvious is the overlap in women's strong and weak ties. Women who relied on family and friendship ties as well as business contacts frequently reported that the two were one and the same. Family members who were business executives offered business advice, while business contacts became friends in the course of helping new business owners. Sometimes women hired kin and friends to perform tasks for which the owner was unskilled. As many women in the study demonstrated, social resources provided avenues through which skills were gained that were unavailable in educational or job settings.

Traditional rational choice theories of economic activity contribute little to an understanding of women's accumulation of human capital through social ties. Becker's (1964, 1975, 1993 editions) theory of human capital as investment in self applies somewhat to professionals who take continuing education classes to comply with licensing, but these women are required by law to do so. A more accurate theory of investment would be society's investment in professionals' training as a means to continue to profit from their public services. Focusing more on choice and economic actors' decision-making processes, rational choice adds little to explanations of women entrepreneurs' human resource mobilization. Feminist theories contribute little more, focused as they are on environments in which actors make decisions.

Social capital and social embeddedness theories contribute much more to an understanding of how women gain additional human resources for business operations. Coleman's (1988, 1990) notion of organizations providing social capital beyond services they were intended to provide is directly relevant to women's experiences in this study. Granovetter's (1973, 1982, 1992) theories of social embeddedness provide a starting point for understanding entrepreneurs' human resource mobilization, but need to be redefined to fit *women* business owner's experiences. While Granovetter's job seekers found weak business ties to be most helpful, women in this study used both weak and strong ties. Often, strong ties were to business leaders who could provide needed information and skills assumed by social embeddedness theorists to come only from weak business ties. Thus, women in personal relationships to men gained weak tie information from strong tie relationships.

Women's use of strong ties to provide weak tie information, and their patterns of non-hierarchical learning imply an organic, "seamless" model in which women exist in webs of complex relationships and circumstances, responding to and using resources in the webs around them. Conventional rational choice theory presents an atomized model of action based on personal profit motives unconnected to circumstances and relationships surrounding the actor. In contrast, social embeddedness theory provides a more organic model of social relationships in which the actor initiates and responds to opportunities and constraints that exist as a natural outcome of the web of relationships in which the actor is embedded. This generally fits the experiences of women in this study.

NOTES

[1] By hiring technicians, she also, in effect, hired outsider knowledge to perform the entire occupational side of her business. She and her husband were left to do the administrative and marketing ends of the business.

CHAPTER 9

Social Ties and Financial Capital

Social contacts played important roles in financing women's businesses in this study. Whether co-signing loans or offering gifts and loans, women's families, friends, and business contacts provided help with funding businesses. Social contacts provided three main types of help. First, they facilitated the commercial loan process. Second, they provided private sources of funding. And third, they helped reduce costs, minimizing the need for funding.

Most commonly, husbands, companions, or friends would co-sign loans, provide steady incomes, or pay the bills at home. Small Business Development Centers, minority business organizations, and other businesses provided backing, financial assurances, or advocacy in the loan application process. Sometimes social contacts led to options for innovative financing. Sometimes social contacts encouraged women to build cash flow slowly and without debt. Social capital was an especially important asset for African American women and women in rural areas. In Grafton and Stanley, minority advocacy organizations were an important social resource. When women met obstacles applying for loans, these organizations helped write business plans, complete paperwork on loan applications, and served as advocates.

Black women and those in rural areas used social networks to reduce the amount of funding needed for start-up and drew upon social relationships as substitutes for financial resources in business operations. For example, owners recruited friends and family members to work for the business, mostly without pay. This support took several forms. African American women used help in renovation and preparation of the business space; family members worked in the business to keep labor costs down; and family and other employees worked for reduced pay at the start of the business.

European American women had help from friends and kin with building renovation and maintenance, but they also received direct financial help from relatives more often than African American women. Male involvement in financial matters was more likely to occur in European American women's businesses. A male benefactor, such as a father or husband, might donate a rent-free building, pay for needed equipment, or negotiate favorable loan or rental agreements.

INTERNALLY MOTIVATED BUSINESS OWNERS

The internally motivated owners used both family/friendship "strong" ties and weaker business contacts to finance their businesses, the latter providing personal loans and gifts. Family members helped reduce costs by paying bills and donating labor, but the Professional women also found ways to reduce costs through business relationships.

Women from different groups used different strategies to provide assurance of reliability in obtaining commercial loans. Across all groups, most women receiving loans had co-signers, usually family members. Two black women, a Professional and an Entrepreneur, had social ties to bankers, in one case a bank president. Two African American Trades women and two black Retirement Planners sought help from minority advocacy organizations. One European American Entrepreneur sought advocate help from the SBA, while one of the white Professionals received extensive help from male family members in negotiating loans.

Two women in Bingham, one black Entrepreneur and one white Professional, had difficulty obtaining loans because they competed with white male owners in the community. One was a black female establishing a business on the main street in town. The other was a white female establishing a dental office in competition with a white male dentist's practice. Social capital in this small, rural town ran against both women.

Some of the Trades women and the Entrepreneurs received monetary aid from family members. Two black Trades women had partners who invested money. The father of one of the white Trades women invested in building renovation and equipment for her business. White women in all groups received loans and gifts from family members, and another received a small loan from a friend.

The most common forms of kin support and cost reduction in which social contacts made significant contributions were 1) husbands or companions who provided more or all financial support at home; and 2) donated labor from kin and friends. Among the internally motivated entrepreneurs, women who were married had husbands who paid home bills. A few were covered by husbands' insurance policies. Two rural women, a black Retirement Planner and a white Trades woman, received donations of supplies and equipment, the first from her community and the second from family.

The Professional women used the most extensive support and cost reduction strategies. These included not only the more common donation of labor and spouse bill payment, but also reduced salaries for employees early in the business and bartering services for rent. Human capital resources were, of course, an important factor in what women were able to barter.

Group 1: Business Planners—Trades Women

The Trades women received help from family and friends both with commercial and personal loans and gifts, and as cost reduction measures. Family co-signed loans, donated buildings, equipment, and physical labor, and provided gifts or loans. Additional help came from partners, community members, and minority advocacy organizations.

Social Capital and Commercial Loans. The Trades women received help with their loans from private and public sources. Four of six women applying for commercial loans had husbands as co-signers. This type of support was the most common private source of aid across all groups. Partnerships also provided extra resources for starting businesses. Ivy's partner, Diane, obtained a personal loan similar to Ivy's.

Two Grafton women, Cynthia and Hazel, received help from a public source of financial aid, the minority loan organization mentioned above.[1] This resource was unique to Grafton and did not help those in rural areas. Thus, none of the Trades women received loans wholly on their own.

Kin and Community as Sources of Financing. The Trades women used family capital and other sources of funding to support and fund their businesses. Carol received a $50 gift from her mother for a countertop. Two white women in the group started their businesses with help from parents or friends. Kathy received financial and labor assistance from her father, who owned and renovated the building that housed her salon. She paid him no rent, and he helped her by purchasing used salon equipment. Linda purchased her business from a man she had known all her life through her church. In addition to a commercial loan, her parents provided a small loan for the down payment. Her benefactor (the previous owner) financed the business through a mortgage. At least half reported that their husbands paid the bills at home. In most cases, this meant women were free to bring home smaller salaries than if they depended solely on their own incomes. Again, this was the most common form of kin support reported in the study.

Cost Reduction Strategies. The Trades women drew upon available social capital to reduce the amount of funding they needed for their businesses. Family and friends of six women helped with renovation and other labor needed to start their businesses. This reliance on family and community labor was a recurrent theme for the African American owners, particularly those in rural areas (see Inman 1996; Inman and Grant 1998).

Group 2: Business Planners—Professionals

The Professional women relied on personal and professional relationships to help finance businesses. Most who received commercial loans had family member co-signers. Several had husbands who provided regular incomes or paid the bills at home. These women also received labor donated by family and friends. Business contacts supplied gifts of a client base and bartered rental space.

Two women, one white and one black, received loans from bankers who knew them. These social ties made significant differences in their experiences getting commercial loans when compared with another white woman who had neither co-signer nor a banker who knew her. Loan agreements came easily for the former, but required significant collateral for the latter.

Social Capital and Commercial Loans. Most Professionals who applied for commercial loans had help in doing so. All but one woman needed collateral or a co-signer to get the loans.[2] Gina reported having a "great relationship with the bank." She explained, "I own stock in the bank, so I had a relationship with the president of the bank." Needing little money for start-up, she did not apply for a loan at first. When she did, she had little trouble securing a line of credit using computer inventory as collateral.

Kin and Commercial Loan Experiences. Two dentists in the group provide examples of how differences in social resources can affect business financing. Three forms of social resources were important in Kirstin's commercial loan application process: 1) family support; 2) her relationship with a banker; and 3) the size of her potential client base. These aspects of social capital interacted to make her application process a positive one. In contrast, Bonnie lacked all of these social resources. She received two loans, but had greater difficulty in the process and had to provide more collateral.

Bonnie: Competition for Clients. Bonnie originally borrowed $40-50,000 to buy equipment and set up her rural Bingham dental practice in a rented building. Later she borrowed more money to buy land and build an office, combining the two loans into one totaling almost $200,000. Two of three banks in town turned down her original loan applications. She feels sure one did so because the only other dentist in town was on its Board of Directors. She believes he influenced the bank's decision to block her practice from competing with his. She received a loan without a co-signer or collateral from a third bank, but was required to purchase life insurance to repay the loan in the event of her death.

Kirstin: Male Mediation. Kirstin's experiences in financing her dental practice in Grafton were significantly different, perhaps because of family ties. Her father negotiated and co-signed her first loan at a bank where he conducted business and knew the banker. In the process of applying for her first loan, Kirstin met her husband-to-be, who worked for the bank. After her father stopped co-signing loans, her husband continued to negotiate loans for her, even after he moved to another company. Now she has an "easy" relationship with the bank. She reported, "W. [her husband] calls the bank and says, 'We'll need $25,000.' 'Ok,' [say] the bankers. I've *always* been on time. They've *never* had to call me and [ask] for money. My people get paid first, the bank gets paid second, I get paid last. That's the way it always is."

In contrast to Bonnie, Kirstin had a very positive experience with the bank. Kirstin's bank loan officer introduced her to his son, who was a dentist, and the two became friends. She explained, "A lot of people would think, 'This is competition!' [But] I've always considered him a friend. If I had any question about any type of procedural thing, I can go to this guy and say, '[How] do you do this?' Or 'I ran out of rubber gloves, do you have any?' I've got somebody that I can call on." Because the potential client base was larger in Grafton than in Bingham, Kirstin's experience turned a relationship away from competitive rivalry to collegial friendship.

Kin Support and Cost Reduction Strategies. The Professional women used social resources to cut costs in their businesses and reduce salary needs. Most commonly, husbands or companions earned regular incomes (Marsha, Meg) or paid bills at home (Fern, Marge, Frieda), providing income stability and reducing the need for women to bring home large salaries. Some of the most innovative cost reduction strategies included family mediated loan and rental agreements (see Kirstin's loan experience above) and trading services for rent on office space (Kay and Jackie). Other strategies included accepting gifts and donations of equipment and using equipment purchased in a previous job (Fern). The Professionals also received donated labor from family and friends. The Grafton white women (Kirstin, Marge, and Frances) relied on friends and relatives to help with physical labor in setting up their businesses, while Barbara, the Stanley black psychologist, said that her sister helped her plan the business financially. This was an interesting racial reversal. In other groups, European American women usually received planning and financial help from relatives, while African American women solicited donated physical labor from kin. Fern and Carla had employees who worked for little pay during business start-up.

Group 3: Business Planners—Natural Entrepreneurs

The Entrepreneurs relied largely on business contacts to ensure commercial loans. One white woman sought advocacy from the SBA, while the black women relied on loan histories with bankers. Most women, both black and white, had family members who co-signed. Family loans and income provided an additional source of financing, and husbands provided additional support by paying home bills. For the African American owners, cost reduction also came in donated physical labor.

Social Capital and Commercial Loans. Two women in the group who applied for the largest commercial loans reported difficulties in the application process. Karen sought help at the beginning of the application process from a nearby Small Business Development Center. Thus, the aid she received was commonly available through a socially structured business organization. Rachel encountered problems in the middle of a complex loan application process. Lacking certain racially ascribed social capital (whiteness), she felt the bank wished to deny her access to a major business location by only partially funding her project. She relied on family members, primarily her husband, to help her renovate her building. She then abandoned her plans for a sporting goods store and instead rented out space to make payments and began a small silkscreen T-shirt business.

Two other women relied on social ties to aid them with loans. Drawing on long-term social capital, Diane returned to her hometown to apply for a loan where the banker knew her. Eleanor's husband co-signed her loan, even though she was the primary borrower. She explained,

> When we went over that day to the bank, the guy at the bank said, "Mr. B., you wanta sign?" I'm looking at him tryin' to think, "No, no, no!" And I'm trying to do a gentle "no" to my head, and he ignored my shake of the head and he signed it. I'm going, "That's men-folk for you!" It was my idea, and it was like he was infringing on my idea that he didn't really want anything to do with. And all of a sudden, just because a mean ol' guy at the bank looked at him, he up and said, "Ok."

Eleanor feels she would have gotten the loan without her husband's co-signature, because she had borrowed money "a number of times" before from the same banker.

Social Capital and Non-Commercial Financing. Two women, Trish and Melissa, relied on family loans to start their businesses. Trish received help from her husband, and Melissa's father lent her $5,000 to start her children's taxi business. Rachel's husband's income was as much a source of financing for the business as her own employment earnings.

Cost Reduction Strategies. Almost all women relied upon indirect savings to reduce costs of business ownership. Three businesses were home-based. Husbands of married women provided them support via living expenses, reducing the need for their incomes. Eleanor received insurance coverage through her husband's policy at work. All the African American women, but none of the whites, relied on donated labor from friends and family members to help them set up businesses, and sometimes family and friends helped with business operations. This reliance on family and community labor was typical of the rural African American owners, but Trish, a Stanley owner, also used donated labor (see Inman and Grant 1998).

Group 4: Business Planners—Retirement Planners

The Retirement Planners relied solely on business contacts for help with commercial loans. These included prior relationships with bankers and aid from representatives of minority advocacy organizations. The Retirement Planners also received loans and gifts from family members in addition to commercial loans and their own savings and investments.

With more financial assets than younger African American owners, Retirement Planners depended less on family and community labor. They more often compensated helpers. This was partly a function of location. Rural owners solicited donations of supplies from the community, while two of the three black Stanley women worked with family members as paid workers.

Social Capital and Commercial Loans. Two of the Retirement Planners, one rural black woman and one Stanley white woman, needed little help with commercial loan applications. Both had recent loan histories and established relationships with their bankers. Two other black owners, however, one from Grafton and one from Stanley, encountered difficulties in applying for loans. Both women sought help from minority advocacy organizations.

African American Use of Agency Intervention. As a result of repeated rejection of their loan applications, Betty and Trudy both sought aid in making loan requests. Even though her income from continued full time employment could easily cover the monthly note payment, Betty had difficulty convincing banks to lend her money and finally sought help from the NAACP. With their help, she was able to get a loan.

Trudy was denied loans at first, so she started her bulk mailing service with her retirement money and funds from her husband. She initially leased equipment. After five years of operation, she applied for and received an equipment loan for $240,000, relying on the help of a consultant from a minority development organization.

Social Capital and Non-Commercial Financing. Both black and white women reported receiving money from family and/or friends for their businesses. Trudy, Rosalind, and Amanda received money from family members. A friend loaned Emily $50 for her first licensing fee. Amanda, Maggie, and Trudy (from Stanley) all said that their husbands supported them, reducing the amount of income they needed to bring home.

Cost Reduction Strategies. Both black and white women from rural areas reported cost savings from several sources. Local teachers and other community members donated toys and educational materials to Rosalind for her daycare center. These donations reduced her initial expenses. Amanda and Maggie operated businesses out of their homes, eliminating office rental costs.

Although donated family labor typically came from the rural black communities, two Stanley black women (Trudy and Helen), one Grafton black woman (Betty), and one rural white woman (Amanda) mobilized friends and/or family to help them in starting and operating their businesses. Trudy's whole family worked in the business off and on. Her son and daughter were working as business partners at the time of the interview. Likewise, Helen's husband and son helped her in the business, her husband taking responsibility for all of the marketing. Unlike the family labor donated to rural black businesses, the urban labor was on-going and was a mixture of paid and unpaid work. Betty, the Grafton beauty supply store owner, received donated labor in renovation and start-up, but also on-going labor from her family. One rural white woman, Amanda, also reported that her husband helped her in the business without pay.

EXTERNALLY MOTIVATED BUSINESS OWNERS

Since all of the externally motivated owners had worked in the past, many had significant personal funding or credit records, extensive occupational training, and collateral. Most still needed commercial financing, since most started relatively large businesses. The Work Skill Owners relied largely on personal assurances of reliability to obtain commercial loans, although two white women needed family or friends to co-sign. The Community Service Providers also relied on family or friends to co-sign loans.

The Career Problem Solvers' loan experiences varied both by race and by availability of social capital. African American owners reported positive and negative loan experiences. All were from the metro area where banking was less personalized. Women with positive experiences tended to have multiple sources of backing. Those with negative experiences lacked one or more of these resources, and they owned businesses that were atypical in some way. These women overcame obstacles in receiving loans only with difficulty.

The white Career Problem Solvers generally had little trouble obtaining loans. Most had already established their businesses, had other financial resources, and needed only small loans. All but one were located in Grafton or one of the rural communities where banking was more personalized. The single white woman who had problems with her loan had a large, urban, non-traditional business and needed a large line of credit. To get it, she hired a business consultant to help with her loan package. As an alternative to commercial funding, the white Career Problem Solvers found innovative ways to finance their businesses. The Career Solvers and Community Service Providers relied heavily on family and community members for financing. Two black and four white Career Problem Solvers received loans from family members, while two white Service Providers received gifts and loans from family members, as well as a small grant and gifts and loans from community members.

Women from all groups reported that their husbands or companions paid a greater share of living expenses at home, however, only the Work Skill Owners and Community Service Providers received cost-reducing aid from family and community members who volunteered work in their businesses. Some of the Career Problem Solvers reported that both employees and they, themselves, worked for little pay at first, and one woman received alimony that helped pay her bills at home.

Group 5: Serendipitous Owners—Work Skill Owners

The Work Skill Owners relied almost entirely on commercial loans and credit to finance their businesses. Even so, only two women needed co-signers. One reported a partner's loan, along with her own, helped fund start-up. Only two women's husbands paid all everyday living expenses.

Social Capital and Commercial Loans. Two Work Skill Owners reported needing help from social contacts, one a family member and one a friend, to get loans. Because Becky and her husband wanted to open their business within two weeks, the bank required a co-signer. Her husband's uncle signed their loan. Sally, the tavern owner, was the only woman in the group who had difficulty obtaining financing. Neither she nor her male partner could get loans on their own. A friend co-signed her loan of between $8,000 and $10,000, and another friend loaned money to her partner. She said,

> It's very hard to go to a bank to get a small business loan, let alone be a woman, but *especially* for this kind of business. It's pretty much out of the question. Now that was fifteen years ago, you have to remember, so

I don't know how far it's come in fifteen years. But in the bar business and a woman, [it's hard] unless you're going into some kind of franchise that has capital back up. But just for an independent little situation like this, I would say slim and none. Probably none.

Cost Reduction Strategies. A few Work Skill Owners reported having kin support and using family ties to help reduce costs. Camilla and Irene relied on their husbands' incomes for living expenses. Camilla, Becky, and Dee had family members who worked in their businesses. Camilla said her family helped her on occasion when she needed someone to take an insurance premium to the Post Office. Becky's husband started out as a reluctant partner but quit shortly after the business got going. Dee reported that her 12-year-old daughter occasionally worked in the business. Her ex-husband remained on the board of directors and helped with strategy for the business.

Group 6: Serendipitous Owners—Career Problem Solvers

The Career Problem Solvers' experiences afford a unique opportunity to examine how women who were faced with sudden career changes used social ties to obtain financing and reduce costs, even with little advance preparation. Those who could muster multiple forms of credit and backing had little trouble obtaining commercial loans. Those who applied on their own without aid from family or business contacts had more trouble. Women entering non-traditional and otherwise atypical businesses had to hire outside expertise for help with loan packages. Some resorted to anger. Barter and reliance on family ties to pay home bills were the primary ways these women reduced costs.

Social Capital and Commercial Loans. A comparison of loan experiences reveals how credit-worthiness and presentation of self determine outcome in the loan application process. For the women in this group, on almost all counts, success in obtaining loans depended upon social contacts or social capital. Individual social contacts co-signed loans. Organizations and businesses provided social capital in the form of franchise or SBA backing and minority loan programs. For African American women, multiple assurances of reliability resulted in positive loan experiences, particularly when several different types were combined. Thus, women received loans more easily when financial (collateral), personal (a co-signer), human capital (work experience), and social capital assurances (SBA or franchise backing) were combined. Absence of these, in combination with start-up of a non-traditional or atypical business, resulted in negative loan experiences. Having a negative loan experience did not necessarily mean the owner did not receive a loan. Most women in the study who applied for loans received them, however not all their experiences of the application process were positive.

Two African American women in this group sought franchise backing as a ready-made means to achieve public images of good character with immediate name recognition. They also wanted human capital resources provided by a franchise. Each wanted a different type of training, however. One sought occupational training, having already held a high-powered business career. The other, with years of employment in her occupation, sought business training.

In both positive and negative loan experiences, how a woman presented herself affected the loan outcome positively. Yet presentation of self was different in each instance. It was a product of social capital in both cases: in the first, it was a by-product of extensive employment experience; in the second, it was an emotional resource built from an ascribed racial status. In the positive loan experience, presentation of self was used as a positive resource in the loan application process that helped ensure receipt of the loan. In the negative loan experience, presentation of self became a tool with which to gain a hearing.

Below, I present two loan application outcomes for the African American women. To better understand the barriers that women encounter in seeking commercial credit, I look first at the loan experiences of those who did not have difficulty.

Positive Loan Experiences: African Americans. Two African Americans, Candice and Sheila, were backed by franchises that facilitated their loan application processes. Each had additional points in her favor when applying for credit. Candice opened a travel agency with three partners, her husband and another black couple.[3] They all signed for a loan guaranteed by the SBA. This guarantee, along with their franchise backing, ensured receipt of the loan. Candice and her husband also used their house as collateral, and Candice had worked in the airline industry for ten years. She said of the loan process,

> It was pretty much straightforward because [the franchise] had already talked to a bank here in this area. They were out selling franchises so they had set up for different banks to tell them about their programs. When we went in to get the loan, we really didn't have any problem. And they have a minority loan department. So we went through that, I think, coupled with SBA.

Like Candice, Sheila also started a business with franchise backing. She had worked in international banking and had a background in money management. Although she did not have prior experience in operating a temporary employment agency, the franchise trained her and helped her with a business plan and projections. She added her resume to the package and sent it with a cover letter to five banks, two of which expressed interest. She obtained a line of credit with little trouble, with her husband as co-signer.

Sheila believes her banking background convinced the bank to work with her. Not only did it denote her familiarity with financial management, but she also knew how to present her case in a self-confident manner. According to Sheila,

> The way I presented myself and my package was very professional. And I went in with the attitude, "We're gonna make a deal. You're not *handing* me *out* anything. It's a win-win [situation] for both sides. You're gonna get your fees and I'm gonna get the loan, so it's not any type of charity." I didn't go in with my head down. I think [your presentation] has a lot to do with it. And believin' in what you can do, because you have to convince them that you can do what you say you're gonna do, and if you don't come across convincing, they're certainly not going to be convinced. So I think that was one of the advantages that I had.

Thus, Sheila's attitude and her presentation of self helped her succeed in obtaining a loan.

Negative Loan Experiences: African Americans. Others were not so fortunate. Geneva encountered extreme difficulties in obtaining a commercial loan. After selling property to raise money for used manufacturing equipment, she began applying for commercial loans. She went to twelve or thirteen banks before one would listen. As she explained,

> Manufacturing is something that frightens most lenders, number one. Number two, being a woman here in the South is a disaster. They don't want to give you the audience, and then when you talk, they're not listening. . . . This is a distributorship area. Everybody's a distributor. I think if I was having full service I would have done better. But I've had more people take my business plan—and everyone likes my business plan. They marvel: "Oh, this is so interesting!" And that's it. And I call them [back] five times [with no response].

By the time she got to the last bank, Geneva was angry. She explained,

> I just looked at the man, I said, "Look, you *claim* that you do this." And
> I said, "Now, here is [my business plan]. And I want you to tell me why
> this will not work." . . . He couldn't say anything. My credentials were
> intact, my business plan was well written, my performers were there,
> my finances were in order, my credit was *great*. Finally, I said, "Who is
> your boss? I want somebody who runs the bank. I don't wanta talk to
> anybody else. You're a Vice President, but I'm certain that you don't
> treat everybody like this. I'm beginning to take it personally." Then we
> began to get a meeting of the eye and a meeting of the mind.

Geneva finally received a loan for $138,000, significantly less than
the $400,000 for which she had applied. She felt that time and money
were lost because her loan was processed through a minority lending
program. While her application was sent back and forth between branch
office and minority lending center, she could have used the money in the
business. She said, "I was supposed to have my loan finalized in April. I
didn't get it finalized until September. And [in] that time I lost money.
Then I went into a slow season, then I lost the client."

Geneva believed there were many reasons for the problems with her
loan: her status as a minority and a woman; her non-traditional business;
the economic structure of the region favoring distributorships; her re-
fusal to have her husband co-sign the loan. Even though she had an accounting degree and had worked as a financial director in the same type
of business, her experiences with commercial lending institutions were
very different from those of Candice and Sheila. Not backed by a franchise nor guaranteed by the Small Business Administration, Geneva
found the going tough on her own. Even her status as a minority, sometimes seen by whites as an asset for obtaining loans and government set-
asides, caused delays and financial loss.

The same was true for Nora on a smaller scale. Nora reported being
"turned down a lot" when applying for loans. She started her business in
1979, a time when both women and African Americans faced many obstacles applying for loans. As one of the few women, and probably the
only African American woman, in what was then a non-traditional business for women, her application for even a small line of credit met obstacles in most banks. She finally met a woman in charge of a "women's
business division" at a bank and succeeded in getting a line of credit. She
said, "My first loan was co-signed. My mentor did it, and I didn't realize

it until after the fact. He banked there and he had already spoken with them. At the time, I was just glad that I was able to get it." Thus, she did not receive a loan until backed by a social contact, her mentor, a white male business professional.

At the time of the interview, she still had trouble getting commercial financing. She explained,

> Even after having been in business [15 years], I still find it difficult to get a considerable amount of credit. And any credit that I have gotten has always been secured. So it's like my home or something has been used as collateral for the loan. . . . I really have been angered by the difficulty in getting a loan. I remember just threatening to leave the bank. And this was not even for a loan, this was for a letter of credit. For an order that I already had. I still feel that's one of my biggest obstacles, access to credit.

European American Loan Experiences. The main difference between the African American and the European American women's loan experiences was the fact that all of the white women who applied for commercial funding did so after their businesses were started. All of the white women applying for loans had significant personal sources of capital with which to start their businesses. Perhaps because of their existing wealth, they had less difficulty obtaining loans than most of the African American women, even without co-signatures or backing.

Judy and Julie were able to obtain funding fairly easily with collateral. Gail was offered loans she didn't need and got them using inventory as collateral. Unlike Candice and Sheila, these women did not have franchise backing. The fact that their businesses were established and they had personal sources of funding might have contributed to the ease with which these white women received loans. They also lived in smaller communities. Gail certainly had a social relationship with her banker. Judy and Julie did not say what their relationships were with their bankers. Their loan experiences may have been ameliorated, however, by a relatively congenial, small town banking atmosphere.

Living in a large city, Sigrid reported that her partner's father signed their first and second loan. Both were small, short-term loans and were easily paid off. When they approached the bank about a third loan, however, they found they would be required to use Sigrid's house for collateral, a move her partner refused. Instead, they decided to use business profits to buy the new equipment they needed.

Negative Loan Experiences: European American Women. Of all the white women in the group, Valerie had the most difficulty obtaining commercial financing. She started her multi-million dollar petroleum business in 1984 with "impeccable credit" and at first had little difficulty getting loans. As the economic climate cooled and the banking industry tightened, she had more trouble. Her financing difficulties came from the type of business she operated. She explained,

> I'm in a very highly leveraged business. To sell something, my margins are a tenth of a percent. It's a commodities business. In order to have a receivable, which is an asset, I have to have a payable. So the payable is a liability. If I'm doing well, my payables are high, then my debt-to-equity is *always* 8-to-1, 10-to-1. And banks are programmed to want 2-to-1, 3-to-1, 4-to-1. So it has *always* been difficult.

Eventually, she was able to get a $4 million line of credit with the help of a consultant. She said,

> Three years ago, [Bank C] could not make up their mind whether to give me a $120,000 loan. And I've got $4 million today? It's pretty impressive. They say it gets easier when you get up above $400 [thousand], $2 million. That it's the smaller ones that are difficult.

Unlike Geneva, who *was* a professional in finance, Valerie had to *hire* a professional as an advocate. No one has ever co-signed a business loan for her and she still finds borrowing money to be "the biggest challenge to overcome."

Kin as a Source of Financing. The African American women turned to family for funding. Heather's husband lent her money from his construction business, while Nora borrowed money from her brother. Some European American women also received money from family. Judy's mother loaned her money to help re-start her business. Jill's parents lent her money before she used her credit cards to finance her business. Gail's husband contributed 401K retirement money to the start-up of her business. She said her husband continued to invest personal income in the business. Four women (Candice, Sheila, Gail, and Jill) had husbands or companions who paid the bills at home. Sigrid reported that her ex-husband's alimony helped support her while she and her partner were first building the business.

Cost Reduction Strategies. Jill's creative financing (see "Alternatives to Debt" below) reduced her start-up costs considerably. Almost everyone else in the group who used cost reduction strategies (Sonia, Heather, and Sigrid) operated their business out their homes, eliminating rent. Sheila did not take a salary for the first 18 months of operation.

Innovation in Financing: Factoring, Cash Flow, and Credit Cards. Three of the most creative financing solutions in the study came from Sigrid, Valerie, and Jill. Unlike Nora, who had low initial expenses and short turn around, Sigrid and Valerie found cash flow to be a problem. Sigrid found a way to counteract it. Valerie, operating in turnover of thousands of dollars per day, used it to further finance her business. Sigrid explained the cash-flow dilemma this way:

> We are not paid on the spot, because most of our larger customers are big: they're universities, they're banks, they're national companies who have an office here. But they don't just pay cash out of the drawer. It has to go through their accounting process, and they pay you when they wanta pay you. So there's a lag between when we put the money out and when we get money back.

Factoring. Sigrid found an innovative way around this dilemma. She reported,

> There are companies that do something called "factoring" where they actually buy your accounts receivable, and then your customers pay them. But we have such a close relationship with our customers that we didn't feel that that was appropriate for us. Our CPA put us in touch with a company who does something very close to factoring, but actually they trust us to collect the money and to then repay to them what they have in essence loaned us. They don't exactly buy our outstanding invoices, but they do put some money into our bank account on the basis of a certain percentage of those. That has allowed me to level out the ups and downs of what was our income before then.

Several social interactions occurred here. First, a business contact (the CPA) put them together with another business to help with a financial problem. Second, the company structured the transaction in a way that respected Sigrid and her partner's relationships with their clients. They did not take over the business/client payment relationship, but simply eased it with the equivalent of a loan.

Cash Flow: Problem and Solution. Valerie learned how to survive on cash-flow. Much of her early financing came from manipulation of receipts. She explained, "You wanta sell it to the people that pay faster, you wanta reduce your margin to be able to sell more." To get cash flow started, she said,

> I lied. I stole some fuel, is what I did. After I couldn't pull any more
> from P.'s account, I called the hauler and I said, "Pull three loads of
> gasoline and take them to so-and-so. And pull it off of this account."
> Well, I didn't have an account with that petroleum company. So then I
> called the [owner], who I *knew*. I mean, he had been a friend in the in-
> dustry. And I called him, I said, "Oh, the carrier screwed up and pulled
> it off the wrong account. Why don't you just send me an invoice?" So
> he sent me an invoice. And that's how I started building credit.

Valerie's relationship with a "friend in the industry" provided an avenue through which she began building credit, an alternative funding source for her business.

Alternatives to Debt: Family, Credit Cards, and Barter. Jill, too, found alternative means to start her business. Although she operated on a much smaller scale, her genius for the recognition of available resources and her willingness to take risks matched Valerie's unorthodox methods. Like the rural and small city black women who drew financial and work support from their families and communities, Jill sought help from family and friends. In return, she traded services and products.

Jill's parents loaned her what they could afford. She said,

> They were pulling it out of retirement accounts for me. My parents are
> not in a position to be able to lose that kind of money. So I told them,
> "I've got it figured out. *If* it looks like I'm going to have to close the
> doors and I'm not going to make it, and I have to file for bankruptcy," I
> said, "I'll wreck my credit line. But before I go down I'll cash advance,
> pay the personal loans back to [you], and let the rest of it go down with
> the bankruptcy."

Jill also drew support from friends who helped her paint and reno-vate the shop. She charged tools and paint with her credit cards, and she paid the painters with pizza and coke, throwing in free haircuts for a year. She also "traded out" haircuts and hair products for bookkeeping ser-vices.

Debt: To Borrow or Not To Borrow? Libby chose not to borrow money for her business. Instead, she paid as she went. She wasn't sure this was the right thing to do, but a contact in the business reassured her she was on the right track. She explained,

> I have a friend, a man I used to work for. I think it was about the second year of business, I couldn't figure out how in the hell that you can get enough cash flow to not be worried sick all the time about living from hand-to-mouth. And so I called him and we talked about cash flow, and he told me, he said "Libby, that's one of the most difficult situations that small business people have, is being able to acquire and build up cash flow." I thought I was doing something wrong by paying for everything as I went. And he said, "No." He admired what I was doing, he thought that was the best thing to do, that I should just persevere with it. So that made me feel better. And eventually the cash flow did accumulate. It just takes time.

Thus, another "friend in business" helped Libby realize that debt was not necessarily the best way to finance a business. Rather than live hand-to-mouth paying off accumulated debt, Libby chose to wait patiently, over time, for cash flow to accumulate.

Group 7: Serendipitous Owners—Community Service Providers

Kin and community were the base upon which the Community Service Providers founded their businesses. All relied on family and friends both to help finance businesses and to perform work within the businesses. All reported receiving aid from companions or husbands in payment of home bills. Laura also had continuous financial aid from a benefactor. To reduce debt and help pay for the business, she staged many fund raising activities, for which she had extensive community support.

Kin and Community as Sources of Financing. All three of the Service Providers relied on social contacts to help finance their businesses. Bernice's husband co-signed a loan, although both "had good credit." She also received support from her husband's employment and retirement income. Jeannette received financial gifts from family and friends. The greatest help, however, came from donations, loans, and benefit income in support of Laura's bookstore.

Throughout years of operation, the store needed continued injections of money. Neighborhood organizations, Laura's parents, and other supporters all donated funds. Laura reported receiving personal loans from a benefactor, Annie. Laura met Annie in the context of an inner city educational organization, a program to provide training opportunities for disadvantaged youth. Annie gave Laura money to open the bookstore and continued to lend money over the years to help with cash flow, to purchase computers, and to provide a down payment and funds for renovation of a new building when the bookstore needed a larger space. Laura got a credit union loan with Annie's co-signature. According to Laura,

> We wouldn't be here without that help. I wasn't doing a business plan and borrowing money and doing things in a way that I could pay that money back. And so she has offered not only that financial support but an emotional and a real connected kind of support through all these [21] years.

Laura continued to borrow money not only from Annie but also from many other supporters. Laura admitted,

> Every time I save any money, we borrow it from me. We've borrowed money from my son, from his college fund. We've borrowed money from every girlfriend I've ever had. The cash flow problem is a constant problem for us. And so we have borrowed money from a lot of different people. And right now the loans are consolidated so that they are either from me, from my son, from my lover, from [my current business partner], from her daughter, or from Annie. And so we make a lot of loan payments every month. We've never borrowed money from a bank, except our mortgage.

Fund Raising Efforts. Currently, Laura and her business partner work hard to repay the money they owe to Annie. Laura said,

> She was young, she gave us money, and now we're involved in a more business-like thing with her where we are raising money to pay back money to her. We owe her a great deal of money, and she's a kind lender.

They find many ways to do so in addition to book sales. Laura pays the monthly loan note with income from rental of an office space in back of the store. The bookstore hosts workshops and book reading events and sponsors benefit dances and concerts to raise money for the building

fund. This reliance on a supportive community to attend events has allowed them to continue in business and repay their debts.

Community Support Networks. With perhaps the most extensive network of supporters in the study, Laura relied on volunteers for much of
the labor in operating the store. Friends and members of the community
volunteered hours and days to work in the store, especially in the beginning. On the day they moved to their new location,

> There were about a hundred people who volunteered. And we did the
> whole move with volunteers. We moved everything over here, put all
> the books on the shelf, got everything in order, and opened that after-
> noon. And that's a measure of the kind of help that we have.

They continue to rely on volunteer labor for many daily tasks in the
store, both to cut operating costs and to get work done.

> We have a number of people who come in once a week and straighten
> shelves, go to the post office, take the recycling, do whatever needs to
> be done to help the store keep running. And those people have been
> really important to us over the years. It's always different people, but
> there's almost always a few volunteers who are helping to keep things
> going here.

Family Support Networks. Bernice also relied on a network of "very
good family support." Bernice paid her cousin to renovate her house into
a care facility. Her mother and mother-in-law lived in a nearby trailer,
and her aunt moved in next door. All three helped with the business. Bernice said, "My aunt stayed there at night and my mother would do the
meals, 'cause she's right across the road there." Family labor allowed
Bernice to keep her costs to a minimum, eliminating the need to hire and
train outside help. In addition to labor donated from friends and community supporters, the Community Service Providers reduced the need for
personal incomes through relationships at home. Laura's companion
contributed to the bookstore by loaning money and by paying a greater
share of bills at home. Bernice's husband also supported her.

SUMMARY

Perhaps the most important finding in the study was the extent to which
social contacts helped women finance businesses. Across all groups,

family, friends, community members, and business acquaintances aided women in a wide variety of finance-related capacities, indicating the importance of social capital and social embeddedness theories in understanding women's entrepreneurial funding processes. Some aspects of social capital aid were racially linked and locale specific. Urban and small city African American women, primarily in the Trade and Career Problem Solver groups, used minority advocacy organizations to help them with loan applications or obtained funding through minority loan programs. White women received similar aid from Small Business Development Centers. Urban blacks also relied on franchise backing to overcome potential discrimination, take advantage of training opportunities, receive help with financing, and provide immediate name recognition to build client bases quickly. This use of social organizations for unintended purposes corresponds directly with aspects of Coleman's (1988, 1990) social capital theory. The study's focus on black and white women entrepreneurs extends that theory to include women in urban businesses.

In contrast, rural African American women (and one urban black woman) relied on friendships and credit histories with local bankers to obtain loans relatively easily in smaller, more personalized lending atmospheres. They also relied on continued employment earnings to support their businesses and received donated labor and supplies from kin and community members to reduce start-up costs. Clearly, social capital from organizations is more available in larger urban areas, while rural owners must rely on networks of individuals for social resources.

Financing and help with financing was much more diverse for European American women in all locales. Rural women who applied for smaller loans had little trouble and needed little help getting them. As locale or size of loan grew, women encountered more barriers and needed more help. A few of them received help from Small Business Development Centers. White women across all locales had a greater variety of funding than black women in the same areas. Thus, structural constraints and opportunities affected environments in which women sought loans, affecting women differently by race (Gerson 1985; Folbre 1994; Collins 1990).

Women used social contacts somewhat differently depending on their reasons for starting businesses. Those who planned their businesses relied largely on family and business contacts for help with commercial funding, while women who had not intended to own businesses were more self-reliant (Work Skill Owners), sought help from organizations

(Career Problem Solvers), or relied on kin or community ties (Community Service Providers). Family and friends generally contributed gifts, loans, and investments to all women except the Professionals and Work Skill Owners. African American family monetary donations were smaller in rural areas. Larger family loans and investments were given primarily to urban businesses or were earned in urban centers and brought to Grafton. Thus, progress made in African American family wealth (Bradford 1990) may primarily benefit urban families. White women in all locales received family gifts and loans of varying sizes.

As a situational factor influencing women's financial resource mobilization processes, timing played both a positive and negative role and was important in cost reduction and profit financing innovations. As such, it became a tool that some women learned to use pro-actively for their businesses, or it remained an external force shaping their efforts to gain commercial funding. Gerson's (1985) theory of circumstantial contingencies has some relevance here, but must be refined to fit women business owners' experiences. It must include women's abilities to take control of circumstances to benefit their businesses, as Valerie did manipulating cash flow, if it is to be applicable to women entrepreneurs' financing experiences.

Along with using time to stockpile equipment (see Chapter 7), time was a factor in dealing creatively with cash flow problems. Timing hurt business, however, when women needed immediate loans. In one case, a co-signer was needed to receive a loan quickly. In another case, the slow pace of a loan routed through a minority loan program hindered start-up of one woman's business. Timing was a background factor in certain finance strategies. Starting businesses after sudden employment changes, the Career Problem Solvers did not have a long time to plan businesses but had to rely on immediately available personal, family, and/or commercial resources.

European American women used more personal and family resources and turned to commercial sources only after start-up. African American women, however, relied more on commercial funding to start their businesses. When applying for credit, the more collateral and proof of credit-worthiness they could provide the less difficulty they encountered receiving financing. Social ties were critical in providing multiple forms of assurance in this process. In addition, some black women drew on another source of social capital, presentation of self, to convince bankers to hear them and give them loans.

Women in unplanned businesses used social capital to create innovative and sometimes holistic financing strategies for their businesses. In addition to a large loan, one Community Service Provider combined rents, fund raising, and volunteer labor in a holistic approach to raise money and reduce business costs. This strategy of combining alternative funding sources to finance as much of a business as possible outside conventional loan environments again indicates women's commitment to organic solutions to resource mobilization within webs of existing social ties and opportunities.

Others who had not planned to own businesses used innovative strategies to raise funds, reduce costs, and deal with cash flow. While most owners built businesses slowly, a few used factoring and manipulation of receipts in the course of cash-flow itself to cope with cash flow problems in their early years of operation. These high-end methods involved social ties, one to another business (factoring) and one to contacts made in business. Rational choice theories of individual economic actions based on profit motives, when relevant at all, applied most to these women who used weak business ties (social embeddedness) to increase profits or reduce income uncertainty. Low-end innovations (credit cards and bartering) were used to raise money to start businesses and involved both weak and strong social ties. A high-cost option in terms of interest paid, the relatively small amount of cash needed by women starting some businesses made credit cards an easily accessible form of financing. It also afforded a way to repay loans made by family members should the business fail. These innovative finance strategies depended largely on weak business ties. Social embeddedness theories (Granovetter 1973, 1982, 1992) of the importance of weak ties in gaining information are perhaps most relevant to women's business financing with these women.

Women from all the groups in the study, both African American and European American, reported using cost reduction strategies in starting and operating their businesses. Perhaps because they perceived commercial financing to be difficult to attain, many women did not seek loans but instead found ways to reduce their need for outside funding. Even those who obtained commercial loans found ways to cut costs. The most common (and most often cited) methods of cost reduction were starting businesses out of the home. Closely related, reliance on husbands or companions to pay all or part of the bills at home allowed women to limit or forego salaries early in business. Women of all groups and both races reported using these strategies. Less frequently reported cost reduction strategies included donations of materials and supplies; donated or low-cost family labor; volunteer community labor; limiting owner salaries in early months or years of operation; and bartering for goods and/or services.

Most of these strategies involved help from strong social ties to kin and community and suggest the need to reassess the importance of strong ties to business owners. While those seeking jobs might receive better information from weak business contacts (Granovetter 1974 and 1995), business owners need different forms of aid and information that strong kin and community ties can sometimes better provide. Rural African American owners, lacking access to significant family wealth, cashed in on donated physical labor from family and friends, a resource more plentiful in their communities. Urban African American women and European American women from all locations, with access to more family wealth and more family human capital, received more information and financial aid from family and close friends. But all these women relied on strong family and friendship ties for these resources, implying a need to reevaluate the importance of these ties to women entrepreneurs.

NOTES

[1] Cynthia did not apply for a loan right away. She started her business with personal savings.

[2] Carla was the only one who needed neither a co-signer nor collateral for a start-up loan. She reported having a previous loan co-signed by her husband.

[3] At the time of the interview, Candice operated the business full time by herself.

CHAPTER 10

Conclusion: Making Choices with Limited Options

This study explores in depth the experiences of women business owners, a rapidly growing but under-studied segment of American workers. It compares the experiences of African American and European American owners and contrasts the experiences of women who found businesses in three types of communities, rural, small city, and large urban areas. The study focuses on two central questions: what motivates women to start businesses and, once they have decided to become owners, how do women garner resources to carry out their business goals?

THEORETICAL FRAMES

I approached these questions initially through the lenses of rational choice (RC), social embeddedness (SE), social capital (SC), feminist, and minority theories of women's labor market participation. Each of these lines of theory approaches these questions from a slightly different vantage point. RC theories (Becker 1964, 1975, 1993 editions) address most directly the question of why people are motivated to become entrepreneurs rather than seek other forms of work or perhaps, in the case of some women, no work at all outside the home. RC theories trace their roots to neoclassical economics. They assume that individuals exist in relative economic isolation and make economic decisions based primarily on the desire to maximize personal profit. Actors' assessments of available personal resources influence whether or not they decide to start businesses as well as decisions related to further accumulation of resources that make such a goal achievable. For instance, the motivation to maximize profit could influence an entrepreneur's decisions to pay for advanced training that would lead to higher business income, or it could determine the choice of one financing method over another.

Social embeddedness (Granovetter 1973, 1982, 1992) and social capital (Coleman 1988, 1990) theories focus on the ways individuals use social ties or social capital to expand networks. This creates access to other forms of capital, such as information about economic opportunities, opportunities to learn skills or acquire credentials, introductions to influential persons, etc. Although only occasionally applied to entrepreneurship, these theories provide useful perspectives from which to address the central questions about women's motivations for business ownership and their resource mobilization processes. Social embeddedness theories are particularly useful for understanding how women with few resources other than social ties are able to translate these ties into assets that allow them to start businesses with few apparent resources. Neither social capital nor social embeddedness theories have been developed with women in mind, and each has limitations when applied to understanding the decisions and experiences of women business owners.

Feminist theories of women's labor market involvement, as exemplified by Folbre (1994) and Gerson (1985), avoid some of the limitations of RC and SE perspectives by including non-economic motives and the structural constraints and situational contingencies that women face when making labor market decisions. These theories, however, also overlook important aspects of the decision-making and resource mobilization processes for women starting businesses, for instance the community service orientation of many of the African American women (Collins 1990). Sociologists have studied such orientations in the context of other social activities undertaken by African American women (i.e., religion, activism through clubs, voluntary community service work), but only rarely in relation to labor market activities (see Higginbotham and Weber 1992), and never in relation to business ownership. Indeed, on the surface, entrepreneurship and community service may seem incompatible. Women in this study, however, provided strong evidence that the two can be combined to benefit both owner and community. Feminist theories also frequently overlook unique ways entrepreneurs have found to deal with disadvantage. Resource theories of minority entrepreneurship suggest that minorities develop alternative resources when unable to access publicly available funding and human resources (Light and Rosenstein 1995). Women in this study developed innovative alternatives to commercial financing for their businesses, suggesting that such innovation in itself might be considered a resource for women.

LIMITATIONS OF THE STUDY

The women in this study were a diverse group, having many differences with regard to my central questions, but many similarities as well. Since my sample was limited to a single geographic region, I make no claims that it represents other regions or countries. Nor do I claim that it represents all European and African American women entrepreneurs in the communities in which I worked. Nevertheless, the information collected in interviews with these 65 women provides valuable insights into a group of workers about which little is known. It also provides a basis for expanding and synthesizing the theoretical frames outlined above, and for assessing motivations and resource mobilization in business start-up for women of diverse races and residential locales.

Because the study focuses on women, I cannot assess whether the results have any relevance to male business owners. Many of the opportunities and constraints experienced by the women in this study are certainly experienced by men. For instance, some of the social networks available to African American women are also available to African American men. Likewise, economic constraints resulting from the 1991 recession experienced by some women in the study were probably also felt by some men. This study, however, does not include an examination of men's experiences, and I cannot, therefore, generalize the information gained here to male business owners. I leave that undertaking for further research. Much of what I found in this study has not been examined in relation to men-owned businesses, and a study of how these findings apply to male entrepreneurs would add valuable information to existing knowledge on entrepreneurship.

APPLICATIONS OF THEORY TO
WOMEN'S ENTREPRENEURIAL EXPERIENCES

Becker's (1964, 1975, 1993 editions) theory of human capital as an investment in self implies a conscious choice and deliberate action to pursue a path toward a goal, in effect "bootstrapping" oneself up to a higher socio-economic level. This line of thinking is most applicable to women in the study who were highly educated and from urban areas. These women typically had opportunities to further their education or otherwise develop skills leading to formal credentials. They had reasonable expectations that these human capital attributes would be useful for garnering resources for their businesses (for example, qualifying for loans) or in operating their businesses (applying professional skills such as dentistry or chiropractic). However, their choices often did not take into account the dual nature of business ownership, requiring knowledge of both occupational and business skills. This need for two skill sets makes investment in human capital for entrepreneurship more complex and demanding than it would be for employment in the labor market. Most women in this study who pursued training in trades and professions sought little training in business related skills. Pursuing formal training in only one of two areas needed for business ownership meant that their emphasis was on skills and services they would provide in the business, not on the business itself. In contrast, some women sought formal training in business rather than an occupation. Their emphasis was on operating a business rather than on providing a particular skill or service. Again, they sought formal training in only one of the two areas needed for business ownership.

Human capital investment theories were less relevant to women in other locales, for example the owner of the children's taxi service and most of the restaurant owners. These women drew more from experiential knowledge and skills they had learned over time on-the-job than from formal schooling in their occupations. For many of the women in all locales, there was only a loose connection between what typically is regarded as human capital and the types of businesses they operated. Many reported learning either the occupational skills they practiced (for instance, Judy, the security alarm owner) or the business skills their ventures required informally (Becky, in office machinery sales), hit-or-miss (Sally, the tavern owner), or on the job (Dee, the temporary employment owner). Skills learned in employed situations were more a result of the pursuit of financial income and available opportunities than a conscious investment in self. Women whose businesses were externally motivated frequently learned business skills in prior employed situations and later chose businesses based on experiences in their previous work settings. Thus, their human capital investments were not consciously made in order to start businesses, but were built while already earning incomes and only retrospectively applied to business ownership.

Becker's (1964, 1975, 1993 editions) theory of human capital as investment in self only partially fit the experiences of women business owners in this study. Some women consciously chose to invest in formal education directly relevant to their businesses before start-up, and then only in one of the two skill areas needed for business operations. Others gained skills based on available opportunities in employment and only applied those skills to business ownership when compelled by outside circumstances. Feminist theories of structured constraint and situational opportunities entered into how women garnered human resources for their businesses. In this study, conscious investment in self as a rational economic choice was frequently mediated by situational factors presenting barriers or offering opportunities that shaped the choices women made about where to learn skills and what skills they would consequently learn.

Social Capital and Social Embeddedness Theories

Social capital and social embeddedness theories were more broadly applicable to many women in the study, although to accurately reflect women's experiences different interpretations are needed. Coleman's (1988, 1990) theories of social capital, particularly in the form of social organizations, were important in explaining how women in this study built not only human capital but also financial capital. Educational institutions, trade organizations, and organized work settings provided human capital resources to women in this study. In addition, business and minority advocacy organizations helped in obtaining financial resources as well as some human capital. These theories fail to address issues of access, however. Institutions and organizations should provide equal opportunities for training and education to all members, but not all do so. Public educational institutions may be available to all, or they may cater to one race over another, as did the Ludlow public schools. Because almost all whites attended private schools, the public schools served an almost entirely black student population.

In addition, college degrees are frequently out of reach for those with lower incomes. Historically limited educational and employment opportunities due to segregated and poorly funded schools and discriminatory job queues (Thurow 1969) have made college attendance difficult for rural blacks. Lack of employment opportunities in rural areas has limited on-the-job training and made the choice of an occupation or trade with affordable training imperative for black women. Thus, hair styling, a trade requiring one or two years of schooling in a cosmetology institute, would draw women less able to afford a four year professional degree. Trade associations provide opportunities where formal education is lacking and make access to relevant skills more available, but initial access to a given trade or profession would determine what skills are offered and how profitable those human capital skills would be. Again, feminist theories of structured opportunity and constraint suggest a need to modify theories of social capital. To gain access to a broader range of occupations, rural black women need better educational opportunities.

For better educational opportunities, they need more financial resources, more information about occupations, and more role models in those occupations.

Granovetter's (1973; 1974, 1995 editions; 1982) focus on personal ties to individuals would suggest that the business owner is "embedded" in various social structures. Ties to kin in family structures or mentor ties in trade associations provide avenues through which information and resources are transferred. Women in the study who lacked adequate human and/or financial capital gained needed information and skills, raised money for business start-up, gained help in accessing commercial funding, and reduced costs with donations of family labor, all through social ties and social relationships. These business owners were able to translate social capital into human *and* financial capital through socially embedded relationships. Indeed, social capital and social networks were often the raw materials out of which women mobilized significant proportions of their business resources.

Social embeddedness theories, however, do not adequately describe the social networks employed by women in starting businesses. Most studies of women entrepreneurs focus on a separation of public and private networks and assume that women, who are immersed in strong, private family ties, are at a disadvantage compared to men who rely on weaker ties to publicly recognized business associates. Daniels' (1988) findings that women's strong family ties in the private sphere are, in fact, very helpful in furthering their public volunteer activities indicate a need to reexamine these assumptions. The strong family ties that Granovetter (1973, 1982) and others (Fischer and Oliker 1983; Lin 1982) dismiss as being too narrow to provide much useful support or information might be cornerstones on which women build businesses. Such ties were essential to many women in this study who relied on kin not only for financing (Gail, Kathy, Carol, and Kirstin) and volunteer labor (Ivy and Diane, Rosalind, Trudy, and Rachel), but also as teachers from whom they learned their business occupations (Judy and Rachel). These findings suggest that, rather than dismiss women's strong kin ties as limited or assume they offer no help to business owners, future research should focus on how these ties affect women's decisions and their resource mobilization processes in starting businesses.[1]

Knowledge of public figures in private life leads to a blurring of the boundaries between public and private arenas. Actors who depend on privately known individuals for public resources are less likely to keep those boundaries in sharp focus. Women's tendencies to blur these boundaries and view the world as a web of non-hierarchical relationships calls into question theories that make clear distinctions between public and private spheres. In addition, definitions of "public" and "private" spheres might change in different contexts. In rural areas, public life is more tightly tied to private relationships. At the same time, separation of racial groups may result in different understandings by race. For blacks, "public life" may mean "white life," while the entire black community may constitute an extended private sphere. Rural whites may hold a ringside seat to the public life of the town. In larger cities, private life may be more narrowly defined as immediate family and friends, and the public arena may remain at a greater distance, making access difficult.

These differences suggest the need to reevaluate theories based on traditional definitions of public and private life. Women entrepreneurs who remain in direct, personal relationships with men who are public figures enter business ownership in the public sphere with advantages from their private lives. In contrast, black women who have few white male contacts must build public relationships (for instance, to bankers or trade association mentors) to gain such advantage. This does not mean, however, that black women have no personal relationships to whites, nor that their personal relationships with black men are devoid of advantage. Work in traditional occupations historically brought black women into the private sphere of white families as domestic workers and nannies. Help from supportive white employers has given selected black women advantages they would not otherwise have had. This is not the current norm, however, and black women as a whole can rely on fewer advantages from white men than white women receive. Their relationships to black men might provide alternative advantages, depending upon the skill, knowledge, and contacts of the men involved. Thus, clear separations between public and private spheres remain problematic for social embeddedness theories involving gender, especially when race and location are added in.

Feminist and Minority Theories

The value of feminist theories such as Folbre's (1994) and Gerson's (1985) lies in their examination of macro-structural disadvantages women face in their decisions for employment and business ownership. In exploring how situational contingencies, discrimination, family responsibilities, and other factors largely external to women's control affect women's decisions, they clarify how non-economic contingencies affect women's decision-making processes in ways not taken into account by rational choice and social embeddedness theories. They also provide better-fitting frames in which to examine women's choices for business ownership. While more traditional theories address issues such as direct acquisition of resources, feminist theorists broaden the examination to include external factors and disadvantages that affect access to resources and available opportunities. Environments in which women in this study made decisions for business included forced departure from paid employment; gender discrimination in certain occupations, making self-employment the only alternative to unemployment; and age discrimination, making business ownership the highest income-generating activity for some older women. These barriers affected availability of opportunities and influenced women to start businesses.

Feminist theories may explain women's choices given structural and situational opportunities and disadvantages, but they remain limited in their ability to conceptualize how women actually deal with disadvantage. For women entrepreneurs in particular, they lack a solid depiction of how women garner resources for start-up despite limited options. Light and Rosenstein (1995) found that minorities who face discrimination in lending develop alternative funding sources and other ethnically based resources available to them as a group. Findings from this study indicate that women entrepreneurs sometimes develop similar kinds of resources in the ways they innovate to fund businesses. Rather than product or market innovations more common to high-growth, men-owned businesses (Schumpeter 1934 and 1988), women in this study developed innovative funding strategies to start and keep their businesses going. Given the difficulty many women have in obtaining commercial financing for their businesses and the high failure rates of businesses in general, this focus on survival rather than profit is not surprising and is a natural avenue for women starting new businesses.

Although feminist theories mention the pushes and pulls of multiple group membership, they provide little explanation of some issues found in this study that are relevant to African American women. For example, black women in all locales, but primarily in rural areas, combined entrepreneurship with community service work to address both personal and community needs. In addition, several urban black women produced public images of good character to obtain commercial funding in what they perceived were unfriendly lending atmospheres. These strategies of African American business owners suggest that Folbre's (1994) and Gerson's (1985) work better fits the experiences of white than black women. Collins (1990) provides more insight on African American women's experiences that can be applied to business ownership, although she does not explicitly examine labor markets or women entrepreneurs. She includes emphasis on community service as an aspect of community "othermothering" across a range of decisions black women make in their lives. She also discusses black women's strategies of resistance and empowerment when faced with racism and structural disadvantages and the strategies they actively construct to get around these obstacles. These strategies clearly have been adopted by many women in the study to circumvent barriers to mobilizing resources for their businesses.

COUNTER-INTUITIVE FINDINGS
AND THEIR APPLICATION TO THEORY

Theories of disadvantage based on gender, race, and age clearly pinpoint issues affecting many women in the study. These theories do not, however, address the conjuncture of race and locale and the limited opportunities available to rural black women in the South, nor do they provide solutions to conflicting demands based on multiple group memberships that women business owners have found. The experiences of black women starting businesses are different in urban versus rural settings. Racial segregation still persists to a greater degree in rural communities than in urban centers, limiting educational and employment opportunities for rural black residents. Black women who found businesses in rural areas contend not only with a smaller client base, but may have fewer business and occupational skills and fewer options in the types of business available to them. Aid from advocacy organizations is largely unavailable in small towns, and adequate financial resources needed for start-up are limited, depending on the type of business founded.

These factors work together in limiting rural black women's options for business ownership and resources, but they also result in unexpected achievements. Therefore, I look more closely at some of the unexpected findings of the study that pertain to rural black women and to women with multiple demands and responsibilities. By examining these women's choices and actions in light of existing empirical literature, I expand rational choice theory and synthesize it with feminist, black feminist, and minority theories of structured constraint, situation-based decision-making, and alternative strategies of resource mobilization.

Race, Locale, and Black Women's Resources

Several rural black women's experiences in obtaining commercial capital were surprisingly successful. Though limited in occupations, older black women combined work expectations with traditional work opportunities and carefully planned credit histories to obtain small business loans relatively easily. Having survived so long in disadvantaged circumstances, these women used deeply anchored skills and strategies that limited threat to white business owners to obtain funding and succeed in business ownership.

These women's experiences go against traditional assumptions made about availability of loans to rural black women, especially in the past, as experienced by the older women in this study. These women are often assumed to have limited access to commercial funding sources because of lack of collateral, low human capital resources, or racial discrimination in lending practices. Application of an expanded rational choice theory to these women's experiences leads to similar conclusions. According to Folbre (1994), existing social conditions should constrain and limit rural black women's resources based on their membership in a racially disadvantaged group. Social embeddedness theory suggests that black women should have limited access to white male business networks and therefore little access to commercial capital controlled by white male business establishments. Because of this, according to resources theory, black women are more likely to depend on ethnic resources developed in response to structured disadvantages in seeking loans. They should go to their communities for business funding.

In the study, rural black women did depend on their families and communities for help with financing, but much of that help was physical labor to help reduce costs. Although this labor might be described as an ethnic resource available to rural black women for their businesses, their monetary funding most frequently came from banks. To better understand this, I turned to the empirical literature on African American entrepreneurship. Research shows that black women expect to work more than middle-class white women and their incomes make an important contribution to family income (Burlew 1982; Murrell et al. 1991). At the same time, lack of employment opportunities has limited the types of work black women can do and their access to job training and experience even more than for white women. Discrimination in hiring has historically affected black women's abilities to enter certain fields. When they do obtain jobs, further discrimination limits their ability to advance to higher positions[2] (Thurow 1969, 1972; Reskin and Roos 1990).

If African American women expect to work, yet they have fewer employment opportunities and the jobs they find do not provide security or advancement opportunities, they are more likely than European American women to start businesses to fulfill work expectations and create their own job security. The numbers bear this out. African American women's businesses represent a greater proportion of all black businesses than European American women's businesses are to all white-owned businesses (Table 3.1). In this study, rural black women experienced lack of meaningful job opportunities in their communities. As a result, they chose to start businesses rather than work in low-wage, dead-end jobs.

To understand their dependence on commercial financing, I again turned to empirical literature that has found African American family wealth to be much lower than family wealth of European Americans (Bradford 1990). African American women, therefore, are likely to have access to less family and community funding than European American women. Combining rural black women's expectations for work with their limited family wealth leads directly to their efforts to gain commercial capital for businesses. Without multiplex personal ties to white business leaders, these women employed the only strategies at their disposal: building business relationships with bankers over time to prove reliability and opening businesses that served their own communities or did not otherwise compete with existing white businesses.

These women made rational choices to remain in relatively low-wage service occupations. Based on personal interests and on existing circumstances and barriers in their lives (expectations to work, limited work opportunities, few role models, limited information, and little money for educational opportunities that could provide greater occupational access), they made choices that were reasonable and achievable for them. The fact that they risked self-employment and were able to obtain commercial funding by turning apparent limitations to their advantage indicates a determination and will to succeed. It also indicates recognition of ways to succeed even within very circumscribed boundaries (focus on traditional occupational skills, service to their community, activities that were non-threatening to whites).

Such determination might be considered an ethnic resource (Light and Rosenstein 1995) tapped to create stable, meaningful employment. These women were very innovative in seeking alternative financing methods such as stockpiling equipment and use of voluntary community labor. But they also sought publicly offered financial resources that should have been readily available to them but which might have been more difficult for them to obtain than for others not racially disadvantaged. Unlike immigrant Asian populations, who tend to focus economic energies inward to create revolving loan funds (see Light, Im, and Deng 1990), these rural black women sought commercial financing from established economic institutions. This indicates a need or desire to enter mainstream economic life. Coming from communities with relatively little family wealth, dependence on established bank resources was probably necessary, regardless of the difficulty in obtaining loans.

Recent voluntary immigrants, especially those from Asian countries, frequently maintain ties to relatives in the "homeland" who send money to help establish businesses in the adopted country (Light and Rosenstein 1995; Yoo 1996). In contrast, African Americans have few direct family ties to their ancestral homeland. Arriving in the New World as slaves, they had little chance to build significant financial capital until late in this century. Further, their history of struggle, not only for liberation from slavery but also to gain equal access to housing, education, and job opportunities, indicates a drive to become full and equal participants in mainstream American life. At the same time, they frequently retain a commitment to serve their communities. To do so through business ownership generally requires resources unavailable within the community, hence the need to reach outside to wealthier sources such as commercial banks.

Circumstances under which African Americans arrived in the U.S. have shaped the needs current African Americans have and the choices they make. Compared to modern, voluntary immigrants, African Americans have fewer resources to pool in support of community-based businesses. Lack of resources, combined with their struggles for equality with whites, has led them to seek publicly offered financing rather than build their own ethnically-based resources. This is changing with inputs of wealth from successful new businesses started by blacks in metropolitan areas throughout the 1980s and 1990s. Black communities in larger cities have started revolving loans funds modeled on those used in Asian communities to support new firms (see Pronet Group, Inc. 1996). These resources are not yet available to rural black owners, however. Rural and small city black women's patterns of business ownership and commercial borrowing still reflect limited community wealth and the struggle to gain access to commercial resources for the benefit of community. The ethnic resources available to these women, therefore, are not monetary so much as they are community willingness to give what they have (physical labor, or equipment and supplies) and creative cost saving strategies. In addition, the depth of patience in planning careers based on traditional skills is itself a resource for these women.

Conflicting Responsibilities of Multiple Group Memberships

Dedication to serving community brings up another unexpected finding of the study. Empirical literature suggests that women's business motives differ based on pulls of domestic responsibilities in competition with employment and business responsibilities. If women have children for whom they are the primary caretakers, their domestic responsibilities directly compete for time with their entrepreneurial responsibilities, resulting in lower earnings (for example, Cromie 1987; Goffee and Scase 1985). Folbre's (1994), Gerson's (1985), and even Granovetter's (1973, 1992) theories of women's multiple group memberships, situational decisions, and socially embedded opportunities and responsibilities echo this theme that women are pushed and pulled in different directions by conflicting ties and responsibilities. Although much is made of this, I found few women in the study to be very affected by conflicts between home and business. When true, it was more apt in describing white women's than black women's experiences. As mentioned above, African American women were more often pulled by community ties than by domestic responsibilities (Blauner 1992).

The experiences reported by women in this study suggest that they did not necessarily make exclusionary choices. Several women founded businesses that served both their own needs and the needs of their communities. African American women founded businesses that provided educational, employment, and elder care opportunities for community members while earning incomes for themselves. European American women founded income-generating businesses that furthered women's networking, provided other women with jobs, and provided opportunities for learning and quiet contemplation. Women starting these businesses found ways to address both their own needs for income generation and their communities' needs for care and opportunities.

African American women's responsibility for community service adds a new dimension to feminist theories of conflicting pushes and pulls between work and family. As business owners, African American women found solutions to the conflict between self-promotion as business owners and community service as members of the African American community. This expands black feminist theory on "uplifting the race," and serving community as "othermothers" (Collins 1991) to include business ownership as a vehicle to uplift community members at the same time as providing income for the owner and serving as community othermothers. The way women combined personal goals with goals for the public good is also another indication of the organic or "seamless" quality of women's lives in which private and public aspects of life intermingle and are not easily distinguishable.

THEORETICAL IMPLICATIONS
AND MAJOR FINDINGS OF THE STUDY

Counter-intuitive and theory-expanding cases reveal why traditional rational choice theories are only partially relevant to women's entrepreneurial experiences. Women start businesses for economic *and* non-economic reasons, and their choices are rational based on existing circumstances and cultural expectations. African American women who start businesses that serve community needs or who use their businesses to uplift community members make choices for business that serve both their own needs for income and the needs of others in their communities. This combination of economic and non-economic motives points to a complexity in women's entrepreneurial experiences and demands reevaluation of rational choice theories as applied to women entrepreneurs. Rational choice theories assume that actors choose to directly or indirectly maximize income and/or profits. Expansions to rational choice theory suggest that other non-economic choices are rational given limits of structural constraint and disadvantage based on group membership. For women in this study, making the choice to serve community needs was rational and based on membership in gendered and racial groups and communities that value service, giving of self, and work to improve conditions for the group or community.

What these theories lack is an adequate explanation of how black and white women fund and start businesses *despite* constraints and disadvantages and what resources *are* available to them. The strength of this study lies in its examination of this question and its findings about the complexity of women's strategies for tapping and building resources for business ownership, particularly women's use of widely varying social contacts.

Major Findings

One of the main findings is that the entrepreneurial experiences of women in the study did not entirely fit frameworks of analysis derived primarily from the study of male entrepreneurs. This was not, as the literature on women entrepreneurs suggests, because they were all non-economically motivated for business or because their businesses were small and new. Rather, the theoretical frameworks discussed in Chapter 2 rely largely on indicators of preparedness for business that reflect neither the quantity nor the variety of human and financial resources women in the study accumulated when starting businesses. This is why so many frameworks of analysis are presented and why, I argue, each framework by itself is incomplete in explaining women's entrepreneurial activities.

Use of multiple sources of human and financial capital distinguished the entrepreneurial efforts of women in this study from the male perspectives discussed in Chapter 2. Women from different subgroups sometimes used one source more than another depending on what their needs were, but the group as a whole seemed willing to seek information and financing wherever it could be found and from whatever sources were most available to them. Many of them employed innovative strategies to gain resources that otherwise would be unavailable to them. Just as some of Gerson's (1985) respondents followed careers based on circumstances beyond their control, women in this study were affected by external circumstances and relied on available opportunities to gain resources for their businesses. To a large extent, they relied on social relationships, both to kin and to people met in public work settings, to translate social capital into human and financial capital. Social contacts of all kinds helped these women gain information, learn new skills, access funding, and reduce costs for their businesses.

Translation of Social Capital to Human and Financial Capital. Translation of social capital into human and financial capital lies at the heart of this study. The study provides detailed information about this process of translation and the types of ties used in doing so. These women's abilities to utilize a variety of relationships (strong personal ties to kin as well as strong personal ties to business professionals *and* "weak" business ties to comparative strangers) is consistent with Daniels' (1988) study. There, women use personal ties to public figures and private activities to accomplish public voluntary efforts. Women's use of a variety of relationships in the current study also reflects a holistic style of learning and resource mobilization that is consistent with the work of authors in several disciplines (for instance Cheney 1987; Gilligan 1982; Warren 1987, 1990). According to these authors, a "woman's perspective" tends to be non-hierarchical and contextual, existing within a web of relationships to others. In this study, women's experiences were often consistent with this perspective. They were as likely to use personal kin and friendship ties as turn to public figures to further business goals,

and their personal ties were often with publicly recognized individuals.
This was truer for white women, though urban black women reported
having similar friendship and kin contacts.

Attempts to fit women's lives and experiences into theories that
clearly separate public and private aspects of life are problematic.
Women's tendencies to blur the boundaries between public and private
spheres make demarcation difficult and call for new approaches to the
study of social networks and their effects on economic and business activities. In this study, Granovetter's (1973; 1974, 1995 editions; 1982)
emphasis on weak business ties as more beneficial carriers of economic
activities does not account for these women's strong ties to public and
business professionals. The degree to which women relied on social ties
to individuals and groups from all parts of their lives indicates an unqual-
ified, holistic reliance on all kinds of social ties to accomplish business
goals. This organic quality of women's networking is an important contribution to the literature on women's entrepreneurial activities and one
of the main contributions of this study.

Expansion of Theory

These findings suggest the need to expand social capital and social embeddedness theories when applying them to entrepreneurship. Much of
the research on social ties has focused on specific types of relationships
and how they effect employment and economic activities. Measuring
only the type of tie, however, provides neither an adequate picture of the
fluidity that is possible in such relationships nor what passes between individuals in the relationship. New contacts and pathways to new contacts
are sometimes left unexamined. Social contacts and the processes
through which they aid business owners to access human and financial
capital have been largely ignored.

A dynamic theory of the socially embedded entrepreneur would include the creation of new social ties through participation in various
structural and organizational settings related to business ownership. It
would include existing informal, "strong" family and community ties
that serve a dual (multiplex) purpose: providing relevant services, information, and monetary aid as well as expected emotional support and the
pushes and pulls of personal commitments. It would include racial continuity in informal and business contacts, but would also expect cross-
racial and cross-gender ties to benefit minority and women business
owners. And it would include a definition of the translation of social capital into a broad spectrum of human and financial resources. In this

process, the business owner would use pre-existing and newly formed social relationships as conduits through which to access these resources, and she might apply innovative strategies in doing so.

The size and kind of community would be important in determining the kinds of networks that are available to women entrepreneurs. In larger locales, social capital resources exist for business owners that are not available in smaller cities and rural areas. Racial minorities and owners of different types of businesses have access to organizations that offer specific services, and informal benefits are often discovered, created, or utilized in the process of partaking of formally offered services. Business ties provide more opportunities to innovate in obtaining financial backing in larger communities, while women in smaller communities must rely on cost-saving innovations and financing on a smaller scale. African American communities provide different kinds of strong social ties and resources than European American communities provide. A dynamic theory of the socially embedded entrepreneur would take these factors into account.

NEED FOR FURTHER RESEARCH

Returning to Chapter 2, it is clear that Figure 1 is an incomplete representation of women's experiences in starting businesses. The figure captures the relationships between motivations and processes of resource mobilization, and the dynamic, interlocking nature of human capital, financial capital, and social capital as resources in starting businesses. In it, ascribed characteristics such as race and gender affect childhood experiences, further affecting the types of social, human, and financial capital available to and sought by women making choices to start businesses. Larger societal influences, such as labor markets, economic climates, size, and demographic structures of local communities in which women start businesses, are left out. These operate as background factors to the figure, but they directly affect individuals' experiences. Childhood experiences differed for rural black women in the study compared with black or white women in large cities. Social, human, and financial capital often differed across locale, and changing economic climates offered different opportunities and placed their own constraints on women entrepreneurs as they made choices for business ownership. Thus, macro-structural factors can be seen as the paper upon which the figure is printed. As the paper changes color, economic climates change, labor markets grow or shrink, and community size differs from large urban areas to small rural towns. Each of these changes affects the figure (women's experiences) as it sits on different colored pages (macro-structural factors).

Also left out of the figure are arrows pointing from "Choice for business start-up" *back* to the "Social Capital," "Human Capital," and "Financial Capital" boxes. When women make choices to found businesses, they often return to the resource building process to increase skills and knowledge, find more sources of funding, and make new contacts to help their businesses grow. With arrows returning to close the loop, the figure represents a picture of women's expanding, ever-changing process of growth and choice.

Except in urban areas, African American women owned, for the most part, much smaller businesses than European American women. Inferences made from these results, therefore, are based on comparisons of loosely matched respondents. More work is needed to explore and further elaborate this figure representing women's entrepreneurial experiences and actions. Research should examine the complex, interlocking nature of race, locale, age, education, and occupation and how these affect women's choices and actions in operating businesses. Women's social networks should be examined in greater detail to determine how women gain weak tie information from strong ties, and how new contacts are made that help in garnering resources. Additional work should systematically examine how women translate social capital into human and financial capital.

To refine and test the theoretical synthesis presented here, further study is needed on black and white women who do not start businesses and on women who started businesses but gave them up. An examination of these women's existing kin and business ties, their use (or non-use) of organizations and structured learning opportunities, and their pursuit of new contacts for help in their business would be critical in determining how social ties contribute to successful businesses. If women who give up businesses, or those who decide not to start businesses at all, have fewer ties, more can be learned about the degree to which women use social contacts to access human and financial capital. If these ties provide fewer specific functions, such as accounting tasks or financing of the business, knowledge may be gained about the types of ties and the resources gained from contacts that are most helpful for black and white women starting successful businesses.

To some extent, this study addresses the issue of differing amounts of social capital by including interviews with black and white women in different sized communities. Larger cities have more potential sources of social capital from businesses and advocacy organizations than do rural areas. Still, the women in the study represent business owners who were successful at the time of the interview. The study does not delve into factors that might contribute to later business failure. Nor did I interview women unable to start businesses. Follow-up interviews with the women in this study would make it possible to compare the businesses that survived with those that failed for possible differences in their translation of social capital to human and financial capital. Such a comparison would be invaluable in describing what it is that makes social ties so important to the successful business owner.

Data collected but not analyzed for the study include other aspects of women's entrepreneurial experiences that are vital in operating businesses. Market development, business management strategies, employee hiring and management, and non-traditional businesses are only a few of the issues yet to be examined.

POLICY IMPLICATIONS AND FUTURE RESEARCH

Although the main purpose of this work was not policy analysis, it nevertheless identified some effective and ineffective policies and programs for enhancing business opportunities for African American and European American women. Racial segregation persists in the South, particularly in rural areas. While urban African Americans have made great strides in business ownership, rural black women have had a tougher time. Disadvantages built into segregated systems of education and employment sometimes result in inadequate cultural capital accumulation by black women to take full advantage of available business and economic opportunities. Further, such opportunities are often *not* available to rural blacks because of discrimination. Programs based on urban statistics do not take into consideration these differences in the experiences of rural black women and therefore cannot accommodate their needs. Programs are needed that focus more specifically on the needs of rural African Americans and take into consideration the effects of long-term segregation.

Small Business Development Center programs were helpful to many women in the study, both in planning and organizing their businesses and in facilitating and guaranteeing loans. Some women felt, however, that SBDC programs had little to offer. This was particularly true for rural African American women and women needing micro-loans of less than $10,000.[3] Minority advocacy organizations had more to offer these women, including help with very small loans.

Revision of the Community Reinvestment Act (CRA) will potentially affect women's current and future loan experiences. Greater access to commercial capital resulting from the adoption of these regulations will be a significant consideration for African American women starting new businesses. It will also be a factor to consider in future studies of women's and men's financial resources for businesses, especially for African American women living in poor and rural neighborhoods. Persistent segregation in these areas has limited black women's abilities to take advantage of business opportunities, mobilize resources for business, and attract racially diverse clientele. Increased access to commercial funding will not, by itself, overcome human capital limits or buyer discrimination, but it will open up business opportunities for rural black women who lack capital but are otherwise prepared for business ownership. Future studies should examine how CRA affects African Americans' and other minorities' access to commercial capital and how increased financial opportunities translate into business opportunities.

Continued attention to improving policy and regulations aimed at helping women's businesses is needed to ensure that intended results actually occur and unintended results do not hinder the business owner. Regulations governing set-asides, minority loan programs, and government procurement goals should be examined, including those of local and state governments. Black women in the study who applied for 8(a) status in order to qualify for government set-asides reported that the amount of paperwork they had to fill out was prohibitive. One woman actually lost business because of delays in receiving a loan through minority lending programs. Procurement goals requiring set proportions of women-owned firms can sometimes do more harm than good if the type of business a woman owns provides services that would fill more than the percentage mandated. Two white women experienced rejection when being considered for contracts by local governments with hiring quotas for women-owned businesses set at three percent. Because their architecture firm would lead projects with 50 percent or more of the contract, their firm was passed over while other women's businesses that more closely filled the three percent goal were hired. Setting low hiring goals, therefore, can *structure in* disadvantage for high profile, women-owned firms rather than support them.

IN CONCLUSION

This study provides detailed and updated information on black and white women entrepreneurs, a little studied but rapidly growing group. Analysis of these women's motivations for business and their resource mobilizing processes contributes to the refinement and synthesis of neoclassical economic and sociological theoretical approaches to the study of entrepreneurship as they apply to the perspectives of black and white women. The study provides greater sociological understanding of women's decisions and activities in the labor market and in business start-up. It emphasizes the importance of social networks in transferring human and financial resources to women entrepreneurs, and it suggests future research needs, implications for policy, and improvements in regulations affecting women entrepreneurs.

NOTES

[1] Social relationships also make demands on women's time and attention, though the women in this study reported surprisingly few such demands compared with current literature on women business owners.

[2] Several black women in the study said they had experienced limited advancement in their prior jobs.

[3] SBDCs do not loan money. They provide management assistance and help with loan packages, however, they prefer working with entrepreneurs who apply for larger loans.

Figures and Tables

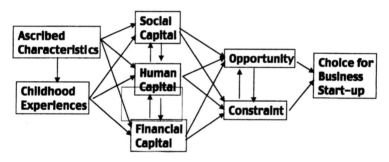

Figure 1. A Model of Resource Mobilization in Business Start-up

Table 1. Business Owners and Business Characteristics

INTERNALLY MOTIVATED OWNERS
Business Planners: Trades Women

Owner	Race	Locale	Business	Owner Age	Business Age
Rural					
Sabrina	Black	Ludlow	Hair salon	early 20s	2.5 years
Carol	Black	Bingham	Sewing/alterations	early to mid 30s	1.5 years
Mabel	Black	Bingham	Hair salon	72	28 years
Kathy	White	Ludlow	Hair salon	21	1 year
Small City					
Cynthia	Black	Grafton	Hair salon	mid- to late 20s	4 years
Ivy	Black	Grafton	Hair salon	33	7 years
Elly	Black	Grafton	Hair salon	62	4 years
Corinne	Black	Grafton	Restaurant	49	2 months
Hazel	Black	Grafton	Alterations	50	2 years
Linda	White	Grafton	Hair/barber shop	39	13 years

Business Planners: Professionals

Owner	Race	Locale	Business	Owner Age	Business Age
Rural					
Bonnie	White	Bingham	Dentist	37	8 years
Small City					
Carla	Black	Grafton	Attorney	35	4.5 years
Kirstin	White	Grafton	Dentist	35	10 years
Marge	White	Grafton	Chiropractor	37	4 years
Frieda	White	Grafton	Interior design	45	3 years
Frances	White	Grafton	Attorney	48	11 years

Business Planners: Professionals (*cont.*)

Owner	Race	Locale	Business	Owner Age	Business Age
Urban					
Fern	Black	Stanley	Corporate attorney	31	2 years
Gina	Black	Stanley	Graphic Design	34	5 years
Olive	Black	Stanley	Attorney	37	1 year
Barbara	Black	Stanley	Psychologist	39	7 years
Kay &	White	Stanley	Architects	40	4 years
Jackie	White			38-ish	
Marsha	White	Stanley	Real estate	43	6 years
Meg	White	Stanley	Video Production	46	15 years
Isabelle	Hispan.	Stanley	Architect	late 50s	11.5 years

Business Planners: Natural Entrepreneurs

Owner	Race	Locale	Business	Owner Age	Business Age
Rural					
Charlene	Black	Bingham	Restaurant	30-ish	1 year
Rachel	Black	Bingham	T-shirts	36	3-4 years
Eleanor	Black	Acorn	Trailer rentals	50-ish	7 years
Karen	White	Ludlow	Restaurant	38	2 years
Small City					
Diane	Black	Grafton	Hair salon	46	7 years
Pam &	White	Grafton	Espresso stand	30/30-ish	6 months
Donna	White				
Melissa	White	Grafton	Kid taxi	30	4 months
Urban					
Trish	Black	Stanley	Monogrammed clothing	47	4 years

Business Planners: Retirement Planners

Owner	Race	Locale	Business	Owner Age	Business Age
Rural					
Rosalind	Black	Ludlow	Daycare center	mid-60s	14 years
Amanda	White	Bingham	Residential design	57	2-3 years
Maggie	White	Ludlow	Real estate	63	12-13 years
Small City					
Betty	Black	Grafton	Beauty supplies	mid- to late 40s	5 years
Lenore	Black	Grafton	Hair salon	47	4 years
Emily	White	Grafton	Financial planning	57	3-4 years
Urban					
Trudy	Black	Stanley	Mailing service	52	8 years
Helen	Black	Stanley	Laser recycling	56	2.3 years
Deborah	White	Stanley	Psychologist	61	5 years

EXTERNALLY MOTIVATED OWNERS
Serendipitous Owners: Work Skill Owners

Owner	Race	Locale	Business	Owner Age	Business Age
Rural					
Camilla	White	Bingham	Insurance	32	2 years
Small City					
Sally	White	Grafton	Tavern	42	14 years
Irene	White	Grafton	Restaurant	45	10 years
Becky	White	Grafton	Business equipment	51	5 years
Urban					
Dee	Black	Stanley	Temporary employment	44	2 years
Nell	White	Stanley	Insurance	65	9 years

Serendipitous Owners: Career Problem Solvers

Owner	Race	Locale	Business	Owner Age	Business Age
Rural					
Judy	White	Bingham	Security Alarms	43	8 years
Gail	White	Bingham	Books/antiques	46	3 years
Small City					
Julie	White	Grafton	Travel agent	45	6 years
Urban					
Sonia	Black	Stanley	Cleaning products	38	3 years
Heather	Black	Stanley	Video production	40	6 years
Geneva	Black	Stanley	Chemical manufacturing	40-45ish	1.5 years
Candice	Black	Stanley	Travel agent	42	5 years
Sheila	Black	Stanley	Temporary employment	42	5 years
Nora	Black	Stanley	Specialty advertising	47	15 years
Jill	White	Stanley	Hair salon	31	13 months
Valerie	Hispan.	Stanley	Petroleum products	35	10 years
Sigrid	White	Stanley	Laser recycling	46	6 years
Libby	White	Stanley	Residential contractor	53	7 years

Serendipitous Owners: Community Service Providers

Owner	Race	Locale	Business	Owner Age	Business Age
Rural					
Bernice	Black	Bingham	Personal care home	60-ish	8-10 years
Small City					
Jeannette	White	Grafton	Women's net-working service	45	3-4 years
Urban					
Laura	White	Stanley	Bookstore	47	21 years

Table 2. Business Owners and Business Clientele

INTERNALLY MOTIVATED OWNERS

Business Planners: Trades Women

Owner	Client Base
Rural	
Sabrina	Black women, some black men
Carol	White and black women and men (majority white women)
Mabel	Black women, some black men
Kathy	White women and men
Small City	
Cynthia	Black women
Ivy (with Diane)	Black women
Elly (with Lenore)	Black women
Corinne	White and black individuals (majority white)
Hazel	Majority white business men and students
Linda	White women and men

Business Planners: Professionals

Owner	Client Base
Rural	
Bonnie	White and black individuals
Small City	
Carla	Black and white individuals
Kirstin	Majority white families and individuals
Marge	Majority white individuals
Frieda	Majority white families and individuals
Frances	Majority white individuals
Urban	
Fern	Corporations

Business Planners: Professionals (*cont.*)

Owner	Client Base
Gina	Local and state governments, corporations, businesses
Olive	Black individuals
Barbara	Majority black individuals
Kay & Jackie	Local and state government, corporations, businesses, few individuals
Marsha	Majority white families & individuals
Meg	Businesses, corporations, non-profits
Isabelle	Governments, corporations

Business Planners: Natural Entrepreneurs

Owner	Client Base
Rural	
Charlene	Black individuals
Rachel	Groups: church, recreational, civic
Eleanor	Majority white families & individuals, some black families & individuals
Karen	Black and white individuals
Small City	
Diane (w/ Ivy)	Black women
Pam & Donna	White and black individuals
Melissa	White families with children
Urban	
Trish	Corporations

Business Planners: Retirement Planners

Owner	Client Base
Rural	
Rosalind	Black families with children
Amanda	Majority white families & individuals
Maggie	Majority black families and individuals

Business Planners: Retirement Planners (*cont.*)

Owner	Client Base
Small City	
Betty	Black women, some black men
Lenore (with Elly)	Black women
Emily	White families & individuals
Urban	
Trudy	Governments, businesses, corporations
Helen	Governments, businesses, corporations
Deborah	Majority white individuals, few blacks

EXTERNALLY MOTIVATED OWNERS
Serendipitous Owners: Work Skill Owners

Owner	Client Base
Rural	
Camilla	White and black individuals
Small City	
Sally	Majority white, some black individuals
Irene	Everyone
Becky	Governments, corporations, businesses
Urban	
Dee	Governments, corporations, businesses (employers). Majority black, some white individuals (employees).
Nell	White individuals

Serendipitous Owners: Career Problem Solvers

Owner	Client Base
Rural	
Judy	White families & individuals
Gail	White and black antique dealers, individuals
Small City	
Julie	Majority white individuals, businesses

Serendipitous Owners: Career Problem Solvers (*cont.*)

Owner	Client Base
Urban	
Sonia	Governments, businesses, schools, public agencies
Heather	Majority black individuals
Geneva	Governments, businesses
Candice	Black and white individuals, businesses
Sheila	Governments, corporations, businesses (employers). Majority black, some white individuals (employees).
Nora	Corporations, businesses, governments
Jill	Majority white women, some white men, few others
Valerie	Governments, corporations, businesses
Sigrid	Governments, corporations, businesses
Libby	White and black families & individuals

Serendipitous Owners: Community Service Providers

Owner	Client Base
Rural	
Bernice	Elderly black men and women
Small City	
Jeannette	Women
Urban	
Laura	Everyone

Table 3.1 Southeastern Business Ownership Statistics, All Firms, 1992

	All Firms	WO Firms	WO % of All Firms	AA WO Firms	AAW % of AA Firms	AAW % of WO Firms	EA WO Firms	EAW % of All WO Firms
AL	227,119	71,466	31.47	6,174	41.98	8.64	64,386	90.09
FL	1,000,542	352,048	35.19	17,533	43.43	4.98	292,925	83.21
GA	425,118	143,045	33.65	16,860	44.06	11.79	121,868	85.20
KY	236,525	74,280	31.40	2,239	43.93	3.01	71,269	95.95
LA	236,589	76,849	32.48	7,832	38.56	10.19	66,034	85.93
MS	135,497	40,879	30.17	5,250	37.32	12.84	35,081	85.82
NC	439,301	142,516	32.44	11,895	40.71	8.35	128,081	89.87
SC	197,330	64,812	32.84	7,288	39.73	11.24	56,507	87.19
TN	325,371	101,134	31.08	6,490	43.50	6.42	93,371	92.32
US	17,253,143	5,888,883	34.13	277,246	44.65	4.71	5,171,448	87.82

Source: U.S. Bureau of the Census, 1992 Economic Census

WO = Woman-Owned

AA = African American

AAW = African American Women

EA = European American

EAW = European American Women

**Table 3.2 Southeastern Business Ownership Statistics,
Firms with Employees, 1992**

	All Firms	WO Firms	WO % of All Firms	AA WO Firms	AAW % of AA Firms	AAW % of WO Firms	EA WO Firms	EAW % of All WO Firms
AL	45,565	11,080	24.32	575	32.43	5.19	10,259	92.59
FL	194,300	66,035	33.99	1,533	28.91	2.32	55,561	84.14
GA	79,785	20,553	25.76	1,223	34.57	5.95	18,399	89.52
KY	43,222	10,648	24.64	171	29.87	1.61	10,184	95.64
LA	40,791	10,760	26.38	586	32.76	5.45	9,684	90.00
MS	28,565	6,566	22.99	498	28.09	7.58	5,933	90.36
NC	82,342	20,324	24.68	1,038	26.34	5.11	18,682	91.92
SC	39,468	9,758	24.72	681	29.84	6.98	8,796	90.14
TN	60,026	13,405	22.33	493	27.40	3.68	12,569	93.76
US	3,134,959	817,773	26.09	20,913	29.24	2.56	727,152	88.92

Source: U.S. Bureau of the Census, 1992 Economic Census

WO = Woman-Owned

AA = African American

AAW = African American Women

EA = European American

EAW = European American Women

**Table 3.3 Southeastern Business Sales (in $1,000s),
All Firms, 1992**

	All Firms	WO Firms	WO % of All Firms	AA WO Firms	AAW % of AA Firms	AAW % of WO Firms	EA WO Firms	EAW % of All WO Firms
AL	41620000	7627704	18.33	130393	24.39	1.71	7364393	96.55
FL	172499^{E3}	39484595	22.89	518332	22.88	1.31	33734134	85.44
GA	82009000	22450439	27.38	443881	26.47	1.98	21547164	95.98
KY	37112000	6763383	18.22	43671	17.41	0.65	6650548	98.33
LA	34217000	11742919	34.32	201617	26.04	1.72	11307475	96.29
MS	19305000	3452070	17.88	166658	33.01	4.83	3232243	93.63
NC	76188000	14365288	18.86	223383	25.00	1.56	13899928	96.76
SC	29217000	5049393	17.28	144207	21.44	2.86	4791557	94.89
TN	59161000	8572522	14.49	162948	29.36	1.90	8258855	96.34
US	33242^{E5}	642484352	19.33	8509656	26.43	1.32	592717839	92.25

Source: U.S. Bureau of the Census, 1992 Economic Census

WO = Woman-Owned

AA = African American

AAW = African American Women

EA = European American

EAW = European American Women

Table 3.4 Southeastern Business Sales (in $1,000s), Firms with Employees, 1992

	All Firms	WO Firms	WO % of All Firms	AA WO Firms	AAW % of AA Firms	AAW % of WO Firms	EA WO Firms	EAW % of All WO Firms
AL	36456000	6646227	18.23	72070	20.99	1.08	6086520	91.58
FL	149089000	33675639	22.59	315621	21.95	0.94	28802992	85.53
GA	71964000	20199478	28.07	254863	23.09	1.26	19567330	96.87
KY	32127000	5821853	18.12	26280	13.26	0.45	5716748	98.19
LA	28893000	10586117	36.64	116289	23.88	1.10	10290503	97.21
MS	16185000	2873490	17.75	110779	36.86	3.86	2719778	94.65
NC	66849000	12494326	18.69	122692	23.12	0.98	12172235	97.42
SC	24845000	4152177	16.71	79743	18.32	1.92	3981290	95.88
TN	51391000	7101593	13.82	88171	26.97	1.24	6897601	97.13
US	2907132^{E3}	550425116	18.93	5391150	23.87	0.98	511840764	92.99

Source: U.S. Bureau of the Census, 1992 Economic Census

WO = Woman-Owned

AA = African American

AAW = African American Women

EA = European American

EAW = European American Women

Table 3.5 Percent of Short-Term Bank Loans Accepted, Early 1980s

Non-minorities	89.9 percent
Asians	96.2
Blacks	61.7
Hispanics	86.6

From Bates, 1993b: 63

Table 4.1 Response Rates of Potential Study Participants

	Agree/Refuse (%)	Agree/Refuse + Unreachable (%)	Agree/All Called (%)
Rural			
Black	8/13 (61.5%)	8/17 (47.1%)	8/21 (38.1%)
White	8/15 (53.3%)	8/19 (42.1%)	8/26 (30.8%)
Grafton			
Black	9/11 (81.8%)	9/16 (56.2%)	9/17 (52.9%)
White	14/16 (87.5%)	14/26 (53.8%)	14/28 (50%)
Stanley			
Black	14/19 (73.7%)	14/34 (41.2%)	14/38 (36.8%)
White	13/18 (72.2%)	13/29 (44.8%)	13/29 (44.8%)

Forms and Questionnaires

CONSENT FORM

I agree to participate in the research titled "Woman-Owned Small Businesses in Georgia", which is being conducted by Kate Inman under the supervision of her advisor, Dr. Linda Grant, Department of Sociology at the University of Georgia, 706-542-3195. I understand that this participation is entirely voluntary; I can withdraw my consent at any time without penalty and have the results of the participation, to the extent that it can be identified as mine, returned to me, removed from the research records, or destroyed.

The following points have been explained to me:

1) The reason for the research is to explore the backgrounds and experience of women business owners in order to better understand the problems and opportunities they face in starting and/or operating their own businesses

The benefits I may expect from the research are to have access to the results of the research in order to learn what factors contribute to growth and failure of woman-owned businesses. I may also gain insights from the experiences of other business women which may be applied to operation of my own business.

2) The procedures are as follows:

I agree to take part in a verbal interview, lasting about one hour, in which the investigator will ask me questions concerning the start-up and operations of my business, business contacts, my attitudes and preferences related to my business and to the economy in general, and my educational and family background. At the end of the interview, I will be given a written survey form with additional questions on the same topics. I will be asked to complete the written survey and return it by mail to the investigator in a self-addressed, stamped envelop provided by the investigator. I understand that I may refuse to answer any question and may discontinue participation at any time.

3) No discomforts or stresses are foreseen.

4) No risks are foreseen.

5) The information I provide will be kept confidential and will not be released in any individually identifiable form without my prior consent, unless otherwise required by law. Audio tapes used to record information during the interview will be transcribed with a coded identification number to protect my identity. The audio tapes will be erased upon written transcription, or no later than December 31, 1995.

6) The investigator will answer any further questions about the research, now or during the course of the project.

_____   _____   _____   _____
Signature of Investigator   Date   Signature of Participant   Date

PLEASE SIGN BOTH COPIES OF THIS FORM. KEEP ONE AND RETURN THE OTHER TO THE INVESTIGATOR.

Research at The University of Georgia which involves human participants is overseen by the Institutional Review Board. Questions or problems regarding your rights as a participant should be addressed to Heidi L. Roof, M.S.; Institutional Review Board; Office of V.P. for Research; The University of Georgia, 604A Graduate Studies Research Center; Athens, Georgia 30602-7411; Telephone (706) 542-6514. Kate Inman, the major investigator, can be reached c/o the Department of Sociology, Baldwin Hall, The University of Georgia, Athens, Georgia 30602-1611; Telephone (706) 542-3195. Her advisor, Dr. Linda Grant, can be reached at the same address; Telephone (706) 542-2421.

WOMAN-OWNED SMALL BUSINESSES
A SURVEY

QUALIFYING QUESTIONS

QQ1   Is this a woman-owned business?   (Definition: more than 50% owned by one or
                                              more women)
        1. Yes --> Go to QQ2   8. Don't know --> Discontinue
        2. No --> Discontinue

IF YES: QQ2. Are you sole owner or do you have one or more partners?
        1. Sole owner   8. Don't know/no response
        2. One partner
          3. Two or more partners

QQ3   Did you start the business yourself?
        1. Yes --> Go to QQ5
        2. No --> Go to QQ4

IF NO: QQ4   How did you acquire the business?
        1. Bought --> Go to QQ5   8. Other --> Use own judgement
        2. Inherited --> Use own judgement

QQ5   Does the business provide you with your main source of income?
        1. Yes --> Go to QQ6   8. Don't know --> Own judgement
        2. No --> Use own judgement

QQ6   Is this business a franchise?
        1. Yes --> Discontinue   8. Don't know --> Go to QQ7
        2. No --> Go to QQ7

QQ7   Do you have any employees?
        1. Yes --> Go to QQ8
        2. No --> Go to QID

IF YES: QQ8 How many employees?
          1. < 500 --> Go to QID
            2. 500 or more --> Discontinue

**WOMAN-OWNED SMALL BUSINESSES
A SURVEY**

INTERVIEWER CHECK LIST

QID _____

Q1   County: _____

Q2   Is respondent the

                1. Owner
                2. Owner/manager
                3. Manager/CEO
                4. Other_____

Q3   Does respondent operate business out of own home?

                        1. Yes   8. Don't know
                        2. No

Q4   Is respondent a minority? Which? _____

                        1. Yes   8. Don't know
                        2. No

Q5   Does respondent have a visible or audible disability?

                        1. Yes   8. Don't know
                        2. No

        Q6   What is it? _____

VERBAL INTERVIEW

I. OPERATIONS

Q7   Please tell me about your business - what do you do, what product you make or service you provide?

Q8   Please tell me about your daily operations - what is your average day at work like?

Q9   Who are your clients or customers? What types of people or organizations buy your product(s) / service(s)?

      PROBE: Q10 Do you serve/sell primarily to (women / a minority?)

[Q   Who is your primary competition?]

II. MOTIVES: CHOOSING A BUSINESS

Q11   What made you decide to start your own business?

      PROBE: Q12   Did you have any interests or experiences in your childhood that might have contributed to your decision to start your own business?

      PROBE: Q13   When you were growing up, did your parents or any relative living near you own their own business?

            IF YES: Q14   What type of business did they own?

                    Q15   Did you spend time there?

                    Q16   Did you work there?

Q17   What made you choose the type of business you did?

      PROBE: Q18   How did you get the idea to do this particular type of business?

      PROBE: Q19   [If followed from job experience:] How did you get started in this line of work?

      PROBE: Q20   When you were growing up, did anyone you know influence you in choosing a career or thinking about having your own business?

III. EDUCATION, TRAINING, AND EXPERIENCE

Q21   What experience or training, if any, prepared you for owning and/or operating this business?

Q22   What about your work history? What types of jobs have you had?

      PROBE: Q23   What was your first job?
      PROBE: Q24   Tell me about the jobs you've had in the last 5 years.
Q25   What was your last job before owning this business?

Q26   Why did you leave it? (get circumstances)

Q27   Have you had previous work experience similar to this business?

      PROBE: Q28   Did your experience in that job help you in founding this business?

      PROBE: Q29   Did anyone there help you form your business?

Q30   Looking back, what training do you feel would have been helpful to have [that you didn't have] in starting and operating your business?

Q   Since starting your business, have you participated in any training or other programs, workshops, or seminars? (Please describe...)

V. STARTING YOUR BUSINESS

Now I am going to ask about the types of support and guidance you've had in starting, owning, and operating your own business. For each person you name in the following section, I am going to ask you five questions.   (SHOW CHART.)

Q31   Who has given you help or support in starting your business? This can be financial support, training, information, encouragement, - any type of support, and as many people as come to mind.

Q32   What is your relationship to each of these people? Are they family, friends, acquaintances, business associates?

Q33   How did you meet them? Are they people you knew from previous jobs, people you met while starting up your business?

Q34   What did they do to help you?

Q35   In what time period did they help you? (Pre-start-up, early operations, etc.)

Q36   Did any of these people help more than the others?

      NOTE: Indicate [with a "*"] those who helped the most.

PERSON	RELATION- SHIP	WHERE MET	HOW THEY HELPED	TIME WHEN HELP WAS GIVEN

Q37   How did your [OTHER] family members (parents, brothers, sisters, husband, children) react to your decision to start your own business? Did they support you? Discourage you?

Q38   Have any of their reactions changed now that you have established your operations?

IF YES: Q39   How did they change?

Q40   Were there any other people or circumstances in your life who/which you feel influenced your decision to own your own business?   Y / N

PROBE: Q41 Who or what?

PROBE: Q42 In what way?

Q43   ...That influenced the type of business you chose to own?

PROBE: Q44 Who or what?

PROBE: Q45 In what way?

Q46   Has there been any one in your life who you've gone to first for information, emotional support, or support for your ideas? (This could be more than one person, for instance going to different people during different periods of your life.)

IF YES: Q47   Who?

             Q48   Where/how did you meet her/him?

             Q49   How has she/he helped you?

Q50   Is there anyone in your life now who comes to you for guidance in the same way?

PROBE: Q51 Who (what gender/age/occupation)?

PROBE: Q52 What type of help/guidance do you give that person?

Q   Has anyone come to you for information or guidance in starting their own business?

PROBE: Q51 Who (what gender/age/occupation)?

PROBE: Q52 What type of help/guidance have you given that person?

IV.   JOB LIMITS AND OPPORTUNITIES

Q53   In any of your previous jobs, do you feel you were discriminated against as a woman?

Q54   ...As an African American?

PROBE: Q55 What were the circumstances?

Q56   Have you faced stereotyping by others in your line of work?

PROBE: Q57 Please explain.

IF YES: Q58 Did this discrimination/stereotyping have an influence on your decision to start your own business?

Q59 How do you feel about this now that you have your own business? Do you still face discrimination?

Q60 Do you feel it is an advantage to be a woman in your business?

Q61 Did you apply for any commercial loans when starting your business?

Q62 Did you close any loans?

   IF YES: Q63 What was your experience with getting the loan?

   IF NO: Q64 What was your experience getting financial backing when starting your business?

VI. BUSINESS ACTIVITIES

Now I am going to ask some questions on your business strategies.

Q65 Do you belong to any business organizations or groups?

   PROBE: Q66 Are you an active member?

   PROBE: Q67 What do you gain from membership?

   PROBE: Q68 What do you give/exchange?

   PROBE: Q69 Who are the other members that you interact with the most? What types of businesses do they have? What is your relationship to them? What do you exchange?

Q70 Do you participate in trade shows? [where? which ones?]

   PROBE: Q71 What have you gained from participation?

   PROBE: Q72 What contacts have you made through these shows? [at which shows?]

Q73 Do you refer clients to other businesses/individuals?

   PROBE: Q74 Who? (What business?)

   PROBE: Q75 For what services/products/information?

Q76 Do other businesses/individuals refer clients to you?

   PROBE: Q77 Who? (What business?)

   PROBE: Q78 For what services/products/information?

Q79 Do you supply goods/services/information to other businesses?

   PROBE: Q80 What business? (type of business, etc.)

   PROBE: Q81 What do you sell?

Q82 Do other businesses/individuals supply you with goods/services/information?

   PROBE: Q83 What business? (type of business, etc.)

   PROBE: Q84 What do you buy?

Q85 Do you trade goods/services/information with other businesses/individuals?

   PROBE: Q86 What business? (type of business, etc.)

   PROBE: Q87 What do you trade?

Q88 How do you advertise your products/services?

   PROBE: Q89 Please describe ...

Q90 If you wanted to try something new with the business [develop a new product or new service/reach a new clientele or market], how would you go about it?

   PROBE: Q91 Where/who would you go to for information?

   PROBE: Q92 ...for financing?

   PROBE: Q93 ...for training?

   PROBE: Q94 ...for materials?

   PROBE: Q95 ..for labor? [employees]

   PROBE: Q96 ...to advertise?

Q97 Are there other things that you've done to build up the business or to gain more customers? (Make new business contacts, do team building with employees, advertise, adopt new technologies, etc.)

   PROBE: Q98 Please describe ...

Q99 Who do you go to for advice on making business decisions?

Q100 Do you have a Board of Directors?

   PROBE: Q101   Who is on it?

   PROBE: Q102   What are their occupations? [Types of businesses owned...]

Q103 If you were sick or had some type of crisis in your life, who would you turn to for help operating the business?

   PROBE: Q104   How did you meet him/her?

   PROBE: Q105   What is your relationship with this person/s?

   PROBE: Q106   How would you reward them? [trade, pay, etc.]

VII. GOALS, SELF IMAGE, SUCCESS

Now I am going to ask you about your goals and visions for the business.

Q107   Do you have any employees? Y / N

> IF YES: Q110   What has been your experience having people work for you?

Q108   Would you like to see your business grow?

> IF YES: Q109 How? (In what way?)

Q113   Do you consider your business to be a success?

> PROBE: Q114   Why? / Why not?
>
> PROBE: Q115   What is your vision of success?

Q116   What have been your greatest challenges in operating this business?   .

Q117   What were your goals and visions when you first started?

> PROBE: Q118 Personal goals
>
> Q119 Business goals

Q120   Has the business become what you expected?

> IF NOT: Q121 How is it different?

Q122   What do you see happening in the next 5 years? Where will the business be?

VIII. FAMILY HISTORY:

Now I'd like to ask you some questions about your family.

Q123   Are you, or have you been, married? Have a companion? Single?

Q124   Do you have any children?

> IF NO CHILDREN ---> GO TO   Q129

> > Q125   How many children do you have? #
> >
> > Q126   What are their ages? _____ years
> >
> > Q127   How are your children cared for while you are at work?
> >
> > Q128   Did you take time off to raise your children, or have you worked most of the time throughout their childhood?

> IF MARRIED/WITH COMPANION etc. AND/OR WITH CHILDREN:

> > Q129   How, if at all, has owning a business affected your family life?

PROBE: Q130   For instance, are there any differences in your daily household routine? Do you eat out more, hire household help, [use more childcare services]?

Q131   How, if at all, has your family life affected your business?

PROBE: Q132   For instance, do you work at home to accommodate childcare? Do you limit business growth in order to accommodate husband's career?

IF MARRIED OR WITH COMPANION:

Q133   Does your husband/companion share in domestic responsibilities?

IF YES: Q134   How much?
1 I do much more   8 Don't know
2 I do more
3 we share equally   .
4 he/she does more
5 he/she does much more
Q135   What does he/she do?

IF MARRIED WITH CHILDREN 12 YEARS OR YOUNGER:

Q136   Does your husband/companion share in childcare ?

IF YES: Q137   How much?
1 I do much more   8 Don't know
2 I do more
3 we share equally
4 he/she does more
5 he/she does much more

Q138   What does he/she do?

IF MARRIED/WITH A COMPANION:

Q139   Has your husband's/companion's income provided you with financial stability to start and/or operate your own business?

Q140   Has your husband/companion co-signed any loans for your business?

IX.   WRAP UP QUESTIONS:

Q141   Is there anything that we haven't covered here that has been important to your experience as a business owner?

Q142   Please explain...

Q143   Would it be alright to contact you again if I need to clarify anything we've talked about today?

1. Yes_____   8. Don't know

2. No

Q144   Do you know of any other women small business owners who might be willing to take part in this study?

PROBE: Name: Business: Phone #:

Survey of Small Business Firms
The University of Georgia
Fall, 1993

Respondent ID _____

Position:

        1. Owner
         2. Owner-Manager
          3. Manager/CEO
          4. Other

I.   **BUSINESS BACKGROUND**

Q2   In what year did you begin operations in this community?
        19_____

Q3   Please describe the major activity of your business.

        _____

        SIC Code (To be coded later):____ ____ ____ ____ ____

Q4   Please indicate the type of industry your firm is located in. **[CIRCLE ONLY ONE]**
        1. Retail
         2. Service
          3. Wholesale
           4. Manufacturing
            5. Construction
             6. Other (Please specify:_____)

Q5   Please identify the legal form of your business.

        1. Sole proprietorship
         2. Partnership
          3. Corporation

Q6   Please circle the description which best indicates this business's status vis a vis related
        establishments.

        1. This business is an independent, single establishment firm.

        2. This business is owned by a multi-establishment firm.

        3. This business owns one or more branch establishments besides the one at this location.

        4. This business is a franchisor which sells the right to use its concept to one or more
        franchisees.

                        8. Don't Know

II.   MANAGEMENT

The next group of questions concerns your experiences and background as the owner or manager
of this business.

Q7   All together, how much experience have you had in the line of work you are now in?
        _____years

Q8   How many years of schooling have you completed?
        _____ years

Q9What is the highest degree, if any, you have completed? (Where two degrees are listed, please circle the degree you have completed.)
       1. High School   8. Other_____
       2. Associate
       3. BA or BS
       4. MA or MS
       5. PhD or MD

Q10   Prior to starting this business, had you owned or operated another small business?
           1. Yes
           2. No

       IF YES: Q11   What type of business?_____

Q12   Are you currently owner or part owner of any other enterprise?
           1. Yes
           2. No

       Q13 Please describe:_____)

Q14   How many hours per week do you work at this business, on average? (If more than one business, how many hours do you work at each business?)

       _____ hours/week

Q15   Do you have another job besides working here?
           1. Yes
           2. No

       Q16 (Please describe_____)

       IF YES: Q17   How many hours per week do you work at this job, on the average? _____hours per week

III.   FINANCING

Approximately what percent of the start-up capital for your business came from the following sources? (Total should add up to 100%.)

      ___% Q18 Personal loans from family or friends
      ___% Q19 Commercial bank
      ___% Q20 Thrift institution (e.g., savings bank)
      ___% Q21 Credit union
      ___% Q22 Commercial investors
      ___% Q23 Personal savings
      ___% Q24 Government program (e.g., Small Business Administration)
      ___% Q25 Sale of corporate stock
      ___% Q26 Private investors
      ___% Q27 Other sources
             (please specify_____)

Approximately what percent of your total capital requirements for your business came from the following sources in the last two years? (Total should add to 100%.)

___% Q28 Personal loans from family or friends
___% Q29 Commercial bank
___% Q30 Thrift institution (e.g., savings bank)
___% Q31 Credit union
___% Q32 Commercial investors
___% Q33 Personal savings
___% Q34 Government program (e.g., Small Business Administration)
___% Q35 Sale of corporate stock
___% Q36 Private investors
___% Q37 Retained earnings
___% Q38 Other sources
       (please specify_____)

Which of the following sources of business assistance have you used in the past three years?
[YOU MAY CIRCLE MORE THAN ONE]

		YES	NO		Don't Know
Q39	Certified public accountant	1	2		8
Q40	Banker	1	2		8
Q41	Lawyer		1	2	8
Q42	Business consultant	1	2		8
Q43	Small Business Development Center	1	2		8
Q44	Trade or professional association	1	2		8
Q45	Relative or friend (unpaid)	1	2		8
Q46	Other (specify)_____	1	2		8

Q47 Have you ever formally negotiated a line of credit with your financial institution?

      1. Yes
      2. No

Q48 Have you had a commercial loan application rejected by a local financial institution in the past three years?

      1. Yes   8. Don't know
      2. No
        3. No loans applied for

IV. PERSONNEL ISSUES

Q49 Does your firm employ any workers who are not members of your immediate family?

      1. Yes
      2. No

Q50 How many full-time employees, including yourself and immediate family members, does your firm have?
      _____ #

Q51 How many part-time employees, including yourself and immediate family members, does your firm have?
      _____ #

Q52   How many employees did your firm have five years ago (total full and part time including yourself and family members)?
_____#

Q53   How many women employees, including yourself, does your firm have now?
_____#

Q54   How many men employees does your firm have now?
_____#

Q55   How many Black employees does your firm have now?
_____#

Q56   How many White employees does your firm have now?
_____#

Q57   How many employees of other racial and/or ethnic backgrounds does your firm have?
_____#

V.   STRATEGY

Please indicate how important these aspects of your competitive strategy are.

	CRITICAL	IMPORTANT	MARGINAL	INSIGNIFICANT	NA
Q58 Lower prices	1	2	3	4	8
Q59 Better service	1	2	3	4	8
Q60 Quality products/services	1	2	3	4	8
Q61 More choices	1	2	3	4	8
Q62 Customize product/service to clients	1	2	3	4	8
Q63 More effective marketing/advertising	1	2	3	4	8
Q64 Fast response to changes in markets	1	2	3	4	8
Q65 Serve those missed by others	1	2	3	4	8
Q66 Superior location/customer convenience	1	2	3	4	8
Q67 Distinctive goods/services	1	2	3	4	8
Q68 Better, more attractive facilities	1	2	3	4	8
Q69 More contemporary, attractive products	1	2	3	4	8
Q70 Utilize new/advanced technology	1	2	3	4	8
Q71 Develop new/advanced technology	1	2	3	4	8

Q72   Is there any other aspect of your competitive strategy that is important?

        1. Yes
        2. No

IF YES: Q73 How important?   1   2   3   4   8

(Please describe:_____)

How important are the following activities to you in operating your business?

		CRITICAL	IMPORTANT	MARGINAL	INSIGNIFICANT	NA
Q74	Making a profit	1	2	3	4	8
Q75	Producing a quality product	1	2	3	4	8
Q76	Providing a service to the community	1	2	3	4	8
Q77	Providing jobs in the community	1	2	3	4	8
Q78	Other	1	2	3	4	8
	(Please specify: _____)					

At the present time, how much do you and/or the company ...

		VERY MUCH	QUITE A BIT	A MODERATE AMOUNT	LITTLE	NONE	DK
Q79	Have formal written business and marketing plan?	1	2	3	4	5	0
Q80	Regularly use, modify, and update plans?		1	2	3	4	5	0
Q81	Set goals, priorities, and follow up to ensure they are attained?	1	2	3	4	5	0
Q82	Accurately forecast operational results?	1	2	3	4	5	0

What percentage of your sales is contracted to ...

Q83 U.S.government: _____%
Q84 state government: _____%
Q85 local government: _____%

VI.   **FINANCIAL INFORMATION**

Please give your best estimate of the financial information requested. Your estimates should be for 1993.

Q86   Gross sales or revenues $_____

Q87   Materials cost $_____

Q88   Wages, salaries, and benefits $_____

Q89   Expenditures overhead, including
        current expenditures for buildings
        and equipment $_____

Q90   Assessed value of fixed assets $_____

VII.   **PERSONAL BACKGROUND**

Q91   Where did you grow up? _____ (City, State)

        IF ELSEWHERE: Q92   When did you move here?_____(year)

What is your ...

         Q93   Age _____

         Q94   Birth order: 1st___ 2nd___ 3rd___ 4th___ 5th___ Youngest_____ Other _____

NOTE: IF YOU WERE NOT RAISED BY YOUR PARENTS OR STEP-PARENTS, PLEASE CROSS OUT "MOTHER" AND WRITE IN THE FEMALE RELATIVE OR PERSON WHO RAISED YOU;

         AND/OR

         CROSS OUT "FATHER" AND WRITE IN THE MALE RELATIVE OR PERSON WHO RAISED YOU.

Q95   What is your mother's ...

        Age ____ Training _____ Highest degree _____

        Occupation (before retirement) _____

Q96   What is your step-mother's ...   (If NOT APPLICABLE, circle: "N/A")

        Age ____ Training _____ Highest degree _____

        Occupation (before retirement) _____

Q97   What is your father's ...

        Age ____ Training _____ Highest degree _____

Occupation (before retirement) _____

Q98 What is your step-father's ...   (If NOT APPLICABLE, circle: "N/A")

Age___ Training _____ Highest degree _____

Occupation (before retirement) _____

NOTE: IF YOU HAVE MORE THAN FOUR BROTHERS, AND/OR MORE THAN
FOUR SISTERS, PLEASE WRITE IN AGE/TRAINING/HIGHEST
DEGREE/EDUCATION FOR EACH ADDITIONAL BROTHER/SISTER BEYOND
THOSE YOU LIST BELOW.

Q99 What are your brothers'...   (If NOT APPLICABLE, circle: "N/A")

Age___ Training _____ Highest degree ___ Occupation _____
Age___ Training _____ Highest degree ___ Occupation _____
Age___ Training _____ Highest degree ___ Occupation _____
Age___ Training _____ Highest degree ___ Occupation _____

Q100 What are your sisters'...   (If NOT APPLICABLE, circle: "N/A")

Age___ Training _____ Highest degree ___ Occupation _____
Age___ Training _____ Highest degree ___ Occupation _____
Age___ Training _____ Highest degree ___ Occupation _____
Age___ Training _____ Highest degree ___ Occupation _____

Q101   Do you have a disability?

           1. Yes   8. Don't know
           2. No

           Please describe: _____

THANK YOU!

Bibliography

Acs, Zoltan, J., and David Audretsch. 1990. *Innovation and Small Firms.* Cambridge: MIT Press.

Aldrich, Howard. 1989. "Networking Among Women Entrepreneurs." Pp. 104–132 in Oliver Hagan, Carol Rivchun, and Donald Sexton, (eds.) *Women-Owned Businesses.* New York: Praeger.

Aldrich, Howard. 1995. "Is Japan Different? The Personal Networks of Japanese Business Owners Compared to Those in Four Other Industrialized Nations." *KSU Economic and Business Review* (Kyoto Sangyo University), 22 (May): 1–28.

Aldrich, Howard and Ellen R. Auster. 1986. "Even Dwarfs Started Small: Liabilities of Age and Size and Their Strategic Implications." *Research in Organizational Behavior,* 8: 165–198.

Aldrich, Howard, Amanda Elam Brickman, and Pat Ray Reese. 1995. "Strong Ties, Weak Ties, and Strangers: Do Women Owners Differ from Men in their Use of Networking to Obtain Assistance?" An unpublished paper.

Aldrich, Howard, John Cater, Trevor Jones, David McEvoy, and Paul Velleman. 1985. "Ethnic Residential Concentration and the Protected Market Hypothesis." *Social Forces* 63, 4(June): 996–1009.

Aldrich, Howard and Pat Ray Reese. 1993. "Does Networking Pay Off? A Panel Study of Entrepreneurs in the Research Triangle." *Frontiers of Entrepreneurship Research* :325–339.

Aldrich, Howard, Pat Ray Reese, and Paola Dubini. 1989. "Women on the Verge of a Breakthrough: Networking Among Entrepreneurs in the United States and Italy." *Entrepreneurship & Regional Development,* 1: 339–356.

Aldrich, Howard and T. Sakano. 1995. "Unbroken Ties: How the Personal Networks of Japanese Business Owners Compare to Those in Other Nations." in *Networks and Markets: Pacific Rim Investigations*, edited by Mark Fruin. New York: Oxford Press.

Aldrich, Howard and Catherine Zimmer. 1986. ""Entrepreneurship Through Social Networks." Pp. 3–23 in *The Art and Science of Entrepreneurship*, edited by D.L. Sexton and R.W. Smilor. Cambridge, MA: Ballinger.

Aldrich, Howard, Catherine Zimmer, and David McEvoy. 1989. "Continuities in the Study of Ecological Succession: Asian Businesses in Three English Cities." *Social Forces* 67, 4(June): 920–944.

American Council on Education. 1988. *Seventh Annual Status Report.* Washington D.C.

Andersen, Margaret L. and Patricia Hill Collins, 1992. *Race, Class, and Gender.* Belmont, CA: Wadsworth.

Ando, Faith. 1988. "Capital Issues and Minority-Owned Business." *The Review of Black Political Economy*, vol. 16 (Spring): 77–109.

Aronson, Robert L. 1991. *Self-Employment: A Labor Market Perspective.* Ithaca, NY: ILR Press.

Bates, Timothy. 1973a. "An Econometric Analysis of Lending to Black Businessmen." *The Review of Economics and Statistics* 55 (August).

Bates, Timothy. 1973b. "The Potential of Black Capitalism." *Public Policy* 21 (Winter).

Bates, Timothy. 1974. "Financing Black Enterprises." *The Journal of Finance* 29 (June): 747–761.

Bates, Timothy. 1975. "Government as Financial Intermediary for Minority Entrepreneurs." *The Journal of Business* 48 (October): 541–557.

Bates, Timothy. 1981. "Black Entrepreneurship and Government Programs." *Journal of Contemporary Studies* vol. 4 (Fall): 59–70.

Bates, Timothy. 1983. "The Potential for Black Business: A Comment." *The Review of Black Political Economy* 12 (Winter): 237–240.

Bates, Timothy. 1985a. "Entrepreneur Human Capital and Minority Business Viability." *The Journal of Human Resources* 20 (Fall): 540–554.

Bates, Timothy. 1985b. "Impact of Preferential Procurement Policies on Minority-Owned Businesses." *The Review of Black Political Economy* 14 (Summer): 51–66.

Bates, Timothy. 1985c. "Minority Business Set-Asides: Theory and Practice." In *Affirmative Action in Employment and Minority Business Set-Asides.* Produced by the U.S. Commission on Civil Rights. Washington, D.C.: Government Printing Office.

Bates, Timothy. 1987. "Self Employed Minorities: Traits and Trends." *Social Science Quarterly* 68 (September).

Bates, Timothy. 1988. *An Analysis of Income Differentials Among Self-Employed Minorities*. Los Angeles: UCLA Center for Afro-American Studies.

Bates, Timothy. 1989a. "Entrepreneur Factor Inputs and Small Business Longevity." (A discussion paper.) Washington DC:U.S. Bureau of the Census, Center for Economic Studies (June).

Bates, Timothy. 1989b. "Small Business Viability in the Urban Ghetto." *Journal of Regional Science* 29 (November).

Bates, Timothy. 1990. "Entrepreneur Human Capital Inputs and Small Business Longevity." *The Review of Economics and Statistics* 72 (November).

Bates, Timothy. 1993a. *Banking on Black Enterprise*: The Potential of Emerging Firms for Revitalizing Urban Economies. Washington, DC: Joint Center for Political and Economic Studies.

Bates, Timothy. 1993b. *Major Studies of Minority Business*. Washington DC: Joint Center for Political and Economic Studies Press.

Bates, Timothy. 1994a. "Social Resources Generated by Group Support Networks May Not Be Beneficial to Asian Immigrant-Owned Small Businesses." *Social Forces* 72, 3(March): 671–689.

Bates, Timothy. 1994b. "Utilization of Minority Employees in Small Business: A comparison of Non-minority and Black-Owned Urban Enterprises." *The Review of Black Political Economy* (Summer): 113–121.

Bates, Timothy and William Bradford. 1979. *Financing Black Economic Development*. New York: Academic Press.

Bates, Timothy and Daniel Fusfeld. 1984. The Economic Dynamics of the Urban Ghetto." Ch. 10 in *The Political Economy of the Urban Ghetto*. Carbondale, IL: Southern Illinois University Press.

Bates, Timothy and Alfred Nucci. 1989. "An Analysis of Small Business Size and Rate of Discontinuance." *Journal of Small Business Management* 27 (October).

Bates, Timothy and Donald Hester. 1977. "Analysis of a Commercial Bank Minority Lending Program: Comment." *Journal of Finance* 32 (December): 1783–1789.

Bates, Timothy and Darrell Williams. 1995. "Preferential Procurement Programs and Minority-Owned Businesses." *Journal of Urban Affairs* 17, 1: 1–17.

Bearse, Peter. 1983. *An Econometric Analysis of Minority Entrepreneurship*. Washington, DC: U.S. Department of Commerce, Minority Business Development Agency.

Bearse, Peter J. 1984. "An Econometric Analysis of Black Entrepreneurship." *Review of Black Political Economy*, 12 (Spring): 117–134.

Becker, Eugene. 1984. "Self-Employed Workers: An Update to 1983." *Monthly Labor Review*, 107 (July): 14–18.

Becker, Gary S. 1957, 1971 editions. *The Economics of Discrimination.* Chicago: University of Chicago Press.

Becker, Gary S. 1964, 1975, 1993 editions. *Human Capital.* Chicago: University of Chicago Press.

Becker, Gary S. 1965. "A Theory of the Allocation of Time." *Economic Journal* 75 (September): 493–517.

Becker, Gary S. 1981, 1991 editions. *A Treatise on the Family.* Cambridge: Harvard University Press.

Becker, Gary S. and H. G. Lewis. 1973. "On the Interaction Between the Quantity and Quality of Children." *Journal of Political Economy* 81, 2: S279–288.

Becker, Gary S. and N. Tomes. 1976. "Child Endowments . . ." *Journal of Political Economy* 84, 4: S143.

Bender, Henry. 1980. *Report on Women Business Owners.* American Management Association.

Berg, Bruce L. 1989. *Qualitative Research Methods for the Social Sciences.* Needham Heights, MA: Allyn and Bacon.

Birch, David L. 1979. "The Job Generation Process." Cambridge, MA: MIT Program on Neighborhood and Regional Change.

Birch, David L. 1981. "Who Creates Jobs?" *The Public Interest* 54:3–14.

Birch, David L. 1987. *Job Creation in America: How Our Smallest Companies Put the Most People to Work.* New York: Free Press.

Bird, Caroline. 1976. *Enterprising Women.* New York: W.W. Norton & Company.

Birley, S., C. Moss, and P. Saunders. 1986. "The Differences Between Small Firms Started by Male and Female Entrepreneurs Who Attended Small Business Courses." Pp. 211–222 in *Frontiers of Entrepreneurship Research—1986.* Wellesley, MA: Babson College.

Blackford, Mansel G. 1991. *A History of Small Business in America.* New York: Twayne Publishers.

Blau, J. 1984. *Architects and Firms.* Cambridge, MA: MIT Press.

Blau, Peter M. and Otis Dudley Duncan. 1967. *The American Occupational Structure.* New York: Wiley.

Blauner, Robert. 1992. "The Ambiguities of Racial Change." Pp. 54–65 in *Race, Class, and Gender*, edited by Margaret L. Andersen and Patricia Hill Collins. Belmont, CA: Wadsworth.

Bonacich, Edna. 1973. "A Theory of Middleman Minorities." *American Sociological Review* 38 (October): 583–594.

Boorman, S. A. 1975. "A Combinatorial Optimization Model for Transmission of Job Information Through Contact Networks." *Bell Journal of Economics* 6: 216–249.

Borjas, George J. and Stephen G. Bronars. 1989. "Consumer Discrimination and Self-Employment." *Journal of Political Economy*, 97: 581–605.

Bowen, Donald D. and Robert D. Hisrich. 1986. "The Female Entrepreneur: A Career Development Perspective." *The Academy of Management Review*, 11, 2 (April): 393–407.

Bradford, William D. 1990. "Wealth, Assets, and Income in Black Households." Afro-American Studies Working Paper, vol.1, no. 1, University of Maryland.

Bregger, John E. 1963. "Self-Employment in the United States, 1948–62." *Monthly Labor Review*, 86 (January): 37–43.

Brewer, Rose. 1988. "Black Women in Poverty: Some Comments on Female Headed Families." *Signs* 13 (2): 331–339.

Brophy, David J. 1989. "Financing Women-Owned Entrepreneurial Firms." Ch. 3 in *Women-Owned Businesses,* edited by Oliver Hagan, Carol Rivchun, and Donald Sexton. New York: Praeger.

Brown, Carolyn M. 1995. "All Talk, No Action: Franchisors Say They Want to Recruit More African Americans. But Are They Willing to Take Affirmative Measures to Ensure Equal Access?" *Black Enterprise* (September): 60–64.

Brown, Charles, James Hamilton, and James Medoff. 1990. *Employers Large and Small.* Cambridge: Harvard University Press.

Brush, C. G.. 1992. "Research on Women Business Owners: Past Trends, a New Perspective and Future Directions." *Entrepreneurship: Theory and Practice* 16:5–30.

Brush, C. G. and R. D. Hisrich. 1985. "Women and Minority Entrepreneurs: A Comparative Analysis." Pp. 566–587 in *Frontiers of Entrepreneurship Research—1985*. Wellesley, MA: Babson College.

Burgess, E. W. and D. J. Bogue, editors. 1967. *Contributions to Urban Sociology.* Chicago: University of Chicago Press.

Burlew, Ann Kathleen. 1982. "The Experiences of Black Females in Traditional and Nontraditional Professions." *Psychology of Women Quarterly* 6, 3 (Spring):312–326.

Carden, Ann D. 1990. "Mentoring and Adult Career Development: The Evolution of a Theory." *The Counseling Psychologist*, 18, 2 (April): 275–299.

Campbell, Karen. 1988. "Gender Differences in Job-Related Networks." *Work and Occupations*, 15, 2 (May):179–200.

Caplovitz, David. 1973. *The Merchants of Harlem: A Study of Small Business in the Black Community.* Beverly Hills, CA: Sage.

Carroll, G.R. and Y.P. Huo. 1986. "Organizational Task and Institutional Environments in Evolutionary Perspectives: Findings from the Local Newspaper Industry." *American Journal of Sociology*, 91:838–873.

Cheney, Jim. 1987. "Eco-Feminism and Deep Ecology." *Environmental Ethics*, 9, 2 (Summer): 115–145.

Clark, T. and F. James. 1992. "Women-Owned Businesses: Dimensions and Policy Issues." *Economic Development Quarterly*, 6, 1: 25–40.

Cohen, Abner. 1969. *Custom and Politics in Urban Africa*. Berkeley: University of California Press.

Coleman, James S. 1988. "Social Capital in the Creation of Human Capital." *American Journal of Sociology* 94 Supplement: S95–S120.

Coleman, James S. 1990. *Foundations of Social Theory*. Cambridge: Harvard University Press.

Coleman, James S. 1994. "A Rational Choice Perspective on Economic Sociology." Ch. 7 in *The Handbook of Economic Sociology*, edited by Neil J. Smelser and Richard Swedberg. Princeton: University of Princeton Press.

Collins, Patricia Hill. 1986. "The Afro-American Work Family Nexus: An Exploratory Analysis." *Western Journal of Black Studies* 10(3): 148–158.

Collins, Patricia Hill. 1990. *Black Feminist Thought*. New York: Routledge.

Committee on Small Business (CSB). 1988. *New Economic Realities: The Rise of Women Entrepreneurs*. Washington, DC: U.S. Government Printing Office.

Cromie, Dr. Stanley. 1987. "Motivations of Aspiring Male and Female Entrepreneurs." *Journal of Occupational Behaviour*, 8: 251–261.

Cromie, Stanley and John Hayes. 1988. "Towards a Typology of Female Entrepreneurs." *Sociological Review*, 36: 87–113.

Crosby, Faye J., editor. 1987. *Spouse, Parent, Worker: On Gender and Multiple Roles*. New Haven: Yale University Press.

Cuba, Richard, David Decenzo, and Andrea Anish. 1983. "Management Practices of Successful Female Business Owners." *American Journal of Small Business*, VIII, 2 (Oct.-Dec.); 40–46.

Cummings, L.L. 1988. "Organizational Decline from the Individual Perspective." Pp. 417–424 in *Readings in Organizational Decline: Frameworks, Research, and Prescriptions*, edited by K. Cameron, R.Sutton, and D. Whetten. Cambridge, MA: Ballinger.

Daniels, Arlene Kaplan. 1988. *Invisible Careers: Women Civic Leaders from the Volunteer World*. Chicago: University of Chicago Press.

Davis, Angela Y. 1981. *Women, Race, and Class*. New York: Random House.

Day, Virginia Kay. 1986. *"My Family Is Me": Women's Kin Networks and Social Power in a Black Sea Island Community*. A PhD dissertation in anthropology submitted to the State University of New Jersey at Rutgers.

DeCarlo, J.F. and P.R. Lyons. 1979. "A Comparison of Selected Personal Characteristics of Minority and Non-minority Female Entrepreneurs." *Proceedings of 39th Annual Meeting of the Academy of Management*, 369–373.

Denzin, Norman K. and Yvonna S. Lincoln, editors. 1994. *Handbook of Qualitative Research*. Thousand Oaks, CA: Sage.

Digest of Educational Statistics. 1997. Washington, DC: U.s. Depeartment of Education.

Dill, Bonnie Thornton. 1980. "'The Means to Put My Children Through': Child-Rearing Goals and Strategies among Black Female Domestic Servants." Pp. 107–123 in *The Black Woman*, edited by La Frances Rodgers-Rose. Beverly Hills, CA: Sage.

Dill, Bonnie Thornton. 1988. "'Making Your Job Good Yourself': Domestic Service and the Construction of Personal Dignity." Pp. 33–52 in *Women and the Politics of Empowerment*, edited by Ann Bookman and Sandra Morgen. Philadelphia: Temple University Press.

Dominguez, John. 1976. *Capital Flows in Minority Areas*. Lexington, MA: Lexington Books.

Duncan, Cynthia M. 1996. "Understanding Persistent Poverty: Social Class Context in Rural Communities." *Rural Sociology* 61, 1 (Spring): 103–124.

Duncan, Otis Dudley. 1961. "A Socio-Economic Index for All Occupations." Pp.109–138 in ed. Albert J. Reiss, Jr., *Occupations and Social Status*.

Duncan, Otis Dudley and Robert W. Hodge. 1963. "Education and Occupational Mobility: A Regression Analysis." *American Journal of Sociology* 68: 629–644.

Eisinger, Peter K. 1988. *The Rise of the Entrepreneurial State*. Madison: University of Wisconsin Press.

Elliehausen, Gregory, Glenn Canner, and Robert Avery. 1984a. "Survey of Consumer Finances, 1983." Federal Reserve Bulletin, vol. 70 (September): 679–692.

Elliehausen, Gregory, Glenn Canner, and Robert Avery. 1984b. "Survey of Consumer Finances, 1983: A Second Report." Federal Reserve Bulletin, vol. 70 (December): 857–868.

Engels, Frederick. 1983. "The Family" from his *The Origins of the Family, Private Property and the State*. Pp. 18–24 in *Women and the Politics of Culture*, edited by Michele Wender Zak and Patricia A. Moots. New York and London: Longman.

Etter-Lewis, Gwendolyn. 1993. *My Soul is My Own: Oral Narratives of African American Women in the Professions*. New York: Routledge.

Evans, David. 1987. "The Relationship Between Firm Growth, Size, and Age: Estimates for 100 Manufacturing Industries." *The Journal of Industrial Economics* 35 (June).

Evans, G. 1948. *Business Incorporations in the United States: 1800–1943*. New York: National Bureau of Economic Research.

Fain, T. Scott. 1980. "Self-Employed Americans: Their Number Has Increased." *Monthly Labor Review*, 103 (November): 3–8.

Farmer, Richard T. 1968. "Black Businessmen in Indiana." *Indiana Business Review* 43 (November): 12–13.

Fischer, Claude and Stacey Oliker. 1983. "A Research Note on Friendship, Gender and the Life Cycle." *Social Forces*, 62: 124–132.

Flora, Cornelia Butler and Jan L. Flora. 1993. "Entrepreneurial Social Infrastructure: A Necessary Ingredient." *Annals*, AAPSS 529: 48–58.

Folbre, Nancy. 1994. *Who Pays for the Kids? Gender and the Structures of Constraint*. London and New York: Routledge.

Foley, Eugene. 1966. "The Negro Businessman: In Search of a Tradition." In *The Negro American*, edited by Talcott Parsons and Kenneth B. Clark. Boston: Houghton Mifflin.

Fontana, Andrea and James H. Frey. 1994. "Interviewing: The Art of Science." Ch. 22, pp. 361–376 in *Handbook of Qualitative Research*, edited by Norman K. Denzin and Yvonna S. Lincoln. Thousand Oaks, CA: Sage.

Fratoe, Frank. 1986. "A Sociological Analysis of Minority Business." *Review of Black Political Economy* 15: 5–29.

Fratoe, Frank. 1988. "Social Capital and Small Business Owners." *The Review of Black Political Economy* 16 (Spring).

Frazier, E. Franklin. 1925. "Durham: Capital of the Black Middle Class." Pp. 333–340 in *The New Negro*, edited by A. Locke. New York: Albert & Charles Boni.

Frazier, E. Franklin. 1957. *The Negro in the United States*. New York: MacMillan (revised edition).

Frazier, E. Franklin. 1963. *The Negro Church in America*. New York: Schocken.

Frazier, E. Franklin. 1967. *Negro Youth at the Crossways: Their Personality Development in the Middle States*. New York: Schocken. (Original work published in 1940).

Frazier, E. Franklin. 1968. *E. Franklin Frazier on Race Relations: Selected Papers* (G.F. Edwards, ed.). Chicago: University of Chicago Press.

Gerson, Kathleen. 1985. *Hard Choices: How Women Decide About Work, Career, and Motherhood*. Berkeley: University of California Press.

Gerson, Kathleen. 1993. *No Man's Land: Men's Changing Commitments to Family and Work*. New York: Basic Books.

Gilligan, Carol. 1982. *In a Different Voice*. Cambridge, MA: Harvard University Press.

Glade, WIlliam P. 1967. "Approaches to a Theory of Entrepreneurial Formation." *Explorations in Entrepreneurial History/Second Series*, 4, 3 (Spring/Summer): 245–259.

Glaser, Barney G. and Anselm L. Strauss. 1967. *The Discovery of Grounded Theory: Strategies for Qualitative Research*. Chicago: Aldine.

Glaser, Barney G. and Anselm L. Strauss. 1974. *The Discovery of Grounded Theory*. New York: Aldine.

Glenn, Evelyn Nakano. 1985. "Racial Ethnic Women's Labor: The Intersection of Race, Gender and Class Oppression." *Review of Radical Political Economics* 17, 3: 86–108.

Gluckman, Max. 1967. *The Judicial Process Among the Barotse of Northern Rhodesia*, second edition. Manchester: Manchester University Press.

Goffee, Robert and Richard Scase. 1985. *Women in Charge—The Experiences of Female Entrepreneurs*. London: George Allen & Unwin.

Goldscheider, Frances K., and Linda J. Waite. 1991. *New Families, No Families? The Transformation of the American Home*. Berkeley and Los Angeles: University of California Press.

Granovetter, Mark. 1973. "The Strength of Weak Ties." *American Journal of Sociology* 78 (May): 1360–1380.

Granovetter, Mark. 1974 and 1995. *Getting a Job: A Study of Contacts and Careers*. Chicago: University of Chicago Press.

Granovetter, Mark. 1982. "The Strength of Weak Ties: A Network Theory Revisited." Pp. 105–130 in *Social Structure and Network Analysis*, edited by Peter V. Marsden and Nan Lin. Beverly Hills, CA: Sage.

Granovetter, Mark. 1992. "Economic Action and Social Structure: The Problem of Embeddedness." Chapter 3 in *The Sociology of Economic Life*, edited by Mark Granovetter and Richard Swedberg. Boulder: Westview Press.

Granovetter, Mark and Richard Swedberg, eds. 1992. *The Sociology of Economic Life*. Boulder: Westview Press.

Green, Shelley, and Paul Pryde. 1990. *Black Entrepreneurship in America*. New Brunswick, NJ: Transaction.

Greene, Richard. 1982. "Tracking Job Growth in Private Industry." *Monthly Labor Review* 105:3–9.

Gutman, Herbert. 1976. *The Black Family in Slavery and Freedom, 1750–1925*. New York: Random House.

Guttman, Peter M. 1977. "The Subterranean Economy." *The Financial Analyst's Journal* 33:26–27.

Haber, Sheldon E., Eugene J. Lamas, and Jules Lichtenstein. 1987. "On Their Own: The Self-Employed and Others in Business." *Monthly Labor Review*, 110 (May): 17–23.

Harrison, Bennett. 1994. *Lean and Mean: The Changing Landscape of Corporate Power in the Age of Flexibility*. New York: Basic Books.

Hartley, Keith and John Hutton. 1989. "Large Purchasers." Ch. 6 in *Barriers to Growth in Small Firms*, edited by J. Barber, J.S. Metcalfe, and M. Porteous. London: Routledge.

Hechter, Michael. 1976. "Ethnicity and Industrialization: On Proliferation of the Cultural Division of Labor." *Ethnicity* 3: 214–224.

Hertz, Rosanna. 1986. *More Equal Than Others*. Berkeley: University of California Press.

Higginbotham, Elizabeth. 1983. "Laid Bare by the System: Work and Survival for Black and Hispanic Women." Pp. 200–215 in *Class, Race, and Sex: The Dynamics of Control*, edited by Amy Smerdlow and Hanna Lessinger. Boston: G. K. Hall.

Higginbotham, Elizabeth. 1985. "Race and Class Barriers to Black Women's College Attendance." *Journal of Ethnic Studies*, 13, 1 (Spring):89–107.

Higginbotham, Elizabeth, and Lynn Weber. 1992. "Moving Up With Kin and Community: Upward Social Mobility for Black and White Women." *Gender and Society*, 6, 3 (September):416–440.

Hisrich, Robert D. 1989. "Women Entrepreneurs: Problems and Prescriptions for Success in the Future." Pp. 3–32 in Oliver Hagan, Carol Rivchun, and Donald Sexton, (eds.) *Women-Owned Businesses*. New York: Praeger.

Hisrich, R.D. and C. Brush. 1983. "The Woman Entrepreneur: Implications of Family, Educational, and Occupational Experience." Pp. 255–270 in *Frontiers of Entrepreneurship Research*, edited by J.A. Hornaday, J.A. Timmons, and K.H. Vesper. Wellesley, MA: Babson College, Center for Entrepreneurial Studies.

Hisrich, Robert D. and Marie O'Brien. 1981. "The Woman Entrepreneur From a Business and Sociological Perspective." Pp. 21–39 in *Proceedings, 1981 Conference on Entrepreneurship*. Babson College.

Hisrich, Robert D. and Marie O'Brien. 1982. "The Woman Entrepreneur as a Reflection of the Type of Business." Pp. 54–67 in *Frontiers of Entrepreneurship Research—1981*. Wellesley, MA: Babson College.

Huberman, Michael A. and Matthew B. Miles. 1994. "Data Management and Analysis Methods." Ch. 27 in *Handbook of Qualitative Research*, edited by Norman K. Denzin and Yvonna S. Lincoln. Thousand Oaks, CA: Sage Publications.

Humphreys, M.A. and J. McClung. 1981. "Women Entrepreneurs in Oklahoma." *Review of Regional Economics and Business*, 6, 2:13–21.

Inman, Katherine. 1996. "Networks and Money: How Women Finance Small Businesses." Richmond, Virginia: paper presented at the annual Southern Sociological Society.

Inman, Katherine and Linda Grant. 1998. "Building from Kin and Community: Business Start-up Strategies of Rural African American Women." San Francisco, California: paper presented at the annual American Sociological Association meeting.

Jones, Jacqueline. 1985. *Labor of Love, Labor of Sorrow: Black Women, Work and the Family from Slavery to the Present*. New York: Basic Books.

Kalleberg, Arne L. 1995. "Sociology and Economics: Crossing the Boundaries." *Social Forces* 73, 4(June): 1207–1218.

Kalleberg, Arne L. and Kevin T. Leicht. 1991. "Gender and Organizational Performance: Determinants of Small Business Survival and Success." *Academy of Management Journal*, 34, 1: 136–161.

Kanter, R.M. 1977. *Men and Women of the Corporation*. New York: Basic Books.

Kaufman, D.R. 1984. "Some Feminist Concerns in an Age of Networking." Pp. 157–164 in *Women Therapists Working with Women: New Theory and Process of Feminist Therapy*, edited by C.M. Brody. New York: Springer Publications.

Kelly, Paul E. 1975. "Educational and Occupational Choices of Black and White, Male and Female Students in a Rural Georgia Community." *Journal of Research and Development in Education* 9, 1:45–56.

Kilson, Marion. 1977. "Black Women in the Professions." *Monthly Labor Review* 100 (May): 38–41.

Kram, K. 1983. "Phases of the mentor relationship." *Academy of Management Journal*, 26, 4:608–625.

Lemkau, Jeanne Parr. 1979. "Personality and Background Characteristics of Women in Male-Dominated Occupations: A Review." *Psychology of Women Quarterly* 4 2 (Winter): 221–240.

Lenzi, Raymond C. 1996. "The Entrepreneurial Community Approach to Community Economic Development." *Economic Development Review* (Spring): 16–20.

Levinson, Darrow, Klein, Levinson, and McKee (1978) and

Lieber, Esther K. 1980. "The Professional Woman: Coping in a Two-Career Family." *Educational Horizons* (Spring): 156–161.

Light, Ivan. 1979. "Disadvantaged Minorities in Self-Employment." *International Journal of Comparative Sociology* 20:31–45.

Light, Ivan. 1984. "Immigrant and Ethnic Enterprise in North America." *Ethnic and Racial Studies* 7: 195–216.

Light, Ivan and Edna Bonacich. 1988. *Immigrant Entrepreneurs; Koreans in Los Angeles; 1965–1982*. Berkeley: University of California Press.

Light, Ivan, Jung-Kwuon Im, and Zhong Deng. 1990. "Korean Rotating Credit Associations in Los Angeles." *Amerasia* 16: 35–54.

Light, Ivan and Carolyn Rosenstein. 1995. *Race, Ethnicity, and Entrepreneurship in Urban America*. New York: Aldine de Gruyter.

Lin, Nan. 1982. "Social Resources and Instrumental Action." Pp. 131–145 in *Social Structure and Network Analysis*, edited by Peter V. Marsden and Nan Lin. Beverly Hills, CA: Sage.

Lofland, J. and L. H. Lofland. 1995. *Analyzing Social Settings: A Guide to Qualitative Observation and Analysis* (3rd ed.). Belmont, CA: Wadsworth.

Loscocco, Karyn A., Joyce Robinson. 1991. "Barriers to Women's Small Business Success in the United States." *Gender and Society*, 5, 4 (December): 511–532.

Loscocco, Karyn A., Joyce Robinson, Richard H. Hall, and John K. Allen. 1991. "Gender and Small Business Success: An Inquiry into Women's Relative Disadvantage." *Social Forces*, 70, 1 (September): 65–85.

Loury, G. 1977. "A Dynamic Theory of Racial Income Differences." Chapter 8 of *Women, Minorities and Employment Discrimination*, ed. P.A. Wallace and A. Le Mund. Lexington, MA: Lexington Books.

Loury, G. 1987. "Why Should We Care About Group Inequality?" *Social Philosophy and Policy* 5: 249–271.

Luttrell, Wendy. 1997. *Motherwise, Streetwise:* . New Brunswick, NJ: Rutgers University Press.

Malizia, Emil. 1996. "Two Strategic Paths to Competitiveness." *Economic Development Review* (Spring): 7–9.

Malson, Michelene Ridley. 1983. "Black Families and Child Rearing Support Networks." *Research in the Interweave of Social Roles: Jobs and Families* 3: 131–141.

Malveaux, Julianne and Phyllis Wallace. 1987. "Minority Women in the Workplace." Chapter 10 in *Working Women: Past—Present—Future*, edited by Karen Shallcross Koziara, Michael H. Moskow, and Lucretia Dewey Tanner. Washington, DC: The Bureau of National Affairs.

Marshall, Nancy L. and Rosalind C. Barnett. 1992. "Work-Related Support Among Women in Caregiving Occupations." *Journal of Community Psychology*, 20 (January): 36–42.

Martin, Elaine and Barbara Keyes. 1988. "Professional Women: Role Innovation and Sex Role Conflict." *Michigan Academician*, 20, 2 (Spring): 139–152.

Martin, Elmer and Joanne Mitchell Martin. 1978. *The Black Extended Family*. Chicago: University of Chicago Press.

Martinelli, Alberto. 1994. "Entrepreneurship and Management." Ch. 19 in *The Handbook of Economic Sociology*, edited by Neil J. Smelser and Richard Swedberg. Princeton: University of Princeton Press.

Marx, Karl. 1965. *Capital, Vol. I*. Moscow: Progress Publishers.

Mayer, K. and S. Goldstein. 1961. *The First Two Years: Problems of Small Firm Growth and Survival*. Washington DC: U.S. Government Printing Office.

McAdoo, Harriette Pipes. 1978. "Factors Related to Stability in Upwardly Mobile Black Families." *Journal of Marriage and the Family* 40:761–776.

McGarry, E. 1930. Mortality in Retail Trade. Buffalo, NY: University of Buffalo Press.

McLanahan, Sara and Gary Sandefur.1994. *Growing Up with a Single Parent*. Cambridge, MA: Harvard University Press.

Mergenhagen, Paula. 1996. "Black-Owned Businesses." *American Demographics* June:25–33.

Michael, R. T. and G. S. Becker. 1973. "On the New Theory of Consumer Behavior." *Swedish Journal of Economics* 75, 4: 378–396.

Miller, James. 1990. "Survival and Growth of Independent Firms and Corporate Affiliates in Metro and Nonmetro America." *Rural Development Research Report No. 74*. Washington, D.C.: USDA/ERS.

Miller, Jon, James R. Lincoln, and Jon Olson. 1981. "Rationality and Equity in Professional Networks: Gender and Race as Factors in the Stratification of Interorganizational Systems." *American Journal of Sociology*, 87, 2: 308–333.

Min, Pyong Gap. 1984. "From White Collar Occupations to Small Business: Korean Immigrants' Occupational Adjustment." *The Sociological Quarterly* 25:333–352.

Min, Pyong Gap and Charles Jaret 1985. "Ethnic Business Success: The Case of Korean Small Business in Atlanta." *Sociology and Social Research* 69: 412–435.

Morse, Janice M. 1994. "Designing Funded Qualitative Research." Chapter 13 in *Handbook of Qualitative Research*, edited by Norman K. Denzin and Yvonna S. Lincoln. Thousand Oaks, CA: Sage Publications.

Mullings, Leith. 1986. "Uneven Development: Class, Race, and Gender in the United States Before 1900." Pp. 41–57 in *Women's Work: Development and the Division of Labor by Gender*, edited by Eleanor Leacock and Helen Safa. South Hadley, MA: Bergin & Garvey.

Murrell, Audrey J., Irene Hanson Frieze, and Jacquelyn L. Frost. 1991. "Aspiring to Careers in Male- and Female-Dominated Professions." *Psychology of Women Quarterly* 15:103–126.

Myers, Robert E. 1983. "Immigrant Occupational Achievement: A Comparative Case Study of Koreans, Soviet Jews, and Vietnamese in the Philadelphia Area." PhD dissertation, University of Pennsylvania.

Park, Robert E. 1925/1967. "The City: Suggestions for the Investigation of Human Behavior in the Urban Environment." Pp. 1–46 in The City, edited by R. E. Park, E. W. Burgess, and R. D. McKenzie. Chicago: University of Chicago Press.

Park, Robert E.. 1952. *The Collected Papers of Robert Ezra Park: Vol. 2. Human Communities: The City and Human Ecology*. (E. C. Hughes et al., Eds.). Glencoe, IL: Free Press.

Parsons, Talcott. 1951. *The Social System*. New York: Free Press.

Parsons, Talcott. 1958. "Social Structure and the Development of Personality: Freud's Contribution to the Integration of Psychology and Sociology." *Psychiatry* 21: 321–340.

Parsons, Talcott. 1966. *Societies: Evolutionary and Comparative Perspectives.* Englewood Cliffs, NJ: Prentice Hall.

Parsons, Talcott. 1971. *The System of Modern Societies.* Englewood Cliffs, NJ: Prentice Hall.

Parson, Talcott and Edward A. Shils eds. 1951. *Toward a General Theory of Action.* New York: Harper & Row.

Passel, Peter. 1990. "Small Business, Large Mirage." *New York Times*, May 9.

Phillips-Jones, L. 1982. *Mentors and Proteges.* New York: Arbor House.

Pierce, Joseph. 1947. *Negro Business and Business Education.* New York: Harper and Brothers.

Pinkney, Alphonso. 1984. *The Myth of Black Progress.* New York: Cambridge University Press.

Piore, Michael and Charles F. Sabel. 1984. *The Second Industrial Divide.* New York: Basic Books.

Poole, Shelia M. 1993. "Entrepreneurs Find Freedom from Scrutiny." *Atlanta Journal-Constitution*, Monday, October 18: E1.

Poole, Shelia M. 1996. "Women Gain Ground in Owning Businesses." *Atlanta Journal-Constitution*, Tuesday, March 26: D1.

Poole, Shelia M., Gertha Coffee and Holly Morris. 1993. "Gays on the Job: Working Against Fear." *Atlanta Journal-Constitution*, Monday, October 18: E1.

Portes, Alejandro and Rueben Rumbaut. 1990. *Immigrant America: A Portrait.* Berkeley: University of California Press.

Portes, Alejandro, and Alex Stepick. 1985. "Unwelcome Immigrants: The Labor Market Experiences of 1980 (Mariel) Cuban and Haitian Refugees in South Florida." *American Sociological Review* 50:493–514.

Pronet Group, Inc. 1996. *Pronet Newsletter*, vol. I, no. 4, Atlanta, Georgia.

Putnam, Robert. 1993a. "The Prosperous Community." *The American Prospect* 13: 35–42.

Putnam, Robert. 1993b. *Making Democracy Work: Civic Traditions in Modern Italy.* Princeton: Princeton University Press.

Putnam, Robert. 1995. "Bowling Alone: America's Declining Social Capital." *Journal of Democracy* 6: 65–78.

Ragin, Charles C. 1987. *The Comparative Method: Moving Beyond Qualitative and Quantitative Strategies.* Berkeley: University of California Press.

Ragins, Belle Rose. 1989. "Barriers to Mentoring: The Female Manager's Dilemma." *Human Relations* 42 1: 1–22.

Ray, Robert N. 1975. "Self-Employed Americans in 1973." *Monthly Labor Review*, 98, (January): 49–54.

Reskin, Barbara F., and Patricia A. Roos. 1990. *Job Queues, Gender Queues: Explaining Women's Inroads into Male Occupations.* Philadelphia: Temple University Press.

Reynolds, Rhonda. 1995. "Capital Ideas: Business Microloans." *Black Enterprise* (October): 38.

Reynolds, Rhonda. 1996. "Small Business News: Wells Fargo Woos Women Entrepreneurs." *Black Enterprise* (February): 29.

Richey, Cheryl A., Eileen D. Gambrill, and Betty J. Blythe. 1988. "Mentor Relationships Among Women in Academe." *Affilia* 3 1 (Spring): 34–47.

Roberts, Priscilla and Peter M. Newton. 1987. "Levinsonian Studies of Women's Adult Development." *Psychology and Aging*, 2, 2:154–163.

Rollins, Judith. 1985. *Between Women, Domestics, and Their Employers.* Philadelphia: Temple University Press.

Romero, Mary. 1992. *Maid in the USA.* New York: Routledge.

Ronstadt, R.C. 1984. *Entrepreneurship: Text, Cases and Notes.* Dover, MA: Lord Publishing.

Roper Organization, Inc. 1985. *The 1985 Virginia Slims American Women's Opinion Poll.* Stores, CT: The Roper Center, University of Connecticut.

Ross, Doug and Robert E. Friedman. 1990. "The Emerging Third Wave: New Economic Development Strategies." *Entrepreneurial Economy Review* (Autumn): 3–10.

Saint-Paul, Gilles. 1996. *Dual Labor Markets: A Macroeconomic Perspective.* Cambridge, MA: MIT Press.

Scase, Richard and Robert Goffee. 1980. "Home Life in a Small Business." *New Society*, 30:220–222.

Schumpeter, Joseph A. 1934. *The Theory of Economic Development.* Oxford: Oxford University Press.

Schumpeter, Joseph A. 1943. *Capitalism, Socialism, and Democracy.* London: Allen & Unwin.

Schumpeter, Joseph A. 1988. *Essays on Entrepreneurs, Innovations, Business Cycles, and the Evolution of Capitalism.* New Brunswick, NJ: Transaction.

Schumpeter, Joseph A. 1991. "Comments on a Plan for the Study of Entrepreneurship." Ch. 10 in *Joseph A. Schumpeter: The Economics and Sociology of Capitalism*, edited by Richard Swedberg. Princeton: Princeton University.

Scott, Allen J. 1988. *Metropolis.* Berkeley: University of California Press.

Sexton, D.L. and C.A. Kent. 1981. "Female Executives and Entrepreneurs: A Preliminary Comparison." Pp. 40–55 in *Frontiers of entrepreneurship research*, edited by K. Vesper. Wellesley, MA: Babson University Press.

Shapero, A. and L. Sokol. 1982. "The Social Dimensions of Entrepreneurship." Pp. 72–90 in *Encyclopedia of Entrepreneurship*, edited by C.A. Kent, D.L. Sexton, and K.H. Vesper. Englewood Cliffs, NJ: Prentice Hall.

Shapiro, E.C., F.P. Haseltine, and M.P. Rowe. 1978. "Moving Up: Role Models, Mentors, and the 'Patron System'." *Sloan Management Review*, 19 (Spring): 51–58.

Smith-Lovin, Lynn and J. Miller McPherson. 1993. "You Are Who You Know: A Network Approach to Gender." Pp. 223–251 in *Theory on Gender / Feminism on Theory*, edited by Paula England. New York: Aldine de Gruyter.

Sokoloff, Natalie J. 1980. *Between Money and Love*. New York: Praeger.

Sokoloff, Natalie. 1992. *Black Women and White Women in the Professions*. New York: Routledge.

Spradley, James P. 1979. *The Ethnographic Interview*. New York: Harcourt Brace Jovanovich.

Staber, Udo and Howard E. Aldrich. 1995. "Cross-National Similarities in the Personal Networks of Small Business Owners: A Comparison of Two Regions in North America." *Canadian Journal of Sociology* 20, 4: 441–467.

Stein, Barry A. 1974. *Size, Efficiency and Community Enterprise*. Cambridge, MA: Center for Community Economic Development.

Strauss, Anselm and Juliet Corbin. 1990. *Basics of Qualitative Research*. Newbury Park, CA: Sage.

Sudarkasa, Niara. 1981. "Female Employment and Family Organization in West Africa." Pp. 49–64 in *The Black Woman Cross-Culturally*, edited by Filomina Chioma Steady. Cambridge, MA: Schenkman.

Suggs, Robert. 1986. "Recent Changes in Black-Owned Business." A working paper. Washington, DC: Joint Center for Political Studies.

Sway, Marlene. 1988. *Familiar Strangers*. Urbana: University of Illinois Press.

Swinton, David and John Handy. 1983. *The Determinants of the Growth of Black-Owned Businesses: A Preliminary Analysis*. Washington D.C.: U.S. Department of Commerce, Minority Business Development Agency.

Teitz, Michael, Amy Glasmeiser, and Douglas Svensson. 1981. *Small Business and Employment Growth in California*. Berkeley: Institute of Urban and Regional Development.

Terrell, Henry. 1971. "Wealth Accumulation of Black and White Families." *Journal of Finance*, 26 (May).

Thurow, Lester C. 1969. *Poverty and Discrimination*. Washington, DC: Brookings Institute.

Thurow, Lester C. 1972. "Education and Economic Equality." *The Public Interest* 28 (Summer): 66–81.

Thurow, Lester C. 1975. *Generating Inequality*. New York: Basic Books.

Tigges, Leann and Gary P. Green. 1992. "Small Business Success Among Men- and Women-Owned Firms." A paper presented at the 1992 ASA Meetings.

Trent, William. 1984. "Equity Considerations in Higher Education: Race and Sex Differences in Degree Attainment and Major Field from 1976 Through 1981." *American Journal of Education*, 41 (May): 280–305.

University of Georgia. 1992. "Strengthening Community Economic Development in Georgia: Survey of Small Businesses in Rural Georgia." A report produced by the Division of Applied Research, Small Business Development Center, and the Institute of Community and Area Development, Athens, GA.

U.S. Comptroller General. 1981. *The SBA 8(a) Program: A Promise Unfulfilled.* Washington, D.C.: General Accounting Office.

U.S. Department of Commerce and Bureau of the Census. 1991. *1987 Economic Census: Women Owned Businesses.* Washington, DC: U.S. Government Printing Office.

U.S. Department of Commerce and Bureau of the Census. 1996a. *1992 Economic Census: Women Owned Businesses.* Washington, DC: U.S. Government Printing Office.

U.S. Department of Commerce and U.S. Bureau of the Census. 1996b. *Survey of Minority-Owned Business Enterprises.* Washington D.C.: Government Printing Office.

U.S. Small Business Administration. 1984–1992. *The State of Small Business: A Report of the President. Annual Report.* Washington, D.C.: Government Printing Office.

U.S. Small Business Administration. 1988b. *Small Business in the American Economy.* Washington, D.C.: Government Printing Office.

U.S. Small Business Administration, Office of Advocacy. 1994. "Regulatory Agencies: CRA Regulations to Emphasize Performance." *Small Business Advocate*, 13, 3 (March): 1.

Small Business Administration 8(a) Review Board. 1978. *Report and Recommendations on the Section 8(a) Program for A. Vernon Weaver, Administrator.* Washington, D.C.: Small business Administration.

Vidich, Arthur J. and Stanford M. Lyman. 1994. "Qualitative Methods: Their History in Sociology and Anthropology." Ch. 2 in *Handbook of Qualitative Research*, ed. by N. K. Denzin and Y. S. Lincoln. Thousand Oaks, CA: Sage Publications.

Waddell, F.T. 1983. "Factors Affecting Choice, Satisfaction, and Success in the Female Self-Employed." *Journal of Vocational Behavior*, 23: 294–304.

Waldinger, Roger. 1988. "The Social Networks of Ethnic Entrepreneurs." Paper presented at the 1988 Annual Meeting of the National Economic Association, New York City.

Wallace, Phyllis A. 1980. *Black Women in the Labor Force.* Cambridge: MIT Press.

Warren, Karen J. 1987. "Feminism and Ecology: Making Connections." *Environmental Ethics*, 9, 1 (Spring): 3–20.

Warren, Karen J. 1990. "The Power and the Promise of Ecological Feminism." *Environmental Ethics*, 12, 2 (Summer): 125–146.

Watkins, J.M. and D.S. Watkins. 1983. "The Female Entrepreneur: Her Background and Determinants of Business Choice—Some British Data." Pp.

271–288 in *Frontiers of entrepreneurship research*, edited by A. Hornaday, J.A. Timmons, and K.H. Vesper. Wellesley, MA: Babson College Center for Entrepreneurial Studies.

Weber, Max. 1958. *The Protestant Ethic and Spirit of Capitalism*. New York: Scribner's.

Weber, Max. 1978, "Anticritical Last Word on the *Spirit of Capitalism* by Max Weber." Translated by Wallace M. Davis. *American Journal of Sociology* 83:1105–1131.

Weiss, Linda. 1988. *Creating Capitalism*. London: Basil Blackwell.

White, Deborah Gray. 1985. *Ar'n't I a Woman? Female Slaves in the Plantation South*. New York: W. W. Norton.

Williamson, Oliver. 1987. *The Economic Institutions of Capitalism: Firms, Markets, and Relational Contracting*. New York: Free Press.

Williamson, Oliver. 1994. *Comparative Economic Organization: The Analysis of Discrete Structural Alternatives*. San Francisco: ICS Press.

Woodard, Michael D. 1997. *Black Entrepreneurs in America: Stories of Struggle and Success*. New Brunswick, NJ: Rutgers University Press.

Woolf, Arthur. 1986. 1986. "Market Structure and Minority Presence: Black-Owned Firms in Manufacturing." The Review of Black Political Economy vol. 14 (Spring): 79–89.

Yoo, Jin-Kyung. 1996. "Immigrant Entrepreneurs: Social and Family Networks and Ethnic Resources of Korean Immigrants in the Atlanta Metropolitan Statistical Area." A dissertation. Athens, GA: University of Georgia.

Zanna, M.P., F. Crosby, and G. Lowenstein. 1987. "Male Reference Groups and Discontent Among Female Professionals." Pp. 24–41 in *Women's Career Development*, edited by B.A. Gutek and L. Larwood. Beverly Hills, CA: Sage.

Zaretsky, Eli. 1973. *Capitalism, The Family, & Personal Life*. New York: Harper & Row.

Zimmer, Catherine and Howard Aldrich. 1987. "Research Mobilization Through Ethnic Networks: Kinship and Friendship Ties of Shopkeepers in England." *Sociological Perspectives* 30, 4 (October):422–455.

Index

Debt
    alternatives to, 206, 212. *See also*
        financing, alternative
        strategies
    avoidance of, 154, 161–62, 163,
        164, 189, 207, 212
DeCarlo, J.F. and P.R. Lyons, 15, 51,
        62, 67
Decisions, 165, 215–16, 221. *See
        also* Choice
    labor market, 120
    to partner, 98–99
    political influences on, 100
    process of making, 121
    rational, 146
Dee, 112, 138, 158, 159, 177, 199,
        218
Diane, 97, 105, 108, 125, 132, 191,
        195, 220
Digest of Educational Statistics, 66
Dill, Bonnie Thornton, 33
Directorships, 136, 140, 144
Disadvantage, 221
    by class, 75
    in commercial financing, 149
        by race and gender, 162
    dealing with, 36–40, 216, 222,
        223
    and education, 124
    by gender, 164
    and innovation in financing, 164
    labor market, 13, 37, 74–75
        and earnings, 37
        and human capital, 37
    by locale, 75
    in men's informal networks, 68
    by race, 10, 75, 164
    resistance to, 223
    resource, 13
    and restructuring, 10
    structured, 224, 234
Discrimination, 5, 6, 18, 27, 119,
        221, 222

based on age, 159, 222
based on appearance, 159
costs to production, 34
and decisions to start, 120
and educational opportunity,
        123–24
effect on financial capital, 34–35
effect on human capital, 34–35, 37,
        146
and franchises, 92, 210
historical effects of, 37
and job security, 34
and lack of opportunity for rural
        blacks, 233
in loans, 71, 149, 162
on-the-job, 37, 48, 224
as a preference, 18, 34
race- and gender-based, 146, 162,
        222
"Domestics," 65
Dominguez, John, 4
Donna, 104, 105, 107, 134, 156,
        175
Duncan, Cynthia M., 22

Earnings. *See* Income
Economic Opportunity Loan
        Programs (EOL), 58
Economy
    change in, 67
        effect on women's businesses of,
            231
    dual, 4, 14
        definition, 14
    informal, 4
    market conditions and small
        businesses, 53
Education. *See also* Experience;
        Information; Knowledge;
        Learning; Skills; Training
    access to, 219
        by locale, 219
        by race, 66, 219

Kalleberg, Arne L., 68
  and Kevin T. Leicht, 52
Karen, 107–8, 132–33, 154–55, 156,
  165, 194
Kathy, 96–97, 126, 127, 128, 191–92,
  220
Kay, 101, 103, 111, 154, 194
Kelly, Paul E., 67
Kilson, Marion, 5, 61
Kirstin, 130, 153, 193, 194, 220
Knowledge. *See also* Education;
    Experience; Information;
    Learning; Skills; Training
  gained informally, 175
  gained through regulatory
    structures, 170–71
  lack of, 171
  racially linked, 109, 169
  retention of 133
  transfer of, 24, 168

Labor markets
  African American participation in,
    55–56
  and industrial structure, 52–54,
    and African American
    education, 57
  by gender, 52
  barriers and opportunities, 55–56
  characteristics, 52–54
  effect on family income, 55
  historical changes in, 5, 55
  mobility in, 19, 60–61
  public/private sectors, 61
  women's participation in, 5, 48, 67
Laura, 117, 118, 119, 144, 161, 162,
    184, 207, 208–9
Learning. *See also* Education;
    Experience; Information;
    Knowledge; Skills;
    Training
  as a business philosophy, 183–84
  from clients, 183

  from consultants, 181
  incidental, 218
  informal, 183, 185, 218
    definition of, 124
    maximized in ownership, 137
  location of, 218
  nonhierarchical, 173, 183, 185,
    187, 229
  in a nontraditional business,
    182–84
  from other business owners,
    184–85
  patchwork, 133
    and application to ownership,
    134
  structured, 26, 131, 133, 135, 136,
    143, 144, 185
    while doing business, 131
Lenore, 98, 127, 134, 135, 151, 157,
    176
Lenzi, Raymond C., 15
Libby, 114, 116, 140, 141–42, 161,
    207
Licensing, 138, 185
Lieber, Esther K., 63
Life, public/private, 20–21
  blurring of boundaries between,
    70, 220, 230
  and self-concept, 70
  invisible careers and, 20
  meaning of, by race and locale, 21
  racial differences in, 221
  skills learned in, 170
  traditional definitions of, redefined,
    221
Light, Ivan, 37, 38, 39, 64
  and Carolyn Rosenstein, 3, 4, 13,
    36, 37, 38, 40, 64, 69, 164,
    216, 222, 225, 226
  and Edna Bonacich, 37
  and Jung-Kwuon Im and Zhong
    Deng, 38, 71, 225
Lin, Nan, 19, 220

Regulations, unintentional results of, 234
Relationships
  business, 38
  integrating personal and business, 70
  multiplex, 22, 170, 187, 225
    defined, 22
    development of, 167, 186
    and group solidarity, 37–38
    and information flow, 22
  nonhierarchical, 21, 221, 229
  with the oppressor, 31–32
  personal, 22
Research. *See also* Literature; Methodology; Theory
  comparing men's and women's businesses, 6–7
  design and methods, 79–92
  empirical, 47–77
    contributions to study focus, 60–61
  focus of, 43–44, 215
  inferences, 232
  limitations of, 217
  major findings of, 228–29
  need for further, 231–33, 233–34
    on nonowners, 232
  participation in:
    motives for, 81
  regionally integrated, 2
  sampling, 83–87
  theoretical implications of, l228–31
  on women's resources, 7
Reskin, Barbara F. and Patricia A. Roose, 18, 35, 224
Resources, 7. *See also* Cpaital, financial; Capital, human; Capital, social
  access to, 5 ,32, 39, 75
    through social ties, 232
  accumulation of, 10, 41, 215–16

and African American community support, 32
alternative, 16, 39, 223
availability of
  and decisions to start, 215
  by gender, 16, 44
  by group, 162
  by race, 16, 44, 223, 226
  in rural areas, 1, 16, 44, 223
  by type of business, 44, 223
class, 38, 69–70
  and decisions to start, 93–94
  defined, 11
  donated labor, 137
  educational, 75. *See also* Education
  effect on goals/motives/decisions, 93
  entrepreneurial, 38
  ethnic, 22, 38, 69–70, 224, 225, 226
  family/kin, 7, 150. *See also* Family
  family labor as, 117, 213. *See also* Financing, Cost reduction strategies
  financial, 7, 38, 70–74, 75. *See also* Capital, financial
  for business start-up, 2
  formal/informal, 16
  human, 7, 75–76. *See also* Capital, human
  "invisible," 8
  mobilization of, 40, 43, 60, 75, 91, 159, 163, 216, 223, 229
    despite limited options, 222
    innovation in, 229. *See also* Innovation
    by locale, 9, 75
    and motivations for business, 9, 94, 231. *See also* Motivations
    and persistent segregation, 234
    by race, 6, 9, 75, 76